The Labyrinth of the Comic

The Labyrinth of the Comic:

Theory and Practice from Fielding to Freud

Richard Keller Simon

UNIVERSITY PRESSES OF FLORIDA
Florida State University Press
Tallahassee

UNIVERSITY PRESSES OF FLORIDA is the central agency for scholarly publishing of the State of Florida's university system, producing books selected for publication by the faculty editorial committees of Florida's nine public universities: Florida A&M University (Tallahassee), Florida Atlantic University (Boca Raton), Florida International University (Miami), Florida State University (Tallahassee), University of Central Florida (Orlando), University of Florida (Gainesville), University of North Florida (Jacksonville), University of South Florida (Tampa), University of West Florida (Pensacola).

ORDERS for books published by all member presses of University Presses of Florida should be addressed to University Presses of Florida, 15 NW 15th Street, Gainesville, FL 32603

Typesetting by G & S Typesetters, Austin, Texas

Library of Congress Cataloging in Publication Data

Simon, Richard Keller.
    The labyrinth of the comic.

    Bibliography: p.
    Includes index.
        1. English fiction—History and criticism.   2. Comic, The, in literature.   3. Fielding, Henry, 1707–1754—Criticism and interpretation.   4. Comic, The.
    5. Kierkegaard, Søren, 1813–1855.   6. Freud, Sigmund, 1856–1939.   I. Title.
    PR858.C63S56   1985   809'.917   85-6069
    ISBN 0–8130–0831–X (alk. paper)

For Rhoda and Si,
for Kathy,
and for Hermina

Contents

Acknowledgments

I could not have written this book without the assistance of a number of friends and colleagues. Larry Carver, Jack Farrell, Jim Garrison, Louis Mackey, Jane Marcus, and Walt Reed, all of the University of Texas at Austin, read and sometimes read again earlier drafts of the manuscript. Their criticisms and encouragement were of incalculable value. Other members of the Texas faculty, Lance Bertelsen, Tony Hilfer and Wayne Lesser, helped me rethink early versions of individual chapters, while Jim Kaufmann and Rea Keast helped me rethink the basic assumptions of the book as a whole. Donald Wesling and the late Robert C. Elliott, both of the University of California, San Diego, gave me important criticisms on the very first version of this book. My greatest intellectual debts are to Robert Polhemus of Stanford University and Andrew Wright of the University of California, San Diego, who patiently and meticulously evaluated earlier drafts. I owe them a very special thanks for their suggestions, advice and support—more than anyone else, they have led me through the labyrinth of the comic.

Many other individuals have guided my growth as a reader and a writer: my parents, Israel and Rhoda Simon; my grandmother, the late Hermina Keller Weitzenfeld; my mentors at the University of Michigan, Peter Bauland, Kenneth Thorpe Rowe, and Arthur M. Eastman; and my teachers at Stanford University, Thomas Moser, Diane Middlebrook, David Halliburton, and Charles Lyons.

A grant from the Waddell Foundation allowed me to take a one-year leave of absence from the University of Texas to work on this book, and a stipend from the University Research Institute gave me an additional summer of support.

I owe more practical debts to Sarah Williams for typing and correcting the manuscript and to Jeanne Ruppert, Director of the Florida State University Press, for overall guidance and care. My wife, Kathleen J. Waddell, has sustained me with her love, wisdom, and strength.

Rea Keast and Rhoda Simon read the proofs.

"There is nothing like a Theory for blinding the wise."

George Meredith, *The Ordeal of Richard Feverel*

". . . whatever poetry may be, criticism had best be comic."

Kenneth Burke, *Attitudes Toward History*

I

Introduction

THIS BOOK is an interdisciplinary study of comedy and comic theory from the middle of the eighteenth century to the beginning of the twentieth, from Henry Fielding to Sigmund Freud. It is a close reading of four very different kinds of texts: English comic fiction, German and Danish philosophy, Anglo-American psychology, and Austrian psychoanalysis, all of which are preoccupied with the meanings of comedy and the comic, humor, laughter, and mockery. I examine here the parallel development of literary, philosophic, scientific, and philosophic-scientific inquiries into these interrelated subjects: (1) the reflexive study of comedy in the English comic novel, beginning with Fielding in the eighteenth century and continuing with Thackeray and Meredith in the nineteenth, works that are both provocations to laugh and studies of the laugh; (2) the critique of laughter and the comic in German and Danish philosophy in the first half of the nineteenth century, beginning with Schiller, Schlegel, Richter, and Hegel, and culminating with Kierkegaard, whose intricate analysis is as much comic as about the comic; (3) the scientific investigation into laughter in Anglo-American psychology, physiology, and evolutionary biology in the second half of the nineteenth century, from Darwin, Spencer, and Bain, to Dewey, Hall, Sully, and McDougall, essays that are sometimes serious and sometimes wildly comic in their rhetorical strategies; and (4) the consideration of joking and wit in Austrian psycho-analysis at the beginning of the twentieth century, Freud's study of *Witz* and the unconscious, which is both an explanation and a demonstration of psychodynamic play. These are major critical texts in the history of comedy and comic theory. All contain complex arguments about comedy and the comic, and many are simultaneously comic and about the comic—they mock seriousness at the same time that they take mockery very seriously. This study explores both their mockery and their seriousness. It is intended as a contribution to the intellectual history of what Meredith somewhat awkwardly called the idea of comedy and the uses of the comic spirit, and it should be of interest to anyone working on the problems of comedy, humor, and laughter. It privileges no critical vocabulary and studies each discipline on its own terms.

Each discipline does have different primary interests in laughter and the comic—comedy as literary form, the comic as philosophic attitude, laughter as psychological response, joking as psychodynamic play—but in the period covered by this book, with the exception of some of the scientists virtually all of the critics of the comic are generalists. They move widely between considerations of the physiological benefit from laughter, the theological significance of laughter, and the literary provocations to laughter; between forms, attitudes, and behaviors. In the twentieth century, however, with the increasing specialization of academic fields and the development of different critical methodologies, vocabularies, and basic assumptions, the study of the comic has been almost completely fragmented. What has been obscured in the process are the fundamental connections between the different aspects of the comic, what the great critics of the eighteenth and nineteenth centuries were able to explore in detail. This study is an attempt to reverse that tendency in the modern study of the comic by demonstrating the substantial achievements of the critics who, writing before the age of academic specialization, sought to understand a gestalt: the complex configuration of comedy, the comic, and laughter, form, attitude, behavior.

This book is not a survey of comedy or comic theory but a series of readings of major critical texts that are complex, imaginative, and substantial treatments of the subject. It builds on a number of excellent surveys that have already established basic concepts of the comic in some of these fields: Stuart Tave's *Amiable Humorist* for the English theory of the eighteenth century; Robert Martin's *Triumph of Wit* for the English theory of the Victorian period, exclusive of the scientific; and Morton Gurewitch's *Comedy: The Irrational Vision* for the concept of the comic in the modern period considered broadly. Comic theory is an incongruous mixture of approaches and a miscellaneous assortment of arguments, many of them simple repetitions of conventional wisdom or straightforward attacks on the conventional wisdom, some of them extraordinary in their intellectual rigor and imaginative insight. There are as yet no careful or sustained studies of these major critical texts, and it is such a study that I undertake here. The works selected are meant to be representative of the most substantial achievements in the field. From Erasmus's *Praise of Folly* to the present, there is a great richness of critical texts concerned with the comic, and many remain to be studied carefully. This book concentrates on major critical texts in four disciplines, which are meant to be representative of the four broad intellectual approaches that have been taken with the material.

Like Erasmus's *Praise*, these texts are carefully conceived, elaborately developed, and simultaneously comic and about the comic. The exceptions, again, are several of the essays by scientists. Folly herself speaks Erasmus's mock encomium, thereby calling into question everything she says in praise of folly; and because she contradicts herself repeatedly, demonstrating her folly, what she says about folly is difficult to assess. The comic nature of her arguments about the comic creates an elegant comic paradox. We have no general term for this kind of text that is equally theory and practice, although the word *reflexive*

is often used to identify self-conscious literary works. Comedy
has been self-conscious since Aristophanes and the direct address to the audience in the parabasis, and from the Renaissance
to the present it has often contained important metacomic elements. In English comic drama, for example, from Shakespeare's
anatomy of fools and fooling in *Twelfth Night* and Jonson's
study of laughter in *Volpone* to Trevor Griffith's anatomy of
fools and fooling in *Comedians* (1976) and Peter Barnes's study
of laughter in *Laughter!* (1978), comedy has taken itself for subject matter. This is equally true of English comic fiction from
Fielding's *Joseph Andrews* and Sterne's *Tristram Shandy* to Huxley's *Antic Hay*, and in American comic fiction, to West's *Miss
Lonelyhearts*. Comic theory has been self-consciously comic
since Erasmus—*Praise* is an extended comic parabasis, and in
the modern period it has sometimes been elaborately framed
within comic structures and presented in comic styles meant to
provoke laughter from the audience, or at least from that part of
the audience which has understood the jokes. Nietzsche's analysis of laughter is contained in Zarathustra's eccentric speeches in
Thus Spoke Zarathustra, and these provoke laughter from his
listeners. Bergson's essay "Laughter" is characterized by repetition and inversion, techniques that it argues are the essential elements of comedy and meant to provoke laughter.

In Fielding's *Joseph Andrews* and *Tom Jones*, Thackeray's
Vanity Fair, and Meredith's *Ordeal of Richard Feverel* are elaborate studies of the history of comic literature, the meanings of
laughter, and the powers of mockery. There are explicit statements about laughter and the comic—some made by narrators,
some by major characters—and implicit evaluations of those
statements in the action of the plot. The plot itself is both a
comic narrative and a narrative about the comic, about what
Fielding characterized as the shifting "current of laughter," and
about the chronological development of comic forms and styles.
The novels are illustrations, evaluations, and elaborations of theory. And to the extent that the reader is provoked to laugh, then
presented with a statement about laughter, then provoked to
laugh again, then presented with a character who laughs, then

asked to reject laughter, he too participates in the meanings that the text seeks to demonstrate for him.

There is an equally elaborate synthesis of comedy and comic theory in the texts that appear to be straightforward analysis of laughter and the comic. Kierkegaard's extended study is contained within two interconnected comic performances: one is the philosophic clown show conducted by his pseudonyms in the so-called aesthetic authorship, the texts written by Johannes Climacus, Johannes Anti-Climacus, Hilarius Bookbinder, and their friends; the other is conducted by Kierkegaard himself in his journals and autobiographical essays, on the streets of Copenhagen, and in the houses of his friends—an even more elaborate philosophic clown show. The philosopher of the comic lives as a comedian in the world, all the while explaining the meanings of the comic for man in the world. Freud's study of the comic as a form of psychodynamic play is itself a playful book, a series of manifest Jewish jokes that hide Freud's contribution to the subject. This is his own latent Jewish joke, an elegant synthesis of philosophical concepts of play with psychological concepts of sexuality and the unconscious. Freud plays with play. And even some of the Anglo-American psychologists, those with interests in literature as well as science, write in a style that imitates Meredith's comic prose style. They too wish to provoke laughter from the reader, to demonstrate their own significant playfulness.

In all of these texts, comic theory and comic practice are as mingled as the kings and clowns of the hybrid drama of the Renaissance. To study some of these texts as literature and others as theory is to oversimplify the issues they raise and the statements they make. Early in *The Praise of Folly*, Folly tells her followers not to expect a definition or a division into parts of her subject matter, "the path worn by the common herd of rhetoricians." It would be wrong "to circumscribe within the narrow limits of a definition a person whose power extends so widely or to break up into separate pieces someone who enjoys the combined worship of all kinds of creatures" (12, 13). The demonstration is much more adequate to the subject than the definition, and the two together can be said to communicate the paradoxical nature of the material. And in his essay "The Idea of Comedy," Meredith wrote "I do not know that the fly in amber is of any particular use, but the comic idea enclosed in a comedy makes it more generally perceptible and portable, and that is an advantage" (56). When the comic idea is simply enclosed in an essay on comedy, it can be defined, explained, and evaluated, but when the comic idea can be enclosed in a comedy, it can be demonstrated as well, and the readers and spectators, to the extent to which they can be provoked to laugh, can be implicated in the process.

"At their best," Warwick Wadlington has argued, "critical and fictive thinking are not divergent, but convergent" (*Confidence Game*, 23). This study concerns a point of convergence in the history of ideas, between comedy and comic theory, between literature, philosophy, science, and philosophical science. The texts at this focal point are both elegantly conceived and elaborately structured, and the demands they make on the reader are substantial. At their best, critical and fictive thinking about the comic are convergent for another reason as well—they are mutually interdependent forms. Comic theory derives from comedy, makes its generalizations on the evidence supplied by comic drama and comic fiction, but comedy also derives from comic theory, builds its structures on the ideas supplied by comic criticism. One half of this relationship has been obvious to literary critics for a long time—the derivative nature of the theory—but the other half of the relationship is equally important—the derivative nature of the literature. Both *Twelfth Night* and *Volpone* are substantial elaborations and revisions of Erasmus's *Praise* and his three stages of the fool. In *Joseph Andrews* and *Tom Jones* Fielding combines not only Molière and Cervantes but also Hobbes and Shaftesbury, subjecting these theorists to a form of comic agon in which neither is victorious. Sterne's *Tristram Shandy* borrows equally from Fielding and Rabelais and from the major comic critics of the mid-eighteenth century, Morris and Hartley. Austen's *Pride and Prejudice*, as Alistair Duckworth has explained, takes the standard eighteenth-century theoretical arguments about laughter and makes them major aspects of the central characters, who can be seen then as acting out a theoretical problem. Thackeray's *Vanity Fair* and Meredith's *Ordeal of Richard Feverel* are similarly dependent on the comic theory of the mid-nineteenth century, which they expand upon. The complex nature of comic literature cannot be reduced to a handful of critical statements cribbed from the theorists; it must be seen as an elaborate reworking of such critical statements, a fictionalization or dramatization of theory. Between Meredith and the present this is true for a number of comic novels and comic dramas: James's *Portrait of a Lady*, Forster's *Room With a View*, Huxley's *Antic Hay*, Hesse's *Steppenwolf*, West's *Miss Lonelyhearts*, and Beckett's *Waiting for Godot*. Each of these works of literature contains significant commentary on laughter and the comic that is provocative and original, and each borrows substantially from other, much more straightforward commentary on laughter and the comic.

II

IN THE middle of his study of laughter and the laughable, ridicule, comedy, and the comic, their meanings as art, their functions in society, and their values for the individual, Bergson characterizes the comic as a labyrinth, "*le labyrinthe du comique*." His essay has a deceptively simple title—"Laughter," but for Bergson the most obvious fact about the subject is its complexity. "The greatest of thinkers, from Aristotle downwards, have tackled this little problem, which has a knack of baffling every effort, of slipping away and escaping only to bob up again, a pert challenge flung at philosophic speculation" (61). Taking up the challenge of the little problem that has stumped the greatest of thinkers, Bergson argues that he has found the solution, a concept described as a "particular mechanical arrangement" that can be perceived "as through a glass" [*par transparence*] within the limited truths of other explanations. "Disregard this arrangement," he warns the reader, "and you let go the only clue capable of guiding you through the

labyrinth of the comic" (116). The expression indicates intri-
cacy, difficulty, and intellectual adventure, and for those reasons
I have taken it for the title of this book. That the comic is a labyrinth is something that the most sensitive students of the subject
have realized: for some the metaphor simply indicates the comic's
complexity and confusion, while for others the comic is an actual labyrinth on the model of the maze crafted for the king of
Crete—symmetrical, dangerous, captivating—in which lurks
the monster of mockery that destroys all those who come after
it. A labyrinth is not only a tangle of contradictions and inversions, of paths that go nowhere and threads that disappear, but
it is also an order. This book is about the ways in which that
tangle has been ordered, the control that has been imposed on
very difficult material. As part of another philosophic inquiry
into the labyrinth of the comic that includes Baudelaire, Croce,
Pirandello, Breton, Duchamp, Camus, and Sartre, Bergson's essay is outside the scope of this study, but it is valuable for the
clues it provides about the labyrinth of the comic. What can be
perceived as through a glass in Bergson's hyperbole are some important truths about the comic and about the critics of the
comic. The greatest of thinkers have tackled this little problem,
dismissed the explanations offered before them, and confidently
proposed their own explanations, which in their turn have been
dismissed by the critics after them. Like Bergson, they have been
aware of the little subject's great difficulty, and like Bergson, they
have fallen victim to the labyrinth or to the monster that lurks
within the labyrinth, the force of mockery that cannot be described, defined, or otherwise controlled.

Bergson does not use the metaphor of labyrinth casually—it,
too, is a valuable piece of information for the reader, the only clue
capable of guiding him through Bergson's study of the labyrinth,
the essay itself. Inductive, repetitious, and circular, "Laughter"
is a journey into the labyrinth, with Bergson as Ariadne cautiously unraveling the thread of his argument, the particular mechanical arrangement. Starting from a few basic premises, Bergson builds his case slowly, returning again and again to the same
points, the same problems, but each time making increasingly

ambitious and wide-ranging statements about them as he circles toward the center. The middle of the essay contains the most complex parts of his argument. Then he pulls back again, and the points become much more trivial, almost incidental, as he moves toward the exit. At the very end, just as the reader is at the exit, Bergson suddenly indicates that he has failed. Comparing the way a small child grasps after a wave breaking on the beach to the way the philosopher grasps after laughter, he concludes that both find little substance, only bitter-tasting froth. Such a note of renunciation is surprising when the essay is read as straightforward analysis, but not when the essay is read as labyrinth. It is, after all, only a circular return to the very beginning of the essay as through a glass. The pert challenge that has escaped the grasp of the greatest of philosophers has bobbed up again in the metaphor of the wave that eludes the grasp of Bergson.

What is illustrated in this poetic contrast between excessively confident preface and excessively pessimistic conclusion are two techniques that Bergson discusses at length in the essay, repetition and inversion. The failure of all the great thinkers is repeated in the failure of Bergson. The confident Bergson is inverted by the defeated Bergson. Repetition and inversion, Bergson argues in the essay, are techniques of comedy, provocations to laughter. If that is so, then the essay titled "Laughter" is framed by a provocation to laughter and is itself a comic work—the labyrinth of the comic is a comic labyrinth. If we have made our way carefully enough in the labyrinth we should also be laughing. Bergson is testing us, for what is at issue is whether we can exit the labyrinth at all or will remain hopelessly lost in its mazes. But if we are laughing then our task has been hopelessly complicated, for it is by no means clear how much of the essay we should take seriously. For Bergson laughter is ridicule against the rigid and the false. How many other jokes might we find buried within the text? We are now really in the labyrinth of the comic, and there is no Ariadne in sight to guide us. Our guide, in fact, has turned into the monster of mockery that was to be tamed. As we exit the labyrinth at the precise point we have en-

tered, we are reminded again of failure, the impossibility of mas-
tering the material. But the statement of failure is very clever.
Having started with the failure of the greatest of thinkers, Bergson ends with his own and thereby anticipates what he must
know will be the inevitable judgment of history. Not only does
he minimize his readers' criticism in this manner, but by setting
up the repetition and the inversion between beginning and ending he is in fact depending on the statement of failure to reaffirm
his argument. A complex joke is thereby set in motion. If the
reader laughs, then Bergson is affirmed, for what he has had to
say about laughter is correct. And if the reader does not laugh,
does not see the repetition and inversion that encloses the essay,
then Bergson laughs at the reader, who has clearly not understood the argument, and once again, Bergson is affirmed. What
we are finally left with is affirmation/denial, insight/obscurity,
joking/seriousness, an Ariadne who is not trustworthy, and the
possibilities that the reader is laughing at Bergson in rejecting
the theory, that Bergson is laughing at the reader who does not
understand the not-so-hidden joke, or that reader and author
are laughing together if the joke is properly perceived. Bergson's
contribution to the study of the comic is sometimes reduced to
the phrase "something mechanical encrusted on the living" (84),
but that is to take a statement of the clue for the problem it is
meant to explore, the labyrinth itself.

For all of the writers and critics examined in this book, the
comic is either labyrinth or labyrinthine. Like Bergson they
come before the unwary reader as Ariadne, unraveling a strand
of argument, connecting a series of clues, proving their own
adeptness with the material. Almost all of them cannot resist the
temptation to become tricky, to demonstrate mastery of the
comic. The narrator of *Joseph Andrews* tries earnestly to control
the current of laughter, and fails. The narrator of *Tom Jones*, devious and untrustworthy, leads the reader on a merry romp
through an elegantly symmetrical text of mirrors, inversions,
and repetitions—a perfect labyrinth. Kierkegaard and his personas hide behind mirrors, inverting and subverting their positions toward the comic, and tracing out involved labyrinthine

arguments and a thread of clues that can only be recovered with the greatest of difficulty. The narrator of *Vanity Fair* takes up Fielding's project, as does the narrator of *Richard Feverel*, borrowing and mirroring elements of *Tom Jones* to create their own labyrinths, but with very different results. Thackeray's narrator successfully navigates the maze; Meredith's does not. The Anglo-American psychologists attempt to explain clearly what all the others do not, but even some of them get tangled in the labyrinth, and begin sounding more like Meredith than like scientists. Freud's *Jokes and Their Relation to the Unconscious*, with its multiple levels of meaning, its manifest jokes, and its latent joke, is an elegantly structured text, a synthesis of science and aesthetics. The reader cannot fully understand it until he learns, in Freud's specialized sense of the term, to play.

No single metaphor describes a view of the comic shared by all writers and critics, and therefore the title of this book applies more specifically to some of the texts than it does to others. But like Bergson, all of them are in the labyrinth of the comic. Those who fashion themselves as Ariadnes—Fielding, Kierkegaard, Thackeray, and Meredith—continually flash another metaphor at the reader—the mirror. Long associated with comedy—originally attributed to Cicero in the Donatine fragment, "comedy is an imitation of life, a mirror of custom, an image of truth" (Lauter, *Theories of Comedy*, 27)—the metaphor of the mirror is common enough both in comic literature and in comic theory. It is of incidental use to Fielding in *Joseph Andrews* but is a major structuring device in *Tom Jones*, a text that is a fearful symmetry of mirrors—of repeating, inverting, mocking mirrors— which control plot structure and character development. A half century later Schlegel based his conception of romantic irony on a similar concept of the mirror: that romantic poets animated by irony and humor would become "like the epic, a mirror of the whole circumambient world." Hovering on "the wings of poet reflection," this poetry would "raise that reflection again and again to a higher power, . . . multiply it in an endless succession of mirrors" (*Lucinde and the Fragments*, 175). This movement Schlegel characterized as "transcendental buffoonery," the "mimic style of an averagely gifted Italian *buffo*," but also as the greatest achievement of philosophy and of art (148). Whirling in such mirrors, Schlegel proposed, was romantic irony, the stance toward the world that all writers would need to take in order to become poets and that the best philosophers had always known to take in order to find truth. Following Schlegel, Kierkegaard conceived his project as transcendental buffoonery, and whirling in his own set of mirrors, applied the mimic style of the averagely gifted circus clown to the problems of philosophy, literature, and religion. Following Fielding, Thackeray took up the image of the mirror in *Vanity Fair*, turning his text into a reflexive trick of mirror images, and following both Fielding and Thackeray, Meredith turned *Richard Feverel* into an intricate labyrinth of mirrors. For all of these authors the mirror is one of the clues offered to the reader who would make his way into the maze of their texts. And as such it is a tool I have taken from these various Ariadnes to understand the labyrinth myself.

Mirrors of course have important associations in other fields, in theories of mimesis and analyses of narcissism, for example. In Abrams' *The Mirror and the Lamp* there are only two sentences devoted to the connections to comedy. For Lacan, however, in his study of the mirror phase of infantile development, the baby laughs just at the moment when it makes the crucial identification of self in the mirror, and for Sartre, in his study of Flaubert, *L'Idiot de la famille*, the section "*Le miroir et le rire*" is the clue to Flaubert's own psychologically complex development. "Go look in your mirror and tell me if you don't have a great desire to laugh," Flaubert reportedly writes a friend. "So much the worse for you if you don't" (1:681).

III

COMIC THEORY has received relatively little critical attention, far less than theories about more serious subjects. Even in periods when theory occupies a privileged position in academic inquiry, as it does at the present time in literary criticism, there is almost no interest in what the greatest of thinkers have had to say about the comic. There are good reasons for this. Because the critics of the comic dismiss each other's work, begin as Bergson begins because everyone else has failed, it is easy enough to see the field as a 2,500-year tradition of inadequate explanation. Because the most fundamental questions are about the true meaning of laughter and the essential element of the comic, the field can resemble a very contentious contest over a highly specialized topic. Because comic theory appears to be so obviously derived from comic literature, at least from the point of view of literary critics, it has been seen as much less significant than the basic comic texts themselves, to which the critic must return. Because comic theory is perceived as a set of generalizations meant to apply to a great number of comic texts, the lowest denominator of the comic, it can be dismissed as a hindrance to an understanding of the uniqueness of an individual comic text. And because, as Plessner argues in his phenomenological study *Laughing and Crying*, the comic is so "ambiguous and paradoxical," it defies all our abilities to understand it. "We put up with it, but leave it to itself: we don't take it seriously" (88).

By demonstrating the extent to which major comic authors have been involved with their own theoretical inquiries into laughter and the comic, not only in incidental essays but in the best comic novels, and by presenting the complex literary qualities of the major theoretical studies of the comic within other nonliterary disciplines, I mean to make the case for comic theory. It is not marginal, trivial, or highly specialized. To paraphrase Bergson once more, the greatest of thinkers, from Aristotle downward, have been convinced of the little subject's considerable importance. That they have not written as extensively on the comic as they have on the tragic, or as extensively on laughter as they have on grief and despair is an indication that civilization has always placed a greater value on the serious, something many of these thinkers have seen as a tragic mistake. Bakhtin argued in *Rabelais and His World* that by this valuation on the serious, civilization has beaten a free people into submission. And at almost the same time Kenneth Burke was arguing in *Attitudes Toward History* that civilization would finally be destroyed unless it could adopt a comic attitude: a mode of acceptance, accommodation and celebration. "Mankind's only hope," he wrote, "is a cult of comedy" (*Language as Symbolic Action*, 20). And as part of his revaluation of all values, Nietzsche too claimed a great importance for laughter in the destruction of the old Judeo-Christian world order. The overman laughs. What other critics and philosophers have argued for, somewhat less grandly, is the balance of comedy and seriousness at the center of existence. "Existence itself, the act of existing, is both pathetic and comic in the same degree," Kierkegaard wrote in the *Concluding Unscientific Postscript* (84). In *The Eighteenth Brumaire of Louis Bonaparte*, Marx argued that history was a dialectic of tragedy and farce, of revolution and counter-revolution. For him Louis Bonaparte was the comic counter-revolutionary, the farcical repetition of the tragic heroes of the French Revolution and the serious repetition of Falstaff from *I Henry IV*. In *Jokes and Their Relation to the Unconscious*, Freud uncovered the opposition play/seriousness at the heart of the joke, and later he posited the same opposition, pleasure principle/reality principle, at the center of human culture.

For Kierkegaard and for Freud, the comic has one other connection to seriousness, the tie to suffering. "The more one suffers," Kierkegaard wrote in *Stages on Life's Way*, "the more, I believe, has one a sense for the comic. It is only by the deepest suffering that one acquires true authority in the use of the comic" (231). In his essay "Humor," Freud wrote that humor was one of the highest psychical achievements. "Its fending off the possibility of suffering places it among the great series of methods which the human mind has constructed to evade the compulsion to suffer" (163). The German and German-influenced philosophers of the nineteenth century share a conviction of the importance of laughter, humor, and the comic, which originates in their common inheritance from Kant, whose sense of the world as a contradiction between noumena and phenomena and whose definition of the comic as response to contradiction invited those who came after him to make the connection. But this kind of interest in laughter and the varieties of the comic is by no means limited to this century of German philosophy from Kant to Freud. For both Hobbes, who described laughter as a sign of superiority, and Shaftesbury, who described laughter as a sign of sympathy and fellow feeling, the behavior was an indication of human nature. Fielding too urged his readers to learn how to laugh, and in *Joseph Andrews* and *Tom Jones*, where he connects comedy to morality and laughter to Christianity, the correct comic attitude becomes the path to religion. When Carlyle wrote, "How much lies in Laughter: the cipher-key, wherewith we decipher the whole man!" in *Sartor Resartus* (24), he was making explicit what he had learned from English comedy and from German philosophy. For Meredith laughter was the cipher key to personality; and for Herbert Spencer it was the cipher key to physiology. For Bergson laughter was the force that ridiculed mechanical rigidity and thus allowed for the flexibility essential to human life; and for Bakhtin comedy, the least serious form of world literature, revealed the most serious meanings of world history, the destruction of the people's folk humor and with it their freedom. "Laughter has a deep philosophical meaning," Bakhtin wrote in *Rabelais and His World*; "it is one of the essential forms of truth concerning the world as a whole, concerning history and man. . . . Certain essential aspects of the world are accessible only to laughter" (66). And at the end of the book he added, "All the acts of the drama of world history were performed before a chorus of laughing people. Without hearing this chorus we cannot understand the drama as a whole" (474).

IV

IN HIS book on Rabelais, Bakhtin gives prominence to this statement by Alexander Herzen: "It would be extremely interesting to write the history of laughter" (59). This book, too, is a project in that history. There are few simple starting points in the history of laughter and the comic and only two that are relatively straightforward. Plato and Aristotle produced the first important arguments about laughter and comedy, but their commentaries are fragmentary, and Aristotle's poetics on comedy has disappeared altogether, leaving only a single dubious trace, the so-called "Coislinian Tractate." Erasmus produced the first important argument about laughter and comedy in the Renaissance, and the first synthesis of theory and practice, but its meanings are by no means clear, and Erasmus himself had to explain some of his intentions in the book in the letter to Martin Dorp.

I begin this study with Fielding and the shift from comic drama to comic fiction, because it is impossible to understand the great nineteenth-century studies of the comic without first understanding *Joseph Andrews* and *Tom Jones*. These two novels are in their own right the first great studies of comedy and laughter written in English, far more elaborate, considered, and significant than any play with a metacomic subplot or any explicit essay on the subject. They did change the ways in which mockery was understood. When Fielding created the English comic novel he developed what had been clear in Cervantes, the connection between comedy and consciousness, and that has been the preoccupation of the writers and critics who have come after him. Two traditions derive from Fielding: the English comic novel with its reflexive subplot about comedy and laughter, and the study of comedy and laughter in German and Danish philosophy. Both traditions are preoccupied with the ways in which human consciousness is comic, or comic and serious in equal measure.

The rambling narrative voice of Fielding's personas, alternately cranky and polite, exciting and boring, serious and jocular, demonstrated the incongruous nature of human thought processes, what the comic drama by its very nature could neither present nor even uncover. On the stage the author disappears once the prologue has been recited. In the novel the author is present all the time, mediating between reader and action, and what can be comic is both the action and the mediating presence of the narrator. What happened when Fielding, pushed by politics and history, moved from the drama to the novel was this shift to the comic narrator. As the author tells his story he becomes as interesting as the story itself—he stumbles, lies, forgets, changes moods, tries to provoke laughter, tries to provoke tears, comments on himself. His performance is contradictory and incongruous.

During the eighteenth century, as Fielding was writing, the prevailing definitions of the comic shifted from arguments about superiority (the position of Hobbes) and arguments about sympathy (the position of Shaftesbury and Addison) to arguments about incongruity. This was the position of a number of mid-century critics given a grand statement by Kant in the *Critique of Judgment* in 1790. What Fielding made clear in his novels was that neither Hobbes nor Shaftesbury was right—consciousness itself was comic, comic because of its incongruous nature. This is an important moment in the history of laughter, for thereby the subject gains a new status—the comic is neither an unpleasant characteristic of men and women, which reminds us of our baseness, nor an incredibly rosy characteristic, which attempts to convince us of our loving kindness. It is, however, a fundamental quality shared by everyone, an essential attribute of our consciousness, of the patterns of human thought.

Certainly Fielding could not have developed his self-conscious narrators without reference to Cervantes, but in the mid-eighteenth century there was need for a new understanding of the comic, and what Fielding demonstrated was almost immediately appropriated by others, first by Sterne and Smollett, then by Schlegel and the German romantics. In *Satire and the Novel in Eighteenth-Century England*, Ronald Paulson argues that the standard rationale for comedy (which had been the same as for satire), that it ridicules and thereby reforms behavior, was no longer a credible argument by Fielding's time. Paulson argues that Fielding balanced Hobbes and Shaftesbury in his novels, trying to find a mean between them that would give him a new rationale. The point is important. However, in the shift from drama to fiction, the comic necessarily underwent a major re-emphasis. There are other self-conscious comic narrators before Fielding, in Swift as well as in Cervantes, but it is with Fielding that the history of laughter enters upon a new phase, one dominated by the novel, not the drama. Bakhtin argues that novels are basically parodic; that they contain within themselves a strong element of laughter and mockery; that novels lend themselves to the comic to a much greater degree than other literary genres. Unmasking literary codes, they call attention to themselves as works of literature. For Fielding, certainly, the comic novel was a much greater achievement than the drama, and after him the primary form of English comedy is fiction, not drama. Robert Alter begins his study of the self-conscious novel, *Partial Magic*, with Cervantes—his point is that *Don Quixote* initiates the genre, which can be either comic or serious. What I argue here is not that the comic novel is self-conscious, which of course it is, as are the comic drama and the comic oration, but that consciousness itself is comic. It is this point, clearly made by Fielding, that changes the history of comedy and laughter. It is taken up in turn by Sterne and Smollett, by Schlegel, Richter, and Hegel, by Thackeray and Meredith, by Kierkegaard and Freud. Significantly, it is denied by many of the Anglo-American scientists, who have difficulty with the notion of consciousness, and then it is inverted by Freud, who connects comedy to the unconscious.

V

ALTHOUGH most scholarship on the theory and practice of the comic during the eighteenth and nineteenth centuries explains this period in terms of a gradual shift from amiable humor to bitter wit, the texts themselves are not this neat and tidy. Such a relatively uncomplicated linear development obscures at least as much as it explains, in part because it misreads the work of a writer like Fielding, who sought to balance amiability and bitter wit; in part because it focuses attention on what was for the writers and critics involved only one aspect of an extremely complex subject. Between Fielding's *Joseph Andrews* in 1742 and Freud's *Jokes and Their Relation to the Unconscious* in 1905, other issues are at least as important as the matter of amiability and bitterness: the relationship between comedy and consciousness that establishes a new basis for the significance of the subject; the relationship between comedy, morality, and religion that explains the ethical value of the subject; the notion of a shifting current of laughter that turns against the mocker, confounding his ability to master the subject; the metaphor of the comic labyrinth that traps the unwary individual who would understand the subject; the image of the comic mirror that repeats, inverts, and mocks all literary, philosophic, and psychological meanings. A more accurate intellectual history of laughter and the comic can be recovered by following this entire grouping of concepts and metaphors as they are adapted by novelists, philosophers, scientists, and psychologists between Fielding and Freud.

Therefore, no simple model of historical change is imposed on this study, although both the continuity and the change are carefully considered in the chapters that follow. For Fielding, who is preoccupied with all of these concepts, comedy is the essential characteristic of human consciousness, and mockery is the force that must be brought under control by the comic novelist. In *Joseph Andrews* the problem is clearly set out—the narrator attempts to master the shifting current of laughter and fails. In *Tom Jones* the problem is solved—the narrator imposes a set of intricate comic structures onto this shifting current, including an allegory of the history of comic forms and the labyrinth of mocking mirrors. The effect finally is to align comedy with Christian morality and to attempt a balance between Shaftesburian good humor and Hobbesian bad. For Kierkegaard, following Schlegel and the German romantics, comedy is the essential characteristic of all five stages of human consciousness, and mockery is the force that must be brought under control by the philosopher, the poet, and the religious Christian. Each uses mockery for different but equally vital purposes, and Kierkegaard himself, who combines all three, connects his own existence in the world to his mastery of mockery. The mirror remains a crucial image for Kierkegaard, whose pseudonyms enact a labyrinth meant to defy the reader. What was for Fielding a relatively simple shifting current of laughter becomes for Kierkegaard a dazzling demonstration of mockers mocked at all the stages along life's way. For Thackeray and for Meredith the

mirror is once again the central device, and both turn it against
Fielding to rewrite his comic epic. Both refine Fielding's arguments, though in entirely different ways, and both amend his allegory of comic history for their own purposes. In *Vanity Fair*
the comic nature of English history and the history of English
comedy are multiple layers of the novelistic consciousness that
mirror and invert each other. Comedy ridicules English history,
but history also ridicules English comedy—the follies and vices
of each are exposed. In *The Ordeal of Richard Feverel, Tom
Jones* is carefully and mockingly mirrored and inverted. The
current of laughter shifts against Fielding, as bad laughers now
prevail over good, and Christian morality is destroyed, along
with Meredith's narrator and central character. The labyrinth
that Fielding mastered returns in mirrored form and regains
its secret.

In 1859, as Meredith was deconstructing what Fielding had
constructed with such care, thereby announcing the bankruptcy
of such literary visions of the comic, Anglo-American psychologists, physiologists, and evolutionary biologists began offering
their own accounts of laughter and the comic. Far more reductive and pragmatic than the theories of the novelists and philosophers, this scientific discourse is quite different from the other
discourses presented here, but it is just as important. Following
Darwin, laughter is described as a survival instinct, and the
paradigm established by Fielding about comedy and consciousness is altered. With Freud, who relates the comic to the unconscious, it is altered again. What for Fielding was a close tie to
Christian morality becomes for Freud a close tie to Jewish identity. The concepts of the comic have changed dramatically, although the sexual joking remains, along with the conviction
that such joking is ethically meaningful.

Joseph Andrews and *Jokes and Their Relation to the Unconscious* frame this book about comedy and comic theory. Both
alternate between provocations to laugh and studies of the laugh,
and both present systematic challenges to the criticism of the
comic inherited by the authors. For Fielding this criticism is the
theory from classical Greece and Rome, and the British theory

from Sidney to Addison; for Freud it is German aesthetic theory from Kant to Groos, and Anglo-American psychological theory from Darwin to Sully. And just as Fielding established a new emphasis for the understanding of the comic, so did Freud. Contained within the comic novel is an extensive study of the comic; contained within the study of the comic is a demonstration of comic play and of the Jewish joke. The two works perfectly mirror each other.

2

Joseph Andrews: The Current of Laughter

"DO THOU Kindly take me by the Hand, and lead me through all the Mazes, the winding Labyrinths of Nature," the narrator of *Tom Jones* asks in a formal invocation to Genius at the beginning of book 13. Like Jones himself, who has lost his way in book 12 with a guide who does not know the road to Coventry, the narrator feels himself falter as his novel approaches London. His address to Genius is suspect, however, because he has done perfectly well without her up to this point, two-thirds of the way through his story, and because his request follows a mocking invocation to the muses of serious poetry and the Grub Street hacks, an "ill-yoked Pair, this lean Shadow and this Fat Substance," and these two he appears to value equally. When he turns to Genius, however, and identifies her as the source of mockery, the inspiration for Aristophanes, Lucian, Cervantes, Rabelais, Molière, Shakespeare, Swift, and Marivaux, his mockery stops, for even if he can't get the chronological order exactly right he can rattle off the great tradition of mockery in which Fielding clearly wished to place himself. The narrator requests the skill to "strip off" the disguises of men in order to show them what they really are—"the Objects only of Ridicule, for deceiving themselves." But what he first names as ridicule he then renames as humor. "Fill my pages with Humour," he asks her, so that I can teach mankind "the Good-Nature to laugh only at the Follies of others, and the Humility to grieve at their own" (685–86). Any eighteenth-century reader should have been sensitive to the contrasting meanings of ridicule, harsh and rejecting, and humor, sympathetic and good-natured, as indeed Fielding was, but the narrator without explanation simply conflates the two, yoking them by violence together much as he has yoked the muses of poetry and dullness. These contrasting comic styles he also appears to value equally. He wants his novel to teach readers the proper way to laugh, but he can barely explain the nature of the project without getting lost in terminological and conceptual alternatives. Losing control of language, the only tool available to him, the narrator turns understandably to the Genius behind the comic tradition for some guidance, even though it has been from following in the paths of writers like Cervantes, Molière, and Swift, to say nothing of Addison, Shaftesbury, and Hobbes, that he has found himself in this maze to begin with. The distinctions between ridicule and humor that momentarily trap him here are but a small part of the difficulties they present to any writer who would make his way after them into the labyrinth of the comic.

This is a small moment in a very large novel, but it is indicative of the problems that face the narrator throughout, and while there are many layers to the maze and labyrinth that is *Tom Jones*, none is more important to the narrator and thus to the reader than the labyrinth of the comic. He identifies his story as comedy, his style as comic, his purpose to teach proper laughter, much as the narrator of *Joseph Andrews* has done before him, but in the labyrinth of the comic he does not find it easy to make his way. He tells Genius that it is a "winding Labyrinth of Nature," taking no responsibility for its creation, but *Tom Jones* is a greater and more complex novel than that. Fielding created it as a labyrinth. It does not simply reflect the kinds of comic alternatives that Fielding inherited from the traditions of satire and humor—it makes them into a comic labyrinth of intricate shape and proportions, a novel that is simultaneously comic and about the comic, that raises questions about ridicule, humor, laughter and the comic in discussion and in demonstration, contrasting and combining practice and theory, events and concepts, offering a series of tentative answers for the reader whose only guide is not Genius herself but the confused and confusing narrator.

The labyrinth of the comic preoccupied Fielding for most of his productive life—he wrote plays, novels, essays, even poetry about the comic, taking virtually every position, mocking comic playwrights in his plays, comic authors in his novels, comic theorists in his essays, returning again and again obsessively to the nature of mockery. He seems sometimes to be very serious about the comic, sometimes very comic about the serious, sometimes comic about the comic, sometimes serious about the serious. It is not simply that Fielding contradicts himself, a position that critics have argued for some time, but that he takes every possible position toward the comic, sometimes contradicting and sometimes combining, moving between satiric laughter, genial laughter, true laughter, false laughter, and the total absence of laughter; between the position of the mocker and the position of the one mocked. And in the process he is constantly questioning and evaluating the nature of this comedy, wit, humor, raillery, satire, and mockery. As Captain Hercules Vinegar he wrote in a *Champion* essay (no. 52) that he often delighted in turning ridicule against the ridiculer. "I am always apt, at such times, to pity the person who is thus turned into ridicule, and seldom or never join the laugh against him. Nay, it is not unusual with me, to attack the turnspit himself, in which I have been often so successful, that I have turned the whole current of laughter that way" (243). Because Fielding is so expert in turning the current of laughter it is not always easy to decide when his personas speak positions he himself holds, but in this case Vinegar accurately describes the nature of Fielding's comic art, the constant turning of laughter itself, the mockery of mockery. In his "Essay on the Knowledge of the Characters of Men," published under his own name in 1743, Fielding described the way laughter can slowly change "in a good and delicate mind" from harshness to compassion, as the mocker begins to understand how the one mocked may be suffering (287). "No Man is so good a Judge of the true Merits of a Cause, as he who hath been on both sides of it," Fielding wrote as Vinegar in another *Champion* essay (12 January 1739–40, 150–51). If the statement is amended to read "all" sides, for in Fielding the contrasts multiply and in *Tom Jones* they appear to multiply toward infinity, then Vinegar describes the way in which Fielding constructed a great labyrinth of the comic around himself, one that effectively includes all his published literature and literary criticism: the two comic novels; the burlesque, mock heroic, and farcical drama; the satire *Jonathan Wild*; and even *Amelia*, the sentimental melodrama that is the total negation of all ridicule and mockery. Certain texts, however, particularly *Joseph Andrews* and *Tom Jones*, the great comic novels on which Fielding's reputation depends, are more important to an understanding of this comic labyrinth and his claim for joining the tradition of Aristophanes, Lucian, and the others. Of the two novels, *Tom Jones* is the labyrinth at the heart of the labyrinth, itself in miniature a model of the complete works.

Fielding's method in the novels and in the relationships between texts can be described; his dialectical dancing through the maze can be traced and admired, but there are very few conclusions that can be finally drawn about his attitude to the comic beyond the sense that the comic's true value is the process, these wanderings about in the labyrinth. That is the real entertainment. No statement that Fielding ever made about the comic, and he made a great many, is finally reliable, although some certainly seem more convincing and more firmly held. In the essays, for example, he insists again and again on the value of moderation rather than excess, on the mean between extremes, sometimes with special reference to laughter, but in *Tom Jones* it is Blifil who has the speech to make in praise of moderation and Jones himself represents the vitality of excess. And while both novels are full of characters who are too grave or too gay, who laugh too little or too much, virtually no one can manage to find a workable mean between the extremes, least of all the narrators who try valiantly to alternate between comic and serious styles, but in fact get carried off in the seductiveness of their own mockery. The narrators of *Joseph Andrews* and *Tom Jones* repeat a great many critical homilies about laughter and the comic, but even when they appear to speak with Fielding's authority their statements cannot be accepted at face value. In the author's preface to *Joseph Andrews*, the narrator complains that the ridiculous has been "wonderfully . . . mistaken even by Writers who have profess'd it" when they have claimed that true vice can be the proper subject of ridicule (7). Ridicule must be limited to folly and affectation, he insists, and while he appears to speak here as Fielding, before the story starts, he is really jibing at Fielding, who in 1737 had defended "Pasquin" from attack by claiming that laughter was an effective weapon against vice and sometimes the most effective weapon (*Common Sense*, 103–4). It is not simply that Fielding makes fun of his narrators by making them fallible, but that he allows them to make fun of himself as well. In such a labyrinth all authorities are brought into question and anyone who claims to understand the comic finds himself the object of the comic. Later in the novel, the narrator pompously insists that the comic novel is to be a mirror that will allow his readers to contemplate their own deformities in private and so correct them—another bit of conventional wisdom about the comic—but a short time later when he shows Lady Booby and Pamela peering into mirrors, characters who are very much in need of recognizing and correcting deformities, they see nothing. Mirrors apparently don't work after all (294).

We are practiced at identifying texts that mock the serious, at tracing the ways *Joseph Andrews* mocks *Pamela* and mocks Cibber, but we are much weaker at identifying texts that mock the comic; we lack a critical vocabulary even to describe the process, although comic writers turn the mirror onto themselves even as they show us that their characters do not. "I defy the wisest Man in the World to turn a true good Action into Ridicule," Joseph Andrews tells Fanny and Parson Adams; "I defy him to do it. He who should endeavour it, would be laughed at himself, instead of making others laugh" (234). The sentiment echoes precisely the narrator's sentiments in the author's preface, but now the narrator rises to Joseph's challenge and shows that the Parson has fallen asleep listening to Joseph's comic pontifications. The allusion may be to Plato's *Symposium* where Aristophanes falls asleep listening to Socrates define comedy, but even if the reader does not follow Fielding backward into the history of comic texts, he is caught in the changing currents of laughter, the mockery of mockery. That Fielding would finally write a novel like *Amelia* should not then be surprising, for just as the comic has the power to destroy the serious it also has the power to destroy itself. A half century after Fielding, Hegel was to argue exactly such a point in his lectures on art, defining irony as infinite absolute negativity, and comedy as the final form of art, which, after destroying all other forms of poetry, would consume itself. Hegel saw the rise of philosophy replacing it, but for Fielding movement was circular rather than developmental, a journey through a labyrinth without end. "I cannot fairly, I think, be represented as an enemy to Laughter," Fielding wrote in 1752, a year after *Amelia*, "or to all those kinds of writing that are apt to promote it" (*Covent Garden Journal*, no. 10, 112). That statement too should not be surprising nor should the fact that Fielding felt compelled to make it, given the deep ambivalence he felt all his life toward the varieties of mockery. He made it, of course, not as Henry Fielding but as Sir Alexander Drawcansir, a pseudonym he adopted from Buckingham's play *The Rehearsal*. The object of laughter as a character in another's comic drama, Fielding's Drawcansir should have understood its power.

II

JOSEPH ANDREWS is Fielding's first sustained study of laughter and its power, a text that alternates between statements about laughter, ridicule, and the comic, and a story that constantly tests those statements. It begins with an apparently straightforward author's preface, Fielding's most widely read statement about comedy and laughter, which is often used as a guide to the comic nature of the novel. But it is not a reliable guide and does not accurately describe the nature of *Joseph Andrews* or of any of Fielding's other complex comic texts. The first false clue in the first comic epic poem in prose, the preface is a collection of critical homilies about laughter and the comic that the narrator thinks he must follow; but what he discovers when he comes to write the story is the impossibility of following such limiting rules. One of the ways the novel is comic, then, is in its mockery of the precepts about the comic in the preface. The preface is a clue to the novel's meanings, but it is not until the reader has finished the novel that he can properly understand how it functions in the critical/fictional text.

It does appear ordinary enough. Following the pattern of the comic drama, which typically begins with a prologue, the narrator of the novel begins with an author's preface in which he defines the new genre of literature, the comic epic poem in prose; positions it in the context of other more traditional genres—epic, drama, romance, burlesque; describes its subject matter—affectation; and then explains how ridicule functions against that subject matter. He justifies this critical exercise because he tells us he is worried that the "mere *English* reader" will not be familiar with "this kind of Writing, which I do not remember to have seen hitherto attempted in our Language" (3), but the story he is about to tell mimics Cervantes (in books 1, 2, and 3) and Molière (in book 4) so carefully that he must really assume this mere English reader is almost illiterate, someone who has managed to remain unaware of the classics of comic literature. This is curious because at the same time he does assume this reader will know Richardson's *Pamela* and Cibber's *Apology* as well as the standard literary devices of the classical epic, and he also assumes that this reader will be familiar with the uses and abuses of ridicule in literature.

But even if this reader found the genre unfamiliar and needed a guide, if he had had any literary education he would have found the preface all too familiar—it is little more than a collection of the most conventional statements on the comic cribbed from Aristotle, Plato, Cicero, Donatus, Sidney, Jonson, Dryden, Molière, Congreve, Shaftesbury and Addison. In 1751, Dr.

Johnson complained in a *Rambler* essay that the comic was extremely difficult to define, but had he appreciated Fielding more he might have recognized the preface as the closest thing to an encyclopedia entry on the subject that the eighteenth century could have produced. There is virtually nothing original in it *at all*, and it is perhaps for that reason that the narrator hoped his reader would be uneducated. With the exception of Hobbes, whose presence is felt throughout the story oppositionally and against whose views of laughter the narrator argues in the preface, the essay is simply a selection taken from the major critics of comedy, humor, and laughter most accessible to the educated English reader of 1742. While the narrator acknowledges Aristotle and Shaftesbury, though not the extent of his borrowings, he passes the other observations off as his own. Such borrowings are not unusual in the tradition of comic theory—from Cicero to Northrop Frye, critics have stolen from each other with impunity—but the fact that virtually all of the preface is borrowed is important, since it makes it much less likely that the narrator or Fielding believed these statements or could write according to these rules. Given the violent attacks the narrator of *Tom Jones* later makes on critics and their rules, it is difficult to know just how seriously the reader is to take this particular selection from the rules. Mouthing the platitudes of others, the narrator of *Joseph Andrews* does demonstrate mastery of the essay on the comic, but whether this essay should also be taken as comic itself will not be clear until the reader can make his way into his story. Afraid that he will get lost in the labyrinth, the narrator has unrolled a thread for him to follow, but it is of suspicious quality.

Many of the statements this narrator makes either in the preface or in the critical chapters that start the first three books are so common in the history of comic criticism that it would be impossible to identify the first place the concept appears. The notion of comedy as a mirror comes to Fielding from Donatus, who attributes it to Cicero; the notion of comedy as a mean between extremes, used extensively by the narrator in the preface to locate this new genre, comes from Aristotle in the *Ethics*,

though Fielding would also have learned it more recently from
Molière; the notion of comedy as a "true history" derives from
Lucian. Other positions that the narrator takes echo less universal sentiments or occur in texts that Fielding so clearly knew
that attribution is somewhat easier. Following Aristotle in the
Poetics, the narrator limits ridicule to defects that are not painful or destructive, and following Plato in the *Philebus*, he describes the ridiculous as the absence of self-knowledge. He repeats Cicero's argument from *De Oratore* that neither great vice
nor great misery should be made the subjects of ridicule, and Sir
Philip Sidney's argument in the *Defense of Poesie* that men all
too easily laugh at what is deformed and must be taught instead
to mix laughter with a kind of delightful teaching. Like Ben Jonson in the prologue to *Volpone*, the narrator dismisses slapstick
and buffoonery, and like Dryden in his preface to *An Evening's
Love*, he distinguishes between farce and true comedy. Following Molière in the "Critique of the School for Wives," he argues
that comedy is more difficult to compose than tragedy and for
identical reasons: we expect the comic poet to copy nature but
make no similar demands of the tragic poet. Like Congreve in
his "Letter to Mr. Dennis Concerning Humour in Comedy," the
narrator dismisses unnatural grotesques as the proper subjects
of comedy and defines affectation as that which is unnatural in
man and must be made the subject of ridicule. Like Shaftesbury
in the "Essay on the Freedom of Wit and Humour," the narrator
believes one must ridicule folly but recommend wisdom and virtue with pleasantry and mirth—indeed, this becomes his method
of characterizing Parson Adams in the story, and it is a place
where the narrator does write according to the rules. Repeating
Addison in *Spectator* papers 249, 446, and 494, the narrator divides ridicule into comedy and burlesque, discusses the proper
and improper subjects of mirth, and considers the connections
between mirth and religion. In chapter 1, book 1, he talks of instruction mixed with delight, the critical commonplace that derives from Horace's *Art of Poetry*. In chapter 1, book 2, he discusses divisions in writing and compares the spaces between
chapters to inns, resting places for readers, an analogy that de-

rives from a much less well-known fragment of Democritus: "The life without festival is a long road without an inn" (Freeman, *Pre-Socratic Philosophers*, 112). And in chapter 1, book 3, he compares the comic author to the historian, a comparison common in comic criticism since its first statement in Aristotle's *Poetics*. What is true of the narrator throughout *Joseph Andrews* is also true of his central characters when they too become critics of the comic; and when Joseph explains that nothing true can be ridiculed without itself stirring ridicule against the ridiculer, he is simply repeating Shaftesbury.

It is not so much the relatively straightforward content that is valuable in the preface and the three critical chapters as it is the ways in which the narrator and his central characters position themselves within this conventional wisdom. In the preface the narrator contradicts himself once, first dismissing burlesque as the literature of the unnatural and the monstrous, then praising the burlesque at least in diction, because "it contributes more to exquisite Mirth and Laughter than any other; and as these are probably more wholesome Physic for the Mind, and conduce better to purge away Spleen, Melancholy, and ill Affections, than is generally imagined" (5). The narrator here is moving between two mutually exclusive positions toward the comic, much as the narrator of *Tom Jones* moves between ridicule and humor—the current of laughter is shifting in front of us. Neither position is original with the narrator of *Joseph Andrews*: the first he inherits from Shaftesbury, the second from Burton in the *Anatomy of Melancholy* and Udall in the preface to *Ralph Roister Doister*. What is original is the movement between positions and that the movement itself becomes the object of our attention.

There is also a major shift in the preface itself from an objective description of the comic epic poem in prose to an emotionally charged prescription for correct laughter. After we are told about the nature of this new literature we are told how we *must* read it. "Surely he hath a very ill-framed Mind, who can look on Ugliness, Infirmity, or Poverty, as ridiculous in themselves," the narrator warns his mere English reader, and he follows with a set of examples. Were we to see a dirty fellow riding a cart we would find nothing ridiculous, but if he were to emerge from a coach-and-six, we "would then begin to laugh, and with justice." A poor starving family "would not incline us to Laughter (at least we must have very diabolical Natures if it would)," but if the family placed flowers on its empty coal grate or showed other signs of affectation of riches, "we might then indeed be excused, for ridiculing so fantastical an Appearance" (9).

If the narrator intends this comic epic poem in prose to teach us the correct way of laughter then we must first be laughing badly. The prologues of the comic drama typically discuss mirth and laughter—the prologue to *Volpone*, for example, tells us that the comedy will be refined, that the author will respect critical rules, and that our cheeks will be made "red with laughter" so that they will "look fresh a week after." But the narrator of *Joseph Andrews* has a more ambitious project, since he is not only going to instruct and to delight—he is going to instruct in delight. The text is going to force us to laugh in the right way and to give up the wrong, and it is here that the narrator does more than simply repeat the critical tradition—he inverts it.

In 1738 Swift published an *Essay on Polite Conversation*, an ironic collection of conversational dullness passed off as wit by the supposed author, Simon Wagstaff, a self-revealed fool. In the introduction, Wagstaff argues that there is both natural and learned laughter, the first an "involuntary Distortion of the Muscles" and the second "the undoubted Mark of a Good taste, as well as of a polite obliging Behaviour." Convinced that his collection of conversational gems will be "attended with Praise, Laughter, or Admiration," Wagstaff desires to teach his readers the art of correct laughter, a skill not "to be acquired without much observation, long practice, and a sound judgment." Laughter that is natural and involuntary is simply not civilized. "I did therefore once intend," Wagstaff explains "for the Ease of the Learner, to set down in all Parts of the following Dialogues, certain Marks, Asterisks, or Nota Bene's . . . after most Questions, and every Reply or Answer; directing exactly the Moment when one, two, or all the Company are to laugh," but because such a project would have so enlarged his book, Wagstaff admits, that the price would have been adversely affected, he decided to leave these decisions about where to laugh to the ingenuity of his readers (23, 24). Yet before he leaves his readers to their untutored fate he does suggest that a public school be established by "some expert Gentlewoman, gone to Decay," who might teach young girls of quality not only his system of polite conversation, "but above all, to instruct them in every Species and Degree of Laughing, in the proper Seasons at their Wit, or that of the Company" (25).

Wagstaff's various projects are ludicrous—that he is a man without either wit or judgment Swift makes abundantly clear, and thus they are themselves worthy of the reader's laughter, his natural laughter, not the refined and prissy stuff that Wagstaff would teach us. Thus while attacking the idea of instruction in laughter, Swift instructs in laughter. Ten years earlier, Swift had explained, "I expect, and desire no other Reward than that of laughing with a few Friends in a Corner" (*Intelligencer*, no. 3, 34) in return for all the ridicule that he had heaped upon the follies and corruptions of his age. One of these follies was Wagstaff's, the sense that the natural laughter of man was now unacceptable to the new age of refined sensibility coming into existence in the eighteenth century, that Hobbesian laughter could be turned into polite and genteel titters. Fielding's relationship to Swift is complex: he praised Swift, imitated Swift, lived in his shadow, endured some abuse from him, abused him in turn, and to the extent that he was influenced by such Whig humorists as Addison, moved away from the kind of satire that was Swift's special gift. Wagstaff claims he can shift the current of laughter; it is the special movement that fascinated Fielding. Swift mocks the claim; Fielding mocks the mocker.

As Hercules Vinegar, Fielding boasted that he could turn the current of laughter against the turnspit who thought he could control the ridicule, and what he claimed as Vinegar he performed under his own name in 1742 when he answered Swift directly, first in his own "Essay on Conversation" written seriously and meant as a didactic aid to his readers, then in *Joseph*

Andrews written comically but *meant* as serious instruction in laughter. Fielding's "Essay on Conversation" argues for good breeding and in its closing pages it attacks ridicule and raillery unless it is qualified by tenderness and good nature, qualities notably absent in Swift. "And however limited these bounds may appear to some," Fielding wrote, without naming names, "yet, in skilful and witty hands, I have known raillery, thus confined, afford a very diverting, as well as inoffensive entertainment to the whole company" (277). The narrator of *Joseph Andrews* argues the point in the author's preface, then attempts it in the fiction that follows, taking on Simon Wagstaff's abandoned project in all seriousness, instructing the reader in the polite and correct laughter that is consistent with good taste and sound judgment. There are no marks, asterisks, or nota bene's in *Joseph Andrews*, but there are more subtle and equally effective markers in the text that direct the reader away from Swiftian laughter and toward Wagstaffian laughter: from ridicule and raillery to ridicule mediated by tenderness and raillery mediated by good nature. The position Swift lampooned as comic in 1738 Fielding took as the purpose of the comic in 1742—or at least his narrator did. It is simple enough to understand Swift's attitude to the pseudonym Wagstaff but far more difficult to understand Fielding's attitude to his narrator. Following Wagstaff into the labyrinth of the comic, imitating and inverting him, becoming his comic mirror, the narrator does not find the going easy, and while he sometimes succeeds in the project that has defeated Wagstaff, he just as often comes up short. There are times when Fielding turns on this narrator much as Swift turned on Wagstaff. In 1740 as Hercules Vinegar, Fielding urged parents to watch for the appearance of coarse ridicule in their children, and then "to whip this spirit out of their children, the doing which may truly be called a wholesome severity" (*Champion*, no. 52, 241). The cure here seems worse than the disease. The narrator of *Joseph Andrews* has a project of much less vinegar— it is through his words that he would tease us to laugh good-naturedly and shame us from coarse ridicule. Hobbes was only partially right, Fielding wrote in 1743 in his "Essay on the

Knowledge of the Characters of Men," because we can bring harsh laughter under control. If we laugh when we see a well-dressed man fall into a dirty street, it is only because such surges of emotion are not yet subject to our rational control, and when we do feel compassion for the man in the dirt, who may have broken a bone, then "the man, who should continue to laugh, would be entitled to the basest and vilest appellation with which any language can stigmatize him" (287). Simon Wagstaff's argument is here presented with all seriousness by Fielding where it is made over into a critique of pure laughter.

III

EARLY IN *Joseph Andrews* a coach full of respectable people discover a man lying in a dirty street, injured and naked, and while they do rescue him without any enthusiasm, one "Man of Wit" cracks a series of jokes at the expense of this pitiable object (53). The object is Joseph, who has been robbed, beaten, and stripped of all his worldly possessions, and because the man of wit continues to laugh even when the circumstances become known, he does deserve our basest and vilest appellations. Here there is perfect accord between Fielding the essayist and Fielding the novelist. The novel presents the more complicated challenge to the reader, however, because the narrator has encouraged the reader to laugh at Joseph throughout the early chapters, making him ridiculous because of his extreme chastity and the efforts he must go to in order to protect his virtue. Then Joseph is the proper subject of ridicule, but once he is injured we must understand he deserves our compassion. A number of Fielding's most perceptive critics have noted this movement in *Joseph Andrews*, among them, most recently, Wolfgang Iser (*Implied Reader*, 35) and J. Paul Hunter (*Occasional Form*, 109), but none has looked for similar shifts in the current of laughter throughout the novel. This is, after all, the one such movement Fielding made explicit in his "Essay on the Knowledge of the Characters of Men." The novel is composed of such shifts.

The narrator knows what he wants to do in *Joseph Andrews*:

to reform the reader's laughter in this manner and thus to reconcile comedy with Christian morality. Moving back and forth between comic and serious styles the narrator is constantly shifting tones, sometimes provoking to laugh, sometimes warning against the laugn. But in practice it proves to be much more difficult to control the current of laughter than any of his critical pronouncements would indicate, and often he cannot control his own laughter, let alone that of his reader. Hunter notes, "As all writers know, laughter let loose is often difficult to direct precisely, and when we laugh at such conflicting targets as pious men and infidels, good and evil motives . . . we often find it hard to locate the common source of our amusement; if laughter by nature requires fine discrimination, it seldom articulates ingrained distinctions even when it yokes them in violent conflict" (5–6). But in *Joseph Andrews* the narrator demands such fine discriminations of the reader and thus finds himself yoked in the violent conflicts between the various possibilities. His story lurches violently in contradictory directions as the current of laughter shifts and shifts again, and what results are at least two countertexts that are the dialectical negations of each other. The foray into the labyrinth of the comic throws the narrator into a sequence of oppositions almost as if the text was controlled by a mirror that is constantly inverting and subverting the positions he adopts. Mockery comes face to face with its own reflection.

One text, the most obvious one, is the story designed to teach us good-natured laughter and the compatibility of mirth and virtue, of comedy and Christianity. The narrator writes this story much as Addison or Shaftesbury would write it, detailing Parson Adams as a figure of genial humor and provoking our laughter at this figure by a number of devices. Against such a proper object of proper laughter, the narrator includes a number of minor characters who themselves laugh in false mockery, harsh ridicule, and ignorance, such as the man of wit on board the coach. The narrator also interrupts the story to make explicit comments on the nature of the comic and sometimes allows characters to repeat such sentiments, of which the best example is Joseph's comment on the nature of true ridicule already noted. The other text is the dialectical negation of this story. The narrator mocks Joseph's Shaftesburian sentiment, mocks his own statement about comedy as a glass, mocks his own art as a comic writer, sometimes with brief references, once in the figure of the jesting squire who like the narrator turns Adams into a figure of fun for his own love of laughter. If in the first text we are moved from ridicule to humor, in the second we are moved in the opposite direction, from humor to ridicule. When we first meet Parson Trulliber he is introduced as another Falstaff, but he is shortly shown to be a thoroughly bad man worthy only of our contempt and ridicule, and then as that episode ends we meet Trulliber's apparent contrast, a gentleman on the road who laughs in the precise manner spelled out in the author's preface but who is then shown to be even worse than Trulliber. Against this amiable smiling man we are introduced to a jeering innkeeper, and it turns out to be jeering that is the better option. We are sometimes asked to laugh as Shaftesbury would, but other times as Hobbes would, sometimes to identify with the mocker, sometimes with the object of mockery. Nothing escapes this shifting current of laughter in the novel, not a character (although with Fanny only her sexually suggestive name and thus her oppositional pairing to Lady Booby is comic), not the narrator, and not the reader.

The narrator does resolve the plot, of course. Joseph and Fanny do get married, but when he describes the wedding celebration he can say little more than that it was characterized by "the utmost Merriment, corrected by the strictest Decency," and once again a Fielding narrator is caught in an oxymoron (343). Of what such a combination of extremes of merriment and decency might consist, the narrator cannot say, except that Adams "had given a Loose to more Facetiousness than was usual to him" (343). Since none is usual this does not say very much. And then, hurrying through a page of loose ends—of Wilson home with his wife, their son and daughter; of virtue rewarded—the narrator briefly describes the happy future of all the principal characters and then slams his book shut. He ends with a joke on himself—nor will Joseph "be prevailed on by any Book-

sellers, or their Authors, to make his appearance in *High-life*"
(344). What the narrator did to Richardson's Pamela, he will not
allow to be done in turn to Pamela's brother. Joseph must be
killed off as an interesting character for future comic writers,
must be banished to the boredom and happiness of the countryside. By turning the joke against himself and against Joseph,
the narrator prevents others from provoking this current of
mockery against them, and by slamming the story shut, the narrator stops by the only way possible the shifting and slippery
current of laughter that he has never been able to fully or finally
control.

The mocking text and countertext can only be separated from
each other by an act of critical violence—what might be characterized as antiwit, the dialectical negation of wit—but the mere
English reader does find the story breaking up into two other
oppositions: the satire in the style of Cervantes, books 1, 2, and
3, and the comedy in the style of Molière, book 4. Unable to find
a synthesis in styles between the comic and the serious, the narrator simply alternates between them, sometimes yoking them
together by violence as in utmost merriment/strictest decency.
Unable to find a synthesis in comic plots, the narrator simply
alternates between them as well, between prose satire and dramatic comedy. What ties these two plots together (as well as the
two styles) is the obvious continuity of characters and the increasing complexity of the laughing situation, from the initial
contrasts of book 1 to the climax of the jesting squire at the end
of book 3 to the resolution of book 4. The characters are first
trapped in the literary conventions of satire, and then after following Quixote through the comic labyrinth they are suddenly
propelled into comedy, where they experience the demands of
that rival set of conventions and must follow in the paths of the
lovers and the blocking characters from Molière and from Plautus before him. In the first journey through the labyrinth of satire the currents of laughter work at cross-purposes, and the
mockery separates, divides, contradicts, but then in the journey
through the labyrinth of comedy these currents of laughter reverse themselves, and the mockery joins, unifies, and absolves.

The narrator has exercised this much control at least on the broad structures of the plot. It is at the smaller level of the mocking episode that control of the current of laughter is often exceedingly difficult, and the movement is just as often from sympathetic humor to rejecting ridicule.

The text and the countertext are this shifting current of laughter throughout the novel, from the first shift with Joseph naked on the dirty road to the final joke against the narrator in the last sentence. These build in complexity to the end of the satire in book 3 until the narrator finds his one effective weapon against the current of laughter, his ability to shift into different comic genres. It is this shift that rescues his characters from the fate that destroys Don Quixote, and Fielding's mere English reader, from a journey without end through the labyrinth. At the center of his increase in complexity is the long episode of the jesting squire and his comic henchmen, the mirror reflection of the narrator and his readers, who pose the greatest danger to all the actors in the story.

In book 1, the current of laughter starts off simply enough; as long as Richardson is the object of comic reference we are prodded to become mockers of the serious; then when Joseph is discovered naked and we see the man of wit mock falsely, the comic itself becomes the object of serious reference and we are prodded to become critics of the mock. Once Joseph is safely at the inn operated by the comic Tow-wouses, the narrator shifts back to mockery, this time in mock heroic style, forcing the reader once again to laugh at the story. Joseph's predicament is not the direct object of the narrator's mockery, but to the extent that he is making light of what is at this point Joseph's story, what at first appears an easy distinction becomes more and more murky. At dusk a "grave person" comes to the inn and soon finds himself in a heated argument over medical care with the surgeon, who is revealed to be something of a wit. This wit carries the argument by provoking the others to laugh at this grave person, even though it is obvious to the reader that the surgeon argues in ignorance. Our sympathy is entirely with the object of laughter, even more so when we are told the man is Parson Adams. And now, after Joseph and Adams have been mocked, the narrator mocks himself at the end of the following chapter when he invokes Vanity and then admits that the "errant Nonsense" has only been "to lengthen out a short Chapter" (70).

The first movement of laughter is complete; what we have first seen from the position of the mocker we have returned to see from the position of the one mocked, and in the process we have been teased to keep laughing. A second movement, a provocation to us to laugh in a new and more genial way, begins when the parson appears in his odd assortment of ill-fitting clothes. We should not laugh at the parson as the surgeon laughs, but we can laugh at him for his foolish and harmless affectations. No harm is meant and no harm is done. But then the narrator almost immediately subverts this Shaftesburian impulse with a far more mean-spirited jest, one that now validates Hobbes. In an extended discussion with Parson Barnabas on religion, Adams takes the Shaftesburian position that "frequent cheerful Meetings among Members of a Society" promote the true sense of Christianity when they "make Promises of being good, friendly and benevolent to each other" (83). Responding to this provocation, the narrator interrupts Adams with the discovery of the good and friendly Betty, the chambermaid, in a cheerful meeting with Mr. Tow-wouse, but because this meeting takes place in Mr. Tow-wouse's bed and is perhaps a little too friendly, Mrs. Tow-wouse objects. Betty "had Good-nature, Generosity and Compassion," the narrator tells us, mocking Adams (86). The narrator who has earlier sided with Adams against those who would mock him in ignorance then reverses himself and mocks Adams with loving compassion, then reverses himself again and mocks him more severely—for if this is a harmless jest on Adams's sense of Christianity, the result is much more serious for Betty, who is discharged from her employment at the inn. The only person willing to take care of Joseph when he arrives injured, Betty is sacrificed by the narrator in his mischievous compulsion to ridicule Adams. The narrator is slipping into the kinds of laughter and ridicule that he has warned us against in the author's preface.

Book 2 contains the justice of the peace who mocks Adams and Fanny in ignorance; Parson Trulliber, the narrator's mockery of the Falstaffian ideal of mockery; the genial gentleman who offers Adams a parson's living that he does not have to offer, the narrator's mockery of the narrator's own ideal of mockery; an attack on the concept behind Aristotle's definition of the comic, and a suggestion that it is such definitions that are themselves comic; and numerous provocations to the reader to laugh at Adams, who is shown forgetting his sermons, wading through waist-high water because he overlooks a foot path, groaning through the story of Leonora, getting a pan of hog's blood discharged on his head, and outrunning a coach for the sheer challenge of a race. The shifting currents of laughter in book 1 are relatively simple in comparison. But just as we are asked first to laugh at Joseph Andrews in book 1 and then to feel compassion for him, in book 2 we are asked first to laugh at Adams when he gets into a fight at an inn for a trivial cause and is covered with hog's blood and then to feel admiration for him when in his next fight he rescues the helpless Fanny from a rapist. When, just as in book 1, we are then shown a man of wit mocking at Joseph when we have already stopped mocking at Joseph, so here too we are introduced to a crowd of people who laugh at Adams in ignorance. After the fight Adams and Fanny are falsely apprehended by others who believe the story of the culprit, who accuses them of the attack, and they are taken before a justice "in the height of his Mirth," who gets more pleasure out of cracking jokes at Adams and Fanny than at determining truth (145). The justice and his cronies mock Fanny's virtue and Adams's innocence, precisely their most admirable qualities, but Adams nevertheless loses the argument because he can not control the current of laughter. Lacking money to wager on his skills in Latin, Adams is forced to withdraw from the challenge of the wits "which set them all a laughing, and confirmed the Triumph of his Adversary" (147). Instead Adams must be rescued by the kind of surprise recognition scene typical of comedy and must be identified by another traveler. The false mockery stops but only gives way to its opposite, false gravity. A quarrel breaks out between those who have apprehended Adams and Fanny on the road over how they might have divided their reward. "All the Company laughed at this, except *Adams*, who . . . fetched a deep Groan" (150). This is the kind of affectation that the narrator argues is the precisely correct object of ridicule in the author's preface, and thus we have been shifted again—the false laughers have become true laughers; the true grave have become the false grave.

The narrator turns next to major figures and concepts from the comic tradition—Aristotle's definition, Shakespeare's creation of Falstaff—and then closes the book by turning on himself and his definitions. The reference to Aristotle is indirect in the chapter "concerning high People and low People" (156); the distinction that the narrator argues is false. It is people who make such distinctions that are themselves the proper subjects of laughter. "If the Gods . . . made Men only to laugh at them, there is no part of our Behavior which answers the End of our Creation better than this" (158). Comedy, Aristotle explained in the *Poetics*, is "an imitation of characters of a lower type" in contrast to the elevated styles and characters in tragedy. Fielding offered a somewhat different critique in his "Essay on Conversation," arguing there for an inversion of hierarchies. "If men were to be rightly estimated, and divided into subordinate classes, according to the superior excellence of their several natures, perhaps the lowest class of either sex would be properly assigned to those two disgraces of the human species, commonly called a beau, and a fine lady" (265).

From Aristotle the narrator moves on to Falstaff, remaking Shakespeare's figure of genial mockery into a thoroughly evil man. We are introduced to Parson Trulliber, a man "liable to many Jokes" because he is as fat as his hogs, and so addicted to his ale that he is "little inferiour to that of the Beasts he sold" (162). He "could have acted the part of Sir *John Falstaff*," but the narrator makes him act the part of an anti-Falstaff. Like Falstaff who claims in *II Henry IV*, "I am not only witty in myself, but the cause that wit is in other men" (1.2.10–11), Trulliber is not only an object of laughter but himself a laugher, and

when Adams falls into the mire with the hogs, "instead of assist-
ing him to get up," Trulliber "burst into a Laughter." Believing
that Adams has come to purchase hogs he speaks to him with
some contempt, then understands the mistake that he blames on
his wife and apologizes. This is the movement we have come to
expect in the novel: the laugher who renounces it when he understands it is not appropriate, and indeed, after Adams has
cleaned himself off Trulliber is shown only grinning moderately
at Adams's dress. But then the narrator reverses all of this: Trulliber orders his wife serve Adams only the worst ale, then shows
himself to be little more than a hog at table, then becomes the
most boorish and abusive of men, finally denying Adams's request for a loan of seven shillings. The moderation of Trulliber's
laugh has *not* indicated good nature or sympathy. And genial fat
Jack Falstaff, conceived in the eighteenth century as a figure of
amiable humor, has turned into his mirror inversion. This is
Shakespeare as Hobbes would have rewritten him.

The next episode of the novel introduces us to a character
who appears to be the mirror inversion of this mirror inversion,
a generous and amiable gentleman with "so smiling a Countenance" that Adams takes to him at once (171). This gentleman
laughs in the absolutely correct manner prescribed in the author's preface. About the affectation of the local parson, the
gentleman explains, "I often laugh when I behold him on *Sun-
days* strutting along the Church-Yard, like a Turkey-Cock. . . .
But if such temporal Pride is ridiculous, surely the spiritual is
odious and detestable; if such a puffed-up empty human Blad-
der strutting in princely Robes, justly moves one's Derision;
surely in the Habit of a Priest it must raise our Scorn" (172).
This gentleman understands what is laughable and what is perhaps too serious to be simply laughable; the narrator should
also take to this man at once, but in truth the narrator is only
taking the reader in by mocking the position that appears so similar to his own. The gentleman offers Adams this parson's living
but then after Adams has made plans to accept it on the following day, the gentleman disappears. The host of the local inn tells
Adams "with a kind of Jeering-Smile" that "I own, I could not

help laughing, when I heard him offer you the Living; for thereby
hangs a good Jest" (177). The gentleman is a compulsive liar and
trickster who does this sort of thing often, we discover, and his
personal history makes him out to be a far more "wicked Man"
than Trulliber. The narrator has now called his entire project
into question, for there may be no justification for teaching his
reader correct laughter if that laughter has no connection to attitudes toward vanity and hypocrisy. The narrator's ideal, the
amiable smiling gentleman, is false and his standard of harsh
ridicule, the "jeering" innkeeper, is true. The episode ends with
an argument between Adams and this jeering but nevertheless
kind innkeeper over the significance of such smiles. You can not
"give any Credit to a Man's Countenance," the innkeeper maintains (180) (and the narrator has just demonstrated the truth of
what he argues), but Adams replies, "Nature generally imprints
such a Portraiture of the Mind in the Countenance, that a skilful
Physiognomist will rarely be deceived" (182). Adams is wrong
here, but in his "Essay on the Knowledge of the Characters of
Men" written the following year Fielding will reverse himself
and argue that a "glavering, sneering smile" indicates a bad
heart and an "amiable, open, composed, cheerful aspect" a
good one (287).

IV

AT THIS point halfway through the novel the free-floating mockery has moved to subvert every position toward mockery. Evi-
dently the narrator cannot resist the impish temptation to make
fun of everything and in the process his amiable and rational
project slips away from his control. We are at the crisis point of
his story or at least of that aspect of the story concerned with the
problem of the comic. Reasserting control over the text at the
start of book 3, the narrator argues that the story is a glass for
us to hold up in our closets so that we will contemplate and then
reduce our deformities. His project in the author's preface has
been to teach us how to laugh correctly; now his project is re-
defined to teach us how to be the correct objects of laughter.

This is still to be a humane process, we are assured, because the narrator is a satirist, someone who corrects faults for the benefit of the person suffering with them and not a libeler, someone who exposes the person only for the benefit of others. The narrator has ended book 2 by mocking himself, and thus it seems only fair that the reader take his turn. He has already been mirrored into the text on a number of occasions in books 1 and 2, of course, and has been made to confront the nature of his own laughter, but now that process is made explicit. Now the reader is offered two mirror inversions of each other in book 3—Wilson and the jesting squire, the reformed and the unreformed rake—and is asked to find himself in the portraits not of men but of manners.

The contrasting stories of Wilson and the jesting squire dominate book 3, but before the narrator gets to them he tries one more dialectical inversion of the laughing situation: absent laughter. Walking at night in the dark Adams trips and rolls down a hill. Joseph and Fanny see nothing and are frightened, but the narrator assures us that "if the Light had permitted them to see it, they would scarce have refrained laughing" (194). In a fiction where no one misses an opportunity for laughter, the narrator teases us with this provocation to laughter that is denied by the total darkness in which the characters must make their way. And like them, the reader too is now in total darkness unable to laugh, or at least unable to laugh with confidence, given the travails of the first two books of the novel. We march together toward the chance of enlightenment.

Wilson illuminates the darkness, at least for Joseph, Fanny, and Adams, but the story he has to tell them is not comic at all and there are now no opportunities for laughter. His confessions are filled with arguments against vanity and affectation, but because he has put these behind him there is now nothing to be ridiculed, and ridicule, in fact, has nothing to do with his reformation. The love of a good woman and a certain exhaustion and boredom had finally led him to the light. The story is additionally anticomic because it is so similar to the "comedy" of Colley Cibber against which Fielding and his narrator so often rail, the transformation of Restoration rake into sentimental husband, but the story is so sentimental and so complicated and extended that it becomes a parody of itself. And then the narrator has his own Hobbesian joke when the story ends with the "tragical Adventure of the Dog" (225), which is shot gratuitously and then forced to die in front of us. Adams, having missed the meaning of the parable, declares that Wilson and his family live in a Shaftesburian paradise. He remains in darkness. More opportunities for laughter are being missed by the central characters, but whether we are laughing or not now depends on what we have learned following the narrator through the labyrinth. And if we are to laugh at this character and this story, do we laugh kindly, as we laugh at Adams, because Wilson is a good man, or do we laugh with jeering ridicule, as Fielding ridicules Cibber, because Wilson's story is as patently false and as uncomic as Cibber's? There are now no directions in the text to provide assistance.

We are now ready for the story of the jesting squire and his band of comic cronies who are as excessively comic as Wilson is excessively sentimental. Like Wilson, the jesting squire is well aware of vanity and affectation but unlike Wilson, the squire simply glories in it because of the laughter it provides him; what is absent from Wilson and his story, the opportunity for laughter, is here provided us in great measure. Adams, Joseph, and Fanny come upon Wilson after they miss an opportunity for laughter; they are set upon by the jesting squire after they miss an opportunity for a discussion of laughter and ridicule. Once again, the central characters are outside in an open field, but where Adams was first awake in darkness he is now sleeping in the light. Joseph puts him to sleep by discoursing on the nature of true ridicule and the squire wakes him up by making him the object of false ridicule. The squire's hounds catch up with the unfortunate hare they have been pursuing in front of Fanny and destroy it before her eyes—this is the mirror inversion of the tragical history of Wilson's dog. They turn next to Adams's wig and with the encouragement of the squire ("generally said to be a great Lover of Humour" [238]) to the rest of Adams, who has somehow managed to sleep through all the mayhem. But now it is the narrator who is caught in a mirrored relationship with the squire, for as soon as the squire sets his dogs on Adams for some comic entertainment, the narrator shifts styles and adopts the mock heroic, setting his words on Adams for some comic entertainment of his own. And when the squire calls his dogs off, seeing that Joseph is beating Thunder, Plunder, Blunder, and the rest, the narrator calls the muse of humor off as well and reverts to his normal writing style. The squire's jests seem dangerous and excessive, for his dogs have just ripped apart a hare, but the narrator's jests serve to deny the dangers of the squire's jests, since in the mock heroic style nothing appears to be serious or worth taking seriously. The narrator and the squire are here closely allied. And of course no real harm is done.

Then the current of laughter shifts. Unlike Wilson, the squire is a Restoration rake unreformed, and he invites them all to dinner in order to plot a seduction of Fanny. The narrator now scorns the squire and refuses to recount the jests played on his central characters as they travel to the squire's house, even though they "afforded much Laughter and Diversion," what the narrator has praised in the author's preface, but which he now believes "would ill become the Dignity of this History" (244). Repulsed by the squire's mockery, he adopts the style of gravity, but this he cannot sustain for long, and once the entertainments begin at dinner he begins to recount the squire's jests in great and loving detail and to explain the nature of his character. What distinguishes him is "a strange Delight" he takes in everything "ridiculous, odious, and absurd in his own Species" (245), and to feed that delight he has surrounded himself with a cast of natural and artificial fools, a comedia dell'arte troupe of sorts, who have been charged to turn even virtue and wisdom into ridicule. These men quickly recognize Adams as the perfect butt—he is after all also the narrator's favorite butt—and the jokes begin: his chair is pulled out from under him; soup is spilled into his pants; gin is poured into his ale; the lame German dancing master tries to force him to dance. When Adams warns them "not to carry the Jest too far" (247), the reply is a

firecracker set off under his cassock; then when he lectures the
squire on the lack of respect he has been shown, the quack doctor who "could laugh inwardly without betraying the least Symp-
toms in his Countenance" tries the opposite approach, agreeing
with Adams in all earnestness (249). He invites Adams to act in
Socrates' favorite diversion and Adams foolishly agrees: positioned over a tub of water on a blanket between two other players Adams is dunked when the actors rise. Adams pulls the
squire into the water after him and together with Joseph and
Fanny flees the household. He has succeeded, however, in shifting the current of laughter back onto the squire, and the narrator tells us that because the squire did not dry himself carefully enough he caught a fever "that had like to have cost him his
life" (251).

Is this harmless fun? Certainly Adams is betrayed by his own
vanity when he accepts the invitation to act out the part of Socrates, and thus he may deserve something as harmless as a slapstick dunking. But the narrator is so morally indignant that he
would have us believe the squire nearly died from getting dunked.
It is hard now to take him seriously. Certainly these practical
jokes are precisely what the narrator has done to Adams through
the story with mud, water, and hog's blood, sending him off
without his sermons, without his horse, and tripping him so he
rolls down a hill. We are being asked now to see all of these
techniques as mean-spirited and cruel. The story gets more mean-
spirited and cruel when the main characters return to an inn to
discover that Adams's money has been picked from his pocket in
one of the jokes, and then the squire's fools arrive to abduct
Fanny. This is the greatest danger that the trio faces in the
novel—when Fanny has been nearly raped before Adams has
been able to rescue her; when Beau Didapper tries the same in
book 4, Joseph is first able to beat him off, and finally Didapper
wanders into the wrong bedroom. Adams and Joseph are beaten
and tied and Fanny carried off: the story is turning suddenly into
a melodrama worse than Wilson's. The squire is a villain, but the
narrator, so closely tied to him, cannot let us take this villain in
other than a comic light, and so he once again reverts into the

mock heroic. The fight at the inn is ludicrous, played out with mops and chamber pots, and while the situation appears grave when Joseph and Adams are bound together in a room, the narrator breaks the story with a dialogue between a poet and a player on the nature of drama, negating the danger in yet another way. While one comic player, the squire, threatens danger, another, the narrator, denies the danger. The battle in the text between the forces of the squire and the forces of the narrator is mirrored by the battle of comic styles and comic moralities between the squire and the narrator. And as the squire's men win the physical battle, the narrator wins, or appears to win, the struggle over the control of laughter and the comic. What is for Adams, Joseph, and Fanny the greatest danger—physical defeat, rape, humiliation—is also the greatest danger for the narrator: the temptations of the comic, personified here in the squire, and shown to be very close to the narrator's own inclinations. The great danger is that the force of laughter will come to control and imprison consciousness, and this is what has happened to the squire, who lives for the laugh and will do anything to experience the laugh. The danger is that once laughing, the mocker will lose all contact with morality, that he will take nothing seriously but the gratification of his own pleasures, whether these be the physical pleasure of laughter or the physical pleasures that English comic drama was often to celebrate, sexuality. (The history of comedy does imply a connection between laughter and sexuality and it is a connection critics after Fielding were to explore in more detailed ways; Freud, for example, was to suggest in his study of the comic in 1905 that laughter was a sort of psychological ejaculation.)

The narrator beats back the temptations of total laughter, refusing to capitulate to the force against which he has struggled since he started his story. Holding off the tricks of the squire with his own narrative tricks, he brings Peter Pounce onto the scene to rescue Fanny. It proves to be remarkably easy. Adams and Joseph are set free and with Pounce they make the final bit of their journey to Booby Hall. The three books of satire in the style of Cervantes have culminated in the story of the jesting

squire, and here Fielding's borrowings from Cervantes are more
than a matter of style. The jesting squire is an imitation of the
jesting duke and duchess from book 2 of *Don Quixote*, who essentially imprison Quixote and subject him to practical jokes
for their love of laughter. But there is an important difference
between Cervantes and Fielding since Quixote is deluded, crazy,
and Adams is not. The duke and duchess exploit a natural fool
while the jesting squire tries to create an artificial fool. Fielding
raises the ante then, both for the squire and for his narrator,
who share this greater and graver responsibility. Laughing at a
crazy man may not seem acceptable to twentieth-century sensibilities, but it would not have seemed wrong in the Renaissance. Laughing at a naïve but moral Christian on the other
hand and covering him with water and mud and blood for the
sake of laughter is more problematic. In the author's preface,
the narrator insists that there is no harm in such fooleries, but in
the story that follows he shows us the darker side.

Book 3 ends, but not before laughter is set going again. Peter
Pounce laughs at Adams with his "Piss-burnt Beard" and torn
clothing—we are back again in the relative comfort of genial
laughter at the figure of harmless fun (270). Pounce, after all,
has just rescued Fanny, Adams, and Joseph, but no sooner is he a
hero than the narrator turns on him, describes him as a hypocrite of the sort Adams never understood and then shows Adams
finally understanding him. They argue in the coach ride back to
Booby Hall about the nature of charity and when Adams discovers Pounce's total lack thereof he leaps from the moving
coach and walks the rest of the way to Booby Hall. The echo, of
course, is to Adams's earlier race against a carriage when he was
simply comic; now in his walk against the coach he is principled
and worthy only of our admiration. The currents of mockery
keep shifting.

V

BOOK 4 is the narrator's response to the challenge posed by the
jesting squire, a demonstration that a gentleman with a great

love of humor can at least sometimes effectively control the force of laughter. The narrator does it here with the transition from the satire of the first three books to the comedy of the fourth book, for not only do his characters now have different generic conventions to experience but the force of laughter that has divided the characters in the first three books, separating the excessively comic and the excessively grave, the excessively innocent and the excessively experienced, now gives way to its own mirror inversion, a laughter that brings characters together and moves toward harmony. The rationale for satire is here discarded—Pamela and Lady Booby look into mirrors and do not see their deformities; and Fielding, who has started the novel in mockery of Swift's mockery, now just as suddenly confirms Swift's description of the mirror of satire rather than his own narrator's. "Satyr is a sort of glass, wherein Beholders so generally discover every body's face but their own," Swift's narrator wrote in the author's preface to *The Battle of the Books*. But having confirmed Swift the narrator just as quickly turns onto a new butt, introducing Beau Didapper as "a young Gentleman of about four Foot five Inches in height" and so generally repulsive that no woman will have him (312). The mockery, neither gentle nor kind, is of Pope.

We are involved at first in the familiar kind of oppositional mockery of the first three books. As the narrator mocks Didapper, Didapper tells Lady Booby that "as he was entirely well satisfied with his own Person and Parts, so he was very apt to ridicule and laugh at any Imperfection in another" (313). And as Didapper is invited to meet Parson Adams and his family by Lady Booby in order to divert himself with the ridiculous sight, so too is the reader invited to laugh at Booby and Didapper by the narrator. But then satiric laughter gives way to comic laughter and to an entirely new relationship of laughers in the novel. All the principal actors gather at Booby Hall to await information about Joseph and Fanny's relationship—whether they be brother and sister or not—and encouraged by the possibility Lady Booby entertains them all "with great Good-humour at her own Table" (329). And Adams for the first time in the novel begins to joke, trading jokes back and forth with Didapper "chiefly on each other's Dress; there afforded much Diversion to the Company" (329–30). The farce of the night follows, implicating all the characters in a community of laughter that accepts rather than rejects. Joined by the force of laughter, all become fools together, and it is almost as if the laughter provoked from the reader bathes over the action and so alters character. The reader who has learned correct laughter in spite of the temptations along the way and the impossibility of ever adopting one single position can here at least laugh in the right way and be shown the power of this good laughter. We are presented here with a naked Adams at whom we can laugh, unlike the naked Joseph of the first book at whom we could not laugh.

It remains only for the narrator to tie together all the loose ends: the information that Joseph and Fanny are not brother and sister, the reappearance of Wilson as Joseph's father, the comic recognition scenes from Molière, and then the marriage. Adams has to rebuke Pamela and Mr. Booby "for laughing in so sacred a Place, and so solemn an Occasion" (342), and then a day of celebration follows, an oxymoron of utmost merriment and strictest decency. The narrator makes a final joke at his own expense and shuts the book on Joseph before the current of laughter can shift against him again. He has taught us to laugh kindly just as he has promised, but he has also taught us to laugh harshly, to laugh at the kind laugh and to laugh at the harsh laugh. His author's preface now only seems excessively proud, limited, what a critic would say. What a writer learns and what a reader understands is that nothing is that neat or simple. Like the jesting squire the narrator has mocked at everything in his novel, but unlike the squire the narrator has refused to give in to the force of laughter. Fight for control is what we must do to avoid the moral degradation of the squire and his comic players. *Joseph Andrews* is our education in the fight.

3

Tom Jones: The Labyrinth of Mirrors

TOM JONES is a comic epic and an epic about the comic. The solution to the problems posed in *Joseph Andrews*, it demonstrates narrative mastery over the shifting currents of laughter and mockery. Many times more complex than the earlier novel, *Tom Jones* contains a much more elaborate study of the comic, an involved structure taken from the history of comic forms that calls attention to itself, and it contains a fully developed allegory of the history of comic forms that is imposed on the action. Against this are statements by the narrator about laughter, humor, and ridicule, and demonstrations of comic attitudes by many of the central characters. The reader is now in a fully formed labyrinth of the comic, in which the central device is the mirror, mocking, repeating, and inverting.

"One reason why *Tom Jones* is the salient example of literary art in Augustan England," Martin Battestin has argued, "is that Art, in a fundamental and philosophic sense, is its subject" (*The Providence of Wit*, 142). For Battestin the art of the novel is primarily the artifice of the design, a "celebration of the rational values of Art, of the controlling intelligence which creates Order out of Chaos and which alone gives meaning to vitality, making it a source of wonder and of joy" (143). This design provides the novel's central meaning—because art mirrors nature, the elegant

53

rational form imposed on the story by the novelist reflects/reveals the elegant rational form imposed on chaos by divine providence. Looking into Fielding's mirror we see the work of God. From this understanding of the novel's structure, Battestin makes a closely related point about the story contained within the structure. If art is the subject of *Tom Jones*, the novel itself is a very specific form of art, Christian allegory. The novelist is the creator, Jones the pilgrim, Sophia the emblem of true beauty or *sophia*, and the story a progress toward the marriage of *prudentia* and *sophia*. Story mirrors structure. "Unlike Defoe or Richardson, Fielding rejected the methods of 'formal realism' for a mode which verges on the symbolic or allegorical: his characters and actions, though they have a life and integrity of their own, frequently demand to be read as tokens of a reality larger than themselves; his novels may be seen as artful and highly schematic paradigms of the human condition" (151).

In this argument for art as the subject of the novel and for Christian allegory as the art form of the novel, Battestin does not consider the novel's obvious comic characteristics. His interest is in what lies beneath obvious surface content, in the moral basis of Fielding's art and in the aesthetic basis of Fielding's morality. For him Fielding's wit is demonstrated by the symmetry of design; by the striking and provocative connections between characters, events, and layers of meaning; by genius; and not by any explicitly "comic" perspective. However, the narrator of the novel does not make such limited use of the term—for him wit is associated with genius, with judgment, and with humor, and virtue with Christianity and with comedy. In the dedication he explains that wit and humor are to be the means by which he will teach moral values to the reader: "wherein I have endeavoured to laugh Mankind out of their Favourite Follies and Vices" (8). In the novel he reaffirms his purpose to teach right laughter as a part of Christian morality in his invocation to Genius, who is described as the inspiration for the great writers of comedy and satire. "Fill my Pages with Humour; till mankind learn the Good-Nature to laugh only at the Follies of others, and the Humility to grieve at their own" (13.1.686; References to *Tom*

Jones are to book, chapter, and page number.). He accounts for himself and for the novel as "a Writer whose Province is Comedy, or that Kind of Novels, which, like this I am writing, is of the comic Class" (14.1.743). If we can take the narrator at his word for the moment, then what Battestin says about the art of the novel needs to be reconciled with what the narrator says about the art of the novel. One way to do this would be to see the comedy as a layering of delight upon the novel's moral instruction, which the critic/archaeologist can skim off in his search for meaning. But the delight is intimately bound up with the instruction in this novel—they can never be so clearly and cleanly separated. While there is certainly much seriousness beneath the comedy, there is also much seriousness to the comedy. It is not an accidental or an incidental overlay on the novel's structure or its meaning. The reduction of the comedy of the novel to high seriousness must be countered by a return from the high seriousness of the novel back to comedy. The novel is not more trivial than it appears in Battestin's account, but it is far more preoccupied with the interactions of comedy and seriousness, of virtue and ridicule, of wit as genius and wit as comic provocation.

One reason why *Tom Jones* is the salient example of comic literary art in Augustan England is that comic art in a fundamental and philosophic sense is its subject. The novel is both comic and about the comic. Unlike Defoe or Richardson, Fielding rejected the methods of formal and humorless realism for a mode that verges on Christian and on comic allegory. Battestin's insights into the novel can be used to gain access to the seriousness of the comedy. The text is a perfect symmetry of contrasts; Christianity is directly countered by comedy. Battestin has read half the story. The other half is an inquiry into the meanings of the comic—of laughter, wit, humor, ridicule and mockery—many times more complex than the comparable inquiry in *Joseph Andrews*. And while it is an inquiry that most often exists below the surface level of meaning, it sometimes does become an element in the basic plot and characterizations of the novel. It is a major aspect of the novel's design and of the narrator's character. In the Christian allegory Tom is cast out of Paradise Hall, naked before God. The narrator explains: "*The World*, as *Milton* phrases it, *lay all before him*; and *Jones*, no more than *Adam*, had any Man to whom he might resort for Comfort or Assistance" (7.2.331). In the comic allegory Tom comes upon Mrs. Waters, similarly cast out and abused, but actually naked, and clasps her ample bosom to his. She is the comic mirror of Tom; the comedy repeats and subverts the Christianity at the structural center of the novel, and it is in this manner that Fielding joins virtue and mirth in uneasy alliance. Battestin does not reduce the novel to Christian allegory—he is careful to isolate the allegory as one level of the novel's meaning and not as a destruction of its literal sense. Neither do I wish to reduce the novel to comic allegory or to a novel about the comic—this too is but one level of the novel's meaning. Comic art is not the novel's only major preoccupation, but it is nevertheless a significant aspect of the novel's structure and meaning. This reading of *Tom Jones* is designed to supplement, not to replace, the already established meanings of the text. It is also designed to establish the importance of the novel in the tradition of the modern inquiry into the comic.

II

CONTAINED within the central section of *Tom Jones*—the journey from country to city—and somewhat obscured by the seemingly random proliferation of incident is the comic allegory, a history of comic literature from Shakespeare to Fielding. From the first major episodes (Tom's adventure with a company of soldiers, his comic abuse by Northerton and their subsequent fight) to the last (Tom's adventure with a company of gypsies, his subsequent fight with a highwayman, and his comic abuse of Partridge), this journey at the center of the novel is both literal and literary. Tom experiences mid-eighteenth-century public life, the immediate context for Fielding, and learns the ability to distinguish good characters from bad, while the reader experiences a century and a half of literary history, the relevant aesthetic context for Fielding, and learns to distinguish good literature from bad. The journey is told in a chronology of styles beginning with Shakespeare (the bawdy tavern scenes with the soldiers, then Tom's speech on honor that parodies Falstaff's); and continuing with Cervantes (the reintroduction of Partridge as the barber from *Don Quixote*); the Puritan interregnum (the Man of the Hill's high seriousness and the Christian discipline); Restoration comedy (the sexual farce at Upton); sentimental comedy in the manner of Steele or Cibber (Mrs. Fitzpatrick's story); the attack on sentimental comedy (the relapse of the merry andrew after the humorless puppet show); and finally concluding with Fielding (the adventure with the gypsies and the fight with the highwayman, which both parody and affirm the techniques of *Joseph Andrews*). Like Joseph and Fanny's wedding at the end of *Joseph Andrews*, the gypsy wedding near the end of the central section of *Tom Jones* is a marriage of true mirth and absolute decency— but then there is another relapse and Partridge is revealed in a compromising position with a gypsy woman. The incident ends all pretense to decent mirth. The adventure with the sentimental highwayman that follows is another shift in the current of laughter and mockery, the technique that characterizes Fielding's narrator in *Joseph Andrews*. Partridge has been the constant mocker in *Tom Jones*, but here the current of laughter turns against him when he is revealed as a coward, and Jones makes him the object of "some sarcastical Jokes" (12.14.681). Played against Jones's mockery is the narrator's own mockery of the highwayman for his cowardice, and played against these is the narrator's apparent endorsement of Jones's sentimentality.

These are the major episodes of the journey. Between them there are others that do not so clearly belong, and these are devoted primarily to innkeepers whose characters seem relatively unaffected by the march of history. Thus the reader's movement in the text is an alternation between resting places in inns and forward motion in chronological time, and with each episode, more of the pattern of history is revealed to the prudent reader. The narrator has earlier warned about the tasks of discrimination that may be "imposed on Readers of the lowest Class. Much higher and harder Exercises of Judgment and Penetration may reasonably be expected from the upper Graduates in Criticism" (3.1.117). This is one of those exercises for the upper graduates in criticism already familiar with the history of comic literature—what it reveals is that at the center of the comic epic is an epic about the comic. The chaotic comic journey of Tom's present is ordered and controlled by the history of comic literature, Fielding's past. By reducing present tense motion in physical space to past tense motion in historical time, Fielding uses comedy to control comedy.

"Tho' we have properly enough entitled this our Work, a History, and not a Life . . . yet we intend in it rather to pursue the Method of those Writers who profess to disclose the Revolutions of Countries, than to imitate the painful and voluminous Historian" who treats the trivial events with as much care and attention as the important (2.1.75). What the narrator tells us about *Tom Jones,* that it is a history and not a life, has not been taken literally—it is seen as just another of the traditional comparisons between comedy and history designed to justify the importance of the comic novel. But the narrator speaks a greater truth here, for behind the apparently trivial events in Tom's life are the most revolutionary events in comic literary history. Our choice is not between comedy or history, since we are presented with both at the same time. And if this history structures Tom's journey, giving it order and meaning, it is in turn structured by the elegant symmetries of the text, by the art of the comic novelist. The layers of the novel are involved in continual interactions: the revolutions of the history are so artfully ordered by the comic epic that what results is not only a paradox (revolutions/ orders) but a *theory* of literary history. The symmetries of the novel, the balanced repetitions within and between the three large sections—country, journey, city—center at the sexual farce at the inn at Upton. An episode prior to Upton is repeated and inverted in the analogous event after Upton—the Man of the Hill's story, for example, by Mrs. Fitzpatrick's story. Thus in the history of comedy Fielding establishes important connections between authors, demonstrating that history too is a di-

alectical play in the current of laughter. The first half of the journey, from Shakespeare to Cervantes to the Puritans, concludes
with the Restoration comedy at Upton. The second half of the
journey is a precise unraveling of this history—the sentimental
comedy repeats and inverts the Puritan interregnum; the attack
on sentimental comedy does the same to Cervantes; and finally
Fielding appears as the mirrored version of Shakespeare. Renaissance comedy is rewritten in the eighteenth century; the forward movement from Shakespeare to Congreve shifts into a
countermovement from Steele to Fielding, an echoing of pro-
gressively earlier antecedents. By making the history of comic
literature into a dialectic of forward and backward motion,
of text and countertext, Fielding can claim himself to be the
eighteenth-century version of Shakespeare. The chaos of text
and countertext in *Joseph Andrews* is now brought into elegant
control. What frustrated the narrator of *Joseph Andrews* is con-
verted by the narrator of *Tom Jones* into the services of his comedy. The shifting currents of laughter seen from the point of view
of history make clear what they obscure when seen from the
point of view of an individual comic author.

This history of comic literature ends just as Tom arrives in
London, and significantly at this moment the narrator makes his
address to the muses of good literature and bad, asking for assistance in composing his story. Such invocations should come at
the beginnings of epics, but the narrator has not simply mis-
placed this one, as the narrator of *Tristram Shandy* misplaces a
dedication and a preface. Fielding's narrator has just left his history of comedy—he is now on his own without structure or assistance, and he confesses that he is lost. Addressing Genius, he
recites a chronology of comic and satiric literature (Aristophanes, Lucian, Cervantes, Rabelais, Molière, Shakespeare, Swift,
Marivaux), but he makes mistakes, transposing Cervantes and
Rabelais, Molière and Shakespeare. For someone who has just
demonstrated a brilliant control of history, this bumbling is surprising. He goes on to conflate the opposites of harsh ridicule
and amiable humor, treating them as identical concepts, at the
same time that he asks for the ability to teach mankind the cor-

rect way to laugh. The request appears legitimate enough, but because he does not discriminate between terms (he has no judgment about wit), it is yet another example of his apparent confusion. "Lead me through all the Mazes, the winding Labyrinths of Nature" (13.1.685), he asks Genius. He is looking for an Ariadne, but of course he is Ariadne, and his novel is the winding labyrinth of nature into which the reader has been led. If anyone is really lost in the labyrinth it is not the narrator, who here is only pretending to be lost, but the reader. The narrator knows the chronology of comedy perfectly; he knows too the distinctions between harsh satire and amiable humor—contrasts which, like a great many other oppositions in the text, he is yoking by violence together (he has wit about satire and humor).

III

TWO CHARACTERISTICS of the novel have been often discussed: the symmetrical design and the ironic narrator. The structure has been compared to a Palladian mansion, and specifically to the plan for Prior Park, the home of Fielding's patron, Ralph Allen (see Hilles, *Art and Artifice*). The narrator's style has been called irony, double irony, and multiple irony. Objectively the text is elegant neoclassical structure, but subjectively the narration is unreliable eccentric storytelling, a masquerade. The novel is simultaneously an affirmation of Augustan aesthetics and an anticipation of romantic aesthetics, what Hoffman, Poe, or de Quincey might create if asked to rewrite Molière or Congreve. Typically, critics study the structure independently of the narrator, but neoclassical form and subjective eccentric narration are like all the other contraries in the novel intricately bound up with each other. The critic must yoke these incongruities together in order to understand the text.

Tom Jones is a comic labyrinth. Like the original labyrinth at Crete, the novel is elegantly structured, enticing, and dangerous; it is also comic, a play of mockeries, jokes, and tricks. As

Ariadne guided Theseus, providing him with the thread to un-
ravel so that he could locate the Minotaur, destroy it, and find
his way out, the narrator guides us, but the thread he unravels
leads us to a series of missteps and misreadings. What makes
Fielding's labyrinth dangerous is the ironic and tricky narrator
who delights in leading us astray and who mocks us as we
stumble. Our Ariadne is the monster; the mythological oppositions of ally and foe are here yoked together by violence. Significantly, when he does explicitly describe the text as labyrinth, the
monster that he wishes to subdue is the wild force of the comic,
of laughter and mockery, and there is no doubt that on one level
of the novel he does control it. In fact, by the end of the novel he
has renounced wit and humor altogether. Yet what follows this
renunciation is the information that Tom has committed incest,
yet another mockery of the reader. On another level then, the
current of laughter has not been subdued at all.

In his advice to would-be dunces, *Peri Bathous*, Pope wrote,
"His design ought to be like a labyrinth, out of which nobody can
get but himself" (chap. 5). And in *The Dunciad*, Pope wrote:

She sees a Mob of Metaphors advance,
Pleas'd with the Madness of the mazy dance:
How Tragedy and Comedy embrace;
How Farce and Epic get a jumbled race;

(1. 67–70)

If, as I have argued in the previous chapter on *Joseph Andrews*,
Fielding shifts the current of laughter against Swift in his conception of the project for that novel, then, in the conception of
Tom Jones Fielding shifts the current of laughter against Pope.
The behavior of the dunce author is taken over and inverted by
Fielding and made into the behavior of the genius author. Pope's
mockery is mocked in the special dialectical skill that is Fielding's delight. His reference to the labyrinth in *Tom Jones* comes
immediately after the invocation to the muses of great literature
and to Grub Street dullness, to what Pope venerated and what he
despised. The narrator is both genius and idiot at the same time.

Like *Joseph Andrews*, the novel is a dialectic of text and countertext. The narrator struggles to control mockery and is not
wholly successful. But *Tom Jones* is the far more accomplished
and controlled work of art, and this narrator is far more successful than the earlier figure. The comic epic poem in prose is
followed by the comic architectural maze in prose, by a structure so elegantly and elaborately shaped that the order itself is
dizzying, confusing. In *Tom Jones* shifting currents of laughter
and mockery are organized, controlled, and explained, although
they are not destroyed. What is sheer comic chaos on one level
is, on another, *orderly chaos*, the paradoxical synthesis that,
like the synthesis of seriousness and mirth at the end, is part of
Fielding's contribution to the history of comic literature.

Reading *Tom Jones* we are led backward over familiar ter-
ritory; the text is a mirror held up to *Joseph Andrews*. Joseph
has been replaced by Tom, Fanny by Sophia, Adams by Allworthy, Wilson by the Man of the Hill, the jesting squire by Lord
Fellamar, Lady Booby by Lady Bellaston. But our return to the
comic epic is not exactly the same. Tom is more believable than
Joseph—he can be seduced by women, and with increasing ease;
Sophia is more complex than Fanny and must resolve the conflict between her love for Jones and her love for her father; Allworthy is more flawed than Adams and can be tricked into turning on the hero. In place of the casual episodic plot of *Joseph
Andrews* we now have a perfectly balanced symmetrical structure of characters and events. The farce in the night at Booby
Hall, the climax at the end of *Joseph Andrews*, is moved to the
center of *Tom Jones*, where it becomes the farce in the night at
the inn at Upton, the turning point of the story. And significantly, the journey of the central characters is now reversed; the
movement from London to Booby Hall is replaced by the movement from Paradise Hall to London. We journey through the
world in the precisely opposite direction. In the first comic epic,
Joseph explains, "I have been told by other Gentlemen in Livery"
that what the nobility commends in public, they "make sport
and jeer" at in private (234), a behavior that Joseph finds ridiculous. In the second comic epic, the narrator warns, "In reality, a

Footman is often a Wit, as well as a Beau, at the Expense of the
Gentleman whose Livery he wears" (12.7.644).

Tom Jones is the repetition, refinement, and reversal of Joseph
Andrews. We are back again in the shifting currents of laughter.
In place of the long didactic preface to Joseph Andrews, there is
now only a single statement in the dedication about the comic:
"I have employed all the Wit and Humour of which I am Master
. . . wherein I have endeavoured to laugh Mankind out of their
favourite Follies and Vices." But the narrator immediately quali-
fies the statement, leaving it up to his "candid Reader" to determine how well he has succeeded, and asking him not to expect
perfection (8). There will be parts of the novel that will fall
short. How seriously can we take the statement that affirms and
then denies? The narrator is not such a master of wit and humor
as he would have us think, unless he is showing us his mastery
by teasing us to laugh at his apparent lack of mastery.

The narrator of Tom Jones is a master of artifice, of art and of
deception. A far more accomplished writer and trickster (in
Tom Jones one fiction depends on the other), not only can he
control more of the current of laughter than the narrator of
Joseph Andrews, but what he cannot control no longer frus-
trates him. He delights in, and therefore uses, the wild excesses
of mockery, playing with the reader in ways that the narrator of
Joseph Andrews does not. The project of the earlier novel is
abandoned for a new relationship in the current of laughter. "I
am convinced I never make my Reader laugh heartily," we are
told, "but where I have laughed before him, unless it should
happen at any Time, that instead of laughing with me, he should
be inclined to laugh at me. Perhaps this may have been the Case
at some Passages in this Chapter" (9.1.494). Again and again we
are explicitly teased not to take the narrator seriously—there
are no comparable directions in Joseph Andrews. When Allworthy lectures Jenny Jones on sexuality, the narrator titles the
chapter "Containing such grave Matter, that the Reader cannot
laugh once through the whole Chapter, unless peradventure he
should laugh at the Author" (1.7.51). But it is not until the end
of the novel that we get the joke, when Jenny Jones is exposed as

Mrs. Waters. Following Allworthy's lecture, Jenny promises that her future conduct will be exemplary, that she will renounce loose morality. Jenny has been innocent all along; Allworthy's judgment on her precipitates her into the kind of behavior she has been falsely punished for. The narrator is attempting to establish a current of laughter between himself and the reader, a dialectic of countermockeries. Challenging the reader to mock him, he mocks the reader. And should the reader refuse the invitation, he also mocks himself. Alternately comedy and seriousness, fiction and criticism, deception and revelation; simultaneously highly structured form and highly subjective ironic narration, *Tom Jones* is an extremely complex text. A glittering display of mirrors, masquerades, and contrasts, and a demonstration of the ways in which the comic novel can transform the themes of dramatic comedy and of prose satire into something much more elaborate, the novel constantly mocks the reader's wit and judgment. Only by understanding the mockery can the reader learn wit and judgment, and so master the text. In the novel, Partridge is the master of a certain kind of wit and humor, but he does not respond appropriately to art, to *Hamlet*, and is thus laughed at in his turn as the current of laughter shifts onto him. The tragedy of *Hamlet* gives way to the comedy of the naïve spectator. But even the higher graduates in criticism must make mistakes in a first reading of *Tom Jones*. Though they laugh at Partridge's errors, they make other errors themselves, at which the narrator is laughing.

IV

THE NARRATOR is a complex and devious mocker, but the story he has to tell is about a naïve and joyful laugher, Tom Jones. Tom is expelled from Paradise Hall for a variety of imprudent behaviors, but the final damning evidence presented to Allworthy is the fact that he has been mirthful when the house was in mourning for Bridget. Tom is rejected by Sophia at the inn at Upton not because he is in bed with Mrs. Waters, but because of "Instances of a Levity in his Behaviour" (12.8.651). He has apparently

mocked Sophia's name and reputation. That both these moments of rejection turn out to be misunderstandings indicate
just how vulnerable a good man can become when he laughs
without prudence, whether at the hands of an outright villain
like Blifil, who is responsible for the first misunderstanding, or
at the hands of an amiable and jocular friend like Partridge, who
is responsible for the second misunderstanding. Tom laughs
openly, joyously, guilelessly, and this natural passion leads him
into more serious difficulties than his other natural passion, his
sexuality. When Jones is seduced by Molly the narrator explains,
"he was not at this Time perfect Master of that wonderful Power
of Reason, which so well enables grave and wise Men to subdue
their unruly Passions" (5.10.257). For Tom, mirth is analo-
gously out of control.

If Tom's journey from country to city is an allegory of the history of comedy, on a literal level it is a struggle with the current
of laughter and mockery. The first episode of this section is the
meeting with the rowdy company of soldiers, and the jests Tom
must endure about Sophia's virtue. Having been recently expelled from Paradise Hall for his mirth, Jones meets with "Much
Mirth and Festivity" (7.11.369). When Northerton abuses
Sophia's virtue, Jones, "having seen but little of this Kind of Wit,
. . . did not readily understand it," but when he does, he tells
Northerton "Pray, Sir, chuse some other Subject for your Wit:
For I promise you I will bear no jesting with this Lady's Character" (7.12.375). Northerton's mirth contrasts with Tom's. Into
this dialectic enters the narrator, who mocks them both in the
story of their fight, and Tom's subsequent loss of his wit in which
he becomes for the moment like a parody of Falstaff.

The next major episode is the reintroduction of Partridge, a
"Fellow of great Oddity and Humour" (8.4.414). Jones meets
him on the road when he is recovering his wit from the fight
with Northerton, and while the reader has been earlier asked to
sympathize with Jones's position as the object of Northerton's
mockery (if not the narrator's), the reader is now asked to sympathize with Partridge's position as the maker of jests. Because
Partridge jests at others he has experienced "Slaps in the Face,

Kicks in the Breech, broken Bones, etc. For every one doth not
understand a Jest; and those who do, are often displeased with
being themselves the Subjects of it. This Vice was, however, in-
curable in him; and though he had often smarted for it, yet if
ever he conceived a Joke, he was certain to be delivered of it,
without the least Respect of Persons, Time, or Place" (8.4.414).
But while we now see the mocker-mockee relationship from the
opposite perspective, our sympathy with Partridge is shortly to
be revealed as a mistake. Partridge's jests involve Jones in the
tangle of misinformation at Upton that drives Sophia from him.
Believing she has been made the subject of Jones's mockery, Sophia leaves the inn; the irony of course is that Jones has been
involved in a defense of her honor against Northerton's mockery.
Into this dialectic the narrator enters again, and when Sophia
falls upon a landlord who has been helping her dismount from
her horse, the narrator jests with Sophia's character. Because she
falls on top of the landlord, this fall from grace has obvious sexual overtones. She observes an "immoderate Grin" in the by-
standers and suffers "a Violent shock given to her Modesty"
from "the great Injury." The mocking narrator assures his readers that "accidents of this Kind we have never regarded in a comical Light; nor will we scruple to say, that he must have a very
inadequate Idea of the Modesty of a beautiful young Woman,
who would wish to sacrifice it to so paultry a Satisfaction as can
arise from Laughter" (11.2.574). This of course is what the narrator has just done; the irony is itself text and countertext in the
current of laughter, the denial masking the affirmation. The narrator tells us he does not want to make the same kind of mistakes Sophia falsely believes Jones has made, but what he actually does is to subvert Sophia's position. She falls, both literally
and metaphorically.

The opposite position would be to take the dilemma of the
fallen woman seriously—and thus follows Mrs. Fitzpatrick's
story—but it is so solemn and sentimental (and finally revealed
as the fiction of a hypocrite) that at some point the reader is invited to laugh at it too, to mock Mrs. Fitzpatrick as the narrator
has mocked Sophia. First Tom, then the narrator, then also the

reader become involved in the shifts in the current of laughter. The puppet show is the next major shift, "a very grave and solemn Entertainment, without any low Wit or Humour, or Jests; or, to do it no more than Justice, without any thing which could provoke a Laugh" (12.5.638). In short, it lacks precisely what the novel itself has in large measure. The puppet show is designed to promote morality without laughter, and this the narrator of the novel neatly and dialectically inverts, for his story about the puppet show reveals the merry andrew in a sexually compromising position with a woman (comically and theologically named Grace). The narrator promotes morality by laughter, by his ridicule of the attempt to promote morality without laughter.

The sequence culminates in the gypsy wedding. "The Utmost Mirth indeed shewed itself in every Countenance; nor was their Ball totally void of all Order and Decorum" (12.12.667). But because "A young Female *Gypsy*, more remarkable for her Wit than her Beauty," attempts to seduce Partridge, the two are discovered "in a very Improper Manner by the Husband" (12.12.670). The current of laughter that has implicated the somber merry andrew of the puppet show now reverses and implicates Partridge, the master of wit, humor, and jests. But then it is discovered that the true culprit is the husband who has tried to sell his wife's honor. The serious puppet show is followed by the revelation of the merry andrew's hypocrisy, which the narrator ridicules. The mirth and decorum of the gypsy wedding is followed by the revelation of the husband's hypocrisy, which the narrator ridicules. The episode of the puppet show affirms that mirth and decency can coexist; the ethic of the puppet master is false. But the episode of the gypsy wedding affirms that mirth and decency can not coexist; the ethic of the gypsy society is shown to be just as much a lie. The ending of this section of the novel is significant then, for it is moving toward a denial of the basic tenets of Fielding's satire. The final movement is the brief episode with the sentimental highwayman, in which Jones ridicules Partridge for his cowardice. Partridge is in effect ridiculed twice, once in the gypsy wedding, once here. The mocker is no longer subject

to slaps and kicks, to physical abuse from the objects of mockery. If the basic tenet of the text—the alliance of mirth and morality—gets away from the narrator at the end of the journey, so
does the current of mockery escape the mocker's control, and
turn on him in an ordeal of humiliation. Mirth and mockery are
not easy to interpret, the novel maintains in the life of Jones, but
it is that kind of mirth and mockery that the narrator constantly
thrusts at the reader, demanding interpretation. Tom is seduced
by the guiles of women; the reader by the guiles of the narrator,
much of whose guile is his mockery, in the tricks he constantly
plays on the reader's wit and judgment.

V

"WHAT APPEARED confusion, both in the conduct of the story
and in the lives of the characters is, after all, a wise design: the
mighty maze is not without a plan," Battestin argues (*Providence of Wit*, 162). For him the maze is a mirror of divine providence, and the central image within the maze is the mirror itself. When Tom sees Sophia's reflection in a mirror at the end of
the novel, when Tom's eyes meet Sophia's in the mirror at Lady
Bellaston's apartments earlier in the novel, when Partridge suggests to Tom that he use the moon as if it were a mirror to imagine Sophia's reflection, all of these reflect the conception of the
mirror that comes to Fielding from 1 and 2 Corinthians—as
through a glass darkly the ideal Christian is perceived. But there
are an equal number of occurrences in the novel that show a
conception of the mirror that comes to Fielding from the comic
and satiric tradition, and that are comparable to his use of the
mirror in *Joseph Andrews*. It is a commonplace in both comic
theory and comic practice that can be traced to Cicero's statement, which survives only in the Donatine fragment, about
comedy as "an imitation of life, a mirror of custom, an image of
truth" (Lauter, *Theories of Comedy*, 27). When Molly peers
into a glass to admire herself in her finery before the churchyard
brawl, and then when she is forced to look again after the fight;
when Mrs. Honour fails to notice Sophia's countenance during

a discussion of Tom because she is so taken by her own image in the mirror; when Lady Bellaston peers into her mirror while Lord Fellamar discusses female beauty: all of these are uses of the comic Ciceronian mirror.

The comic mirror and the Christian mirror mirror each other, the one reflecting the wise design that is God's order, the other the wise design that is the order of comic literature. The novel's design is comic in this fashion, a multiplication of comic literary structures that Fielding takes from Molière, Congreve, and the comic tradition more generally. The symmetry of the plot reflects the symmetries of plot in Molière and Congreve, and the symmetries of the characters reflect the Aristotelian distinctions between the man who laughs too much, the man who laughs too little, and the perfect mean between them. There are explicit references to these sources thoughout the novel. In Molière's *The Miser*, a play that Fielding had translated and adapted for the London stage, Valère must pretend to urge Élise to marry Anselm, at Harpagon's urgings, to maintain his own deceit. In *Tom Jones* Tom must pretend to encourage Sophia to marry Blifil, at Squire Western's urgings (6.7.297). In Congreve's *Way of the World*, Mirabell pretends to court Lady Wishfort in order to court her niece, Millamant. In *Tom Jones* Tom makes "sham Addresses to the older Lady, in order to procure an easy Access to the Younger" (16.9.867), courting Lady Bellaston in order to court Sophia. All women desire Mirabell in the Congreve play; all women desire Jones in the Fielding novel.

Both *The Miser* and *The Way of the World* are perfectly mirrored symmetries. In the Molière play, the son of Harpagon marries the daughter of Anselm, the son of Anselm the daughter of Harpagon. One family dissolves in rancor on the stage (Harpagon and his children), while the other is magically reassembled (Anselm and his children). In the Congreve play, Mirabell, the true wit, is contrasted to Fainall, the false wit, and both carry on mirrored adulterous relationships: Mirabell with Mrs. Fainall, a good adulteress; Fainall with Mrs. Marwood, a bad adulteress. The true and false wits are in turn mirrored by true and false would-be wits (Wit-Would, Petulant, and Sir Wilful

Witwoud), the good and bad adulteresses by the paragon of virtue, Millamant, and the comic parody of virtue, Lady Wishfort.
Mirabell, grave, is further contrasted to Millamant, gay. This
kind of symmetry is standard enough in comic drama that Fielding could have learned it from other texts as well—in Jonson's
Volpone, for example, the first act is precisely mirrored and inverted by the last. The order in which the three gulls visit Volpone when he is faking illness is reversed in the order in which
they visit him when he is about to have real illness thrust upon
him. Additionally, the three are mirrored by the three "natural"
fools who make up Volpone's household.

What Fielding does to this tradition of comic symmetry and
artifice is to mirror it repeatedly, creating out of it a truly extrav-
agant form. In the basic plot of a typical Molière play, an unrea-
sonable father attempts to prevent the marriage between a head-
strong son or daughter and the true object of their love, until a
raisonneur (typically an uncle, but in *The Miser* the other father) intervenes and brings about a happy ending. In Fielding's
mirroring of this device, we begin with Allworthy and Western
agreeing to separate Tom and Sophia (a doubling of the unrea-
sonable father), then move to a doubling of the entire situation
(the subplot that concerns Nightingale, Nancy Miller, and Nightingale's father); then to the Molière solution (Nightingale's uncle
plays raisonneur); then to a mirror inversion of the Molière solution (the daughter of the uncle elopes with a young man he op-
poses and the uncle is removed from the subplot); then to another mirror inversion (Nightingale's father does finally become
reasonable); and then to a mirroring back into the Tom-Sophia
main plot (with Allworthy now playing raisonneur to Western).
This is replayed again when Sophia refuses Tom, and both Allworthy and Western must plead with her to marry him.

Fielding makes similar playful use of the Aristotelian distinction between grave and gay. Tom (gay) and Sophia (grave), a mirror inversion of the Congreve dichotomy, are raised by mirror-
inverted parent figures: Tom by the grave Allworthy, Sophia by
the rollicking Western. But Tom is also mirrored by his grave
half-brother Blifil, and Sophia by her gay cousin Harriet Fitz-

patrick (raised with her and known as "Miss Giddy" to Sophia's "Miss Grave-airs"). Tom in turn is educated by two tutors, the grave Thwackum and the gay Square. And this is just the beginning. The number of possible symmetries and contrasts from this simple listing grows geometrically: the pairings true gravity/true mirth (Sophia and Tom), excessive gravity/excessive mirth (Allworthy and Western), false gravity/false mirth (Blifil and Harriet), and the false contrast between gravity and mirth (Thwackum and Square, who are revealed to have similarly unsavory characters). These grow in complexity, from the relatively simple contrast Tom/Blifil at the start of the novel (the one who laughs too much/the one who laughs too little), to the far more difficult contrast in the last part of the novel between Tom/Nightingale, both fundamentally good, amiable mockers who sometimes fall into ridicule, both fornicators who get into trouble because they cannot control their passions. Nightingale is the citified man of wit and humor who flirts with women at the theatres and coffeehouses; Jones the country man of wit and humor who is seduced by women. One would abandon the woman he has made pregnant; the other would stand by the woman he believes he has made pregnant. We are being taught wit and judgment about wit and judgment. To see the connections between lack of control of physical passion and lack of control of mental attitude, mirth, is to learn wit, and to see the differences between two such similar men is to learn judgment.

Between Western's "roaring Mirth" and Allworthy's near total absence of mirth; between the constant raillery of Lady Bellaston and Sophia's gravity; between the whimsical humor of Partridge, his mock father, and the sentimentality of Mrs. Miller, who becomes a kind of mother to him; Jones is at the center of contrasting pairs of extremes. Mirrored against Blifil's extreme and false gravity, Jones appears as an emblem of the comic; but mirrored against Nightingale's extreme and false levity, Jones appears as an emblem of the serious. At the center of an elegant symmetry of grave and gay characters is Jones, Fielding's contribution to the history of comedy. Surrounding him are representatives of that history, arranged now not chronologically but schematically in the mighty maze: Western, the country squire and Whig excessively given to hunting (a parody of Addison's Sir Roger de Coverly); Lady Bellaston, the city lady excessively given to intrigues and somewhat too old for it (a parody of Lady Wishfort); Partridge, the oddity from Cervantes; Nightingale, the oddity from Molière; Northerton, the cruel Hobbesian laugher; Mrs. Miller, the humorless sentimentalist from Cibber or Steele; Allworthy, the humorless good man from Shaftesbury.

Reflecting the mirrored symmetries of characters onto the mirrored symmetries of the plot, the narrator composes his text. When Mr. Fitzpatrick first discovers Tom in bed with Mrs. Waters, he mistakenly believes the woman to be his wife and threatens harm to Tom. Jones escapes and Fitzpatrick leaves the inn with Mrs. Waters who will pretend to be his wife, just as the real Mrs. Fitzpatrick flees in another direction where she will meet her mirror reflection, Sophia, also fleeing the inn. Later when Mr. Fitzpatrick meets Tom again, Tom is leaving the house of the real Mrs. Fitzpatrick, and although she has tried to seduce Tom she has not succeeded. Fitzpatrick attacks Jones again, inverting the original provocation, sex with the false wife becoming no sex with the real wife, and now the battle inverts—it is Tom who injures Fitzpatrick, who is not able to run away. This is an elegant neoclassical dance, played out by clowns. The structure of the story is making a mockery of its serious themes.

The closet trick is played out in this manner three times. Molly hides Square in her closet when Jones comes to visit. Jones hides Lady Bellaston in his closet when Mrs. Honour comes to visit. Jones hides Mrs. Honour in his closet when Lady Bellaston comes to visit, then hides them both in the closet when Nightingale enters his room. During the first closet trick, the meaning seems reasonably clear: Tom laughs in honest ridicule at Square, who is positioned in a humiliating way and revealed as a hypocrite, but he bears the man no grudge and promises not to expose him to others. In contrast, the narrator mocks Square much more harshly, all the while asking us to applaud Jones for mocking Square amiably. And when Jones departs after refusing to turn Square into ridicule, Molly turns Jones into ridicule, abusing him to Square. The trick becomes increasingly complicated as it is mirrored and mirrored again. Unlike Square, Lady Bellaston is not exposed in the second closet trick, and thus she can not become the object of ridicule—instead it is Jones who is implicated by the narrator for becoming someone like Molly, a sexual trickster; but at the same time we are being asked to see the closet trick from Jones's new position in the trick, the point of view of someone like Molly. And now it is not nearly so laughable. The third replay doubles everything: Lady Bellaston and Mrs. Honour together in the closet are mirror images of each other, as are Jones and Nightingale outside the closet, and now the ridicule is wide-ranging. Everyone is implicated.

Multiplying the reflections of the comic mirror held up to the comic texts, Fielding creates an epic. And once the principle is established, he allows it to run wild. Every character, episode, and adventure is mirrored in the text, sometimes only once, sometimes many times. The more times it is mirrored, the more comic it becomes. This order is so intricate that the text becomes a maze of increasingly difficult choices for the reader, mocking his attempts to find truth. *Tom Jones* is an eighteenth-century fun house. In his reading of *Don Quixote*, "The Mirror of Knighthood and the World of Mirrors," Robert Alter writes: "The world, in this multiplication of internal parodies, becomes an assemblage of mirrors . . . but since parody is precisely the literary mode that fuses creation with critique, the mirrors are in varying degrees distortive, so that the characters parade through a vast fun-house hall where even the most arresting figures can suddenly swell into monstrosities or shrink to absurdities. . . . Virtually everything, then, is composite, made up of fragmented images, refractions, and reflections of other things" (24–25). Alter's argument is provocative, meant as metaphor for the kinds of processes that go on in *Quixote*. But in *Tom Jones* mirrors are not vague metaphors—they work neatly and precisely, and such workings can be traced carefully.

Trapped in this fun house and controlled by the mirrors, the narrator shifts from pose to pose as his reflection inverts against the walls of the labyrinth, becoming amiable guide, harsh critic,

serious moralist, mocking clown, amiable humorist, harsh railer
with each turn of the text. What creates the neoclassical symmetry also creates the romantic eccentricity. We are in the Hall of
Mirrors of the Palace of Versailles on the night of a masquerade,
and with each spin around the room we notice that our partner's
mask changes. "Every Gamester will agree how necessary it is to
know exactly the Play of another, in order to countermine him,"
the narrator tells us when Sophia has feigned interest in Blifil to
keep her aunt from learning of her true affection for Jones
(6.3.280). If we could know the play of the narrator, we might
similarly be able to countermine him. Tom is invited to a masked
ball by Lady Bellaston, masquerading as the Queen of the Fair-
ies, and there he proves inept at telling the play and the players.
We are in a similar predicament with the narrator, who has at
the beginning of the novel invited us to his feast. And just as
Lady Bellaston teases and seduces Tom, so too are we teased and
seduced—by mockery.

The narrator's special delight is playing tricks on his reader. In
addition to the obvious lies in the text about who Jones's mother
is, there are many others, only slightly more subtle. We are told
that the narrator's special hatred for critics comes because they
make rules, but the narrator claims for himself the right to make
rules; we are told that only the worst of men would cry out
rogue and villain, but then we are shown Blifil as the very worst
of rogues and villains; we are asked as fellow travelers on a stage
coach with the narrator to put aside our jokes and raillery as the
story draws to a close, but then we are tricked with the story of
the incest; we listen when the narrator complains that he does
not have the resources of a comic writer to resolve his plot, has
none of the *deus ex machina* useful to Molière and to Gay, but
then he ties the plot together by equally trite conventions of
comic drama, the happy coincidences. The narrator in his turns
in the labyrinth is sometimes playful, sometimes serious, sometimes loving, sometimes harsh. He shifts from innkeeper to en-
tertainer to coach rider; from wise man to fool; from mocker to
object of mockery. Like Stultitia in Erasmus's *Praise of Folly*,
who metamorphoses in front of us from genial and drunken fool

to satirist and then to fool for Christ, the narrator of *Tom Jones* changes constantly.

VI

NEITHER JONES'S innocent mirth nor the narrator's complex mockery are adequate or reasonable attitudes. In fact none of the comic attitudes presented in the text (and none of the serious attitudes) are unambiguously endorsed. If Tom's weakness is his love of laughter, Sophia's is her fear of laughter, though she seems to provoke it often enough. Her companions laugh at her when as a child she obeys her father scrupulously; Lady Bellaston laughs at her before the action of the story begins when Sophia refuses to travel to London without her father's consent; and in the last third of the novel Lady Bellaston finds a number of opportunities to turn the simple country girl to mockery. When Jones has met Sophia at Lady Bellaston's and none of the players will acknowledge the masquerade, each feigning ignorance, Lady Bellaston laughs at Sophia's interest in Jones. "This Raillery . . . is a little cruel," Sophia complains "affecting a Laugh" (13.12.737), but Lady Bellaston insists "sure you can bear a little Raillery on a Passion," and here the narrator appears to be sympathetic to the position of the city mocker. Later Lady Bellaston tries a more serious trick, passing on the information that Jones had been killed in a duel to demonstrate to Lord Fellamar the extent of Sophia's passion for him. Sophia faints. Lady Bellaston's joke is a bit too excessive for the narrator, yet at the same time the joke is a reflection of what is to come, the misinformation that comes from the narrator and is played off on the reader that Jones has killed a man in a duel. The narrator is caught in the mirror images of his characters. Describing Lady Bellaston's circle as "very good sort of People, and the Fibs which they propagated were of a harmless Kind, and tended only to produce Mirth and good Humour" (15.3. 790), he mocks the mockers. But he, too, fibs in the interests of mirth and humor, and his own desires for wit and ridicule make Lady Bellaston's pale into insignificance. His statement connect-

ing mirth and fibs mirrors his earlier description of Western's
rodomontade at Allworthy's expense. Western's description of
Allworthy as a rake at college is only a lie: "Too apt to indulge
that Kind of Pleasantry," Western is a reminder that "very much
of what frequently passes in the World for Wit and Humour
should . . . receive that short Appellation" (4.11.194). Having
suggested that Western simply lies, the narrator refuses to give it
a name, mocking Hobbes who had described laughter as the
effect of a passion that hath no name.

No laugher or nonlaugher has an altogether acceptable stance
toward the world, and while some mix of the grave and the gay
would appear to be ideal, the narrator's mix of the two is such an
essential part of his masquerade and such a central element of
his deceptions that making such a combination cannot be easy.
The reader is asked to judge from among a series of flawed alternatives. Tom learns to control his mirth just as he learns to control his sexual energy, and when the novel ends at the wedding of
Tom and Sophia, an evening of "true Mirth," the two "appeared
the least merry of the whole Company" (18.13.978). Similarly
the narrator renounces his kind of joking (18.1.913), but what
Jones really effects, the narrator only pretends to do. The renunciation of joking is followed by the information that Jones has
committed incest with his mother, and it is this kind of false information that the narrator has tricked the reader with throughout his story. When the narrator raises the possibility of incest
between Tom and Mrs. Waters, there is a great fuss made in the
novel until Bridget Allworthy is revealed as Tom's true mother.
What passes by almost unnoticed is that Bridget Allworthy has
felt sexual desires for her son, but when the narrator mentions
this in a casual reference early in his story, no reader suspects
the truth. As the novel denies that there was ever a danger of
incest, it affirms that there was a real danger of incest, and this
real danger, about which the narrator makes no fuss, is more
serious than what is denied. Tom and Mrs. Waters would have
been incestuous by accident, but Bridget desired her son knowing their relationship.

Unlike the narrator of *Joseph Andrews*, who could propose a wedding celebration of utmost merriment/strictest decency but be unable to describe it, the narrator of *Tom Jones* does describe the wedding celebration of the gypsies in detail as such an oxymoron. It is only after he describes it that the scene gets away from him—a woman flirts rather too indecently with Partridge, and we are once more in excess. Disillusioned, the narrator backs away from his earlier praise of gypsy society explaining that the form of that society, absolute monarchy, makes its utopian aspects unworkable for other peoples. Later, when Tom and Sophia marry, the evening is spent in "much true mirth" but with Tom and Sophia as "the least merry." The narrator suggests this is because of their great joy that has followed a sudden change of circumstances. We are suddenly propelled into another oxymoron. The scene of course mirrors the gypsy wedding, which erred in the opposite direction toward excess levity. We are back again to the position of the narrator of *Joseph Andrews*—our second tour of the labyrinth ends precisely where our first tour ends—when the oxymoron is finally described, it is shown to be impossible after all. But here at the end of a comic celebratory novel the renunciation of mirth and levity is uncanny. It foreshadows *Amelia*. The narrator's control of the current of laughter is not his apparent renunciation of joking nor his picture of Jones and Sophia as "least merry" at the moment of true mirth. His real control is the ironic artistry that underlies the shifting currents of laughter throughout the novel. On one level mockery has been tamed—but so tamed that it disappears; on another level the mockery remains. An excessively mocking narrator at the start of the novel has been replaced by an excessively somber one. The ending of *Tom Jones* then is not only a repetition of the ending of *Joseph Andrews*, it is also a mirror inversion. In the first comic epic, the current of laughter simply proves to be too powerful for the narrator to control effectively; in the second epic, the current of laughter is elegantly and elaborately brought under control by the narrator, for the services of his comedy.

4

Transcendental Buffoonery: Kierkegaard as Comedian

BETWEEN 1841 and 1848 Søren Kierkegaard published a series of complicated philosophical fictions, which comprise his
so-called pseudonymous authorship. Contained within many of
these texts are extensive but scattered discussions of such aspects of comedy and the comic as the relationship between
laughter and the stages on life's way, the relationship between
comedy and despair, the relationship between irony and ethics,
and the relationship between humor and religious faith. In addition to being examined in these critical discussions, all of these
relationships are demonstrated in the lives of the pseudonyms
themselves as they are revealed to the reader. The pseudonymous
authorship is a clown show, a masquerade of pretense and mockery as well as of existence and despair, as much comic and about
the comic as it is pathetic and about the pathetic. And at the
same time that Kierkegaard was composing these fictions, he
was acting out his own clown show on the streets of Copenhagen, staging a masquerade of pretense and mockery that was
meant to confuse and to enlighten his readers. In his autobiographical essays and journals, none of which were published
in his lifetime, there is a comparable amount of discussion of
laughter and the comic that is meant to describe not merely the
pseudonymous authorship but also the life of the author who

had multiplied himself into these mirrored comic repetitions. As both a philosopher and a devout Christian, Kierkegaard is properly understood as a comedian. His contribution to the study of the comic is in three forms: expository statement, fictional demonstration, existential enactment. What the comedian and his comic masks discuss they also test, against their own statements and against their mutually interdependent comic fictions.

In the mid-eighteenth century Fielding wrote a labyrinthine study of the comic that is an interplay between the consciousness of the narrators and their abilities to construct devious and intricate fictions, both of which are comic. In the mid-nineteenth century Kierkegaard wrote a labyrinthine study of the comic that is an interplay between the consciousness of the pseudonyms, their abilities to construct devious and intricate fictions, the consciousness of the author, and his ability to turn his own life into a devious and intricate fiction. All of these are comic. For Fielding theory and fiction are comic; for Kierkegaard, theory, fiction, and reality. There are no more complex studies of the comic than Kierkegaard's, and reading the documents is not a simple matter. But Kierkegaard has left a number of clues behind—puzzling confessions that both reveal and hide the truth—by which the reader can make his way into the labyrinth.

"And (rightly understood) between me and laughter there is a secret and happy understanding. I am (rightly understood) a friend and lover of laughter, and in a sense (that is, in all seriousness) never more truly so than just at that moment when the others, all these thousands and thousands, became ironical, and I (ironically enough) was the only one that had no understanding of irony." Kierkegaard made this confession in a footnote to "A Word About The Relation of My Work to the 'Individual,'" an essay written in 1847 but not published until 1859, four years after his death (*Point of View*, 123). The immediate reference is to the series of lampoons directed at him in 1846 by the *Corsair*, Copenhagen's satiric journal, caricatures of an eccentric wandering about the city with one trouser leg shorter than the other. The ridicule was picked up by enough of the

public that for a while Kierkegaard was forced to limit his
walks—even children taunted him as "either/or." Yet in a number
of autobiographical confessions that were not published in his
lifetime, Kierkegaard claimed that he had provoked this ridicule
deliberately, in order to confuse the public and make a reading of
his serious works more difficult; in order to expose himself to
that which was most feared by the public, ridicule, and thereby
test himself; in order to demonstrate to the thousands and thousands of others who had made the *Corsair* a publishing success
that they really had no understanding of laughter, comedy, or
irony. If these claims can be believed, then the thousands of
others who mocked him in 1846 did so in ignorance of the fact
that he was both the object and the author of the mockery; his
understanding *was* greater than their understanding, and we
who are privileged to read this confession are let in on the secret. Kierkegaard must mean the statement that he was the only
one with no understanding of irony ironically enough and the
statement that he had a secret and happy relationship with laughter in all seriousness. The parenthetical remarks direct us to the
way in which the confession must be rightly understood. But the
opposite can also be true, and several of Kierkegaard's biographers have argued that the elaborate justifications for the *Corsair* incident are fabrications made up after the fact to hide the
depth of humiliation he suffered and the surprise he experienced
that ridicule directed against him could have such powerful
effects. If this is so then the statement must be read quite differently; what is now seen as ironical is that this friend and lover of
laughter nevertheless had no understanding of irony. How we
read the confession depends entirely on what we bring to it from
our readings of other statements written by Kierkegaard. And
these, of course, are no more reliable.

But it is not necessary to accept either Kierkegaard's interpretation or that of his revisionist biographers in order to understand the secret that the passage reveals in its dialectical maze
of inversions, negations, and repetitions. A secret understanding of laughter is followed by its negation, a lack of understanding of irony; laughter by its negation, seriousness; irony

by, ironically enough, irony, a negation of the sequence laughter/seriousness. We are asked to understand what is defined as a secret understanding, and the final paradox is that the statement can only reveal its secret by maintaining its secret, for otherwise the irony disappears and there is nothing to understand. The obscurity of content is made clear at the level of form, and form and content are in this manner dialectically joined. But a part of the secret remains hidden, and what we cannot know is whether Kierkegaard was simply mocking himself in 1846 when the *Corsair* ridiculed him, because he was the author of the ridicule, or whether he was also mocking himself in 1847 when he claimed that he was the author of the ridicule, because in fact he was not. In the first case he is also mocking his contemporaries in Copenhagen who think that they understand him but are only reading false clues, and in the second case he is also mocking his later critics and biographers who think *they* understand him but are only reading another set, dialectically inverted, of false clues. And because Kierkegaard was fascinated by repetition, the possibility exists that he is tricking both audiences, the first that did not take him seriously and the second that has taken him very seriously. The repetition of false clues in ironic patterns leads us only to ironic repetitions of earlier misreadings, and it is this which Kierkegaard finally invites us to understand as the truth revealed/maintained in the secret.

Buried in the margins of this marginal 1847 discourse is a confession/secret of major importance: the secret and happy relationship with laughter is the most fundamental intimacy of Kierkegaard's work. This is the ironic style of both the life and the authorship. In 1848 Kierkegaard characterized this kind of dialectic as "the performance of a reflective comedian" in yet another short essay never published in his lifetime, "Herr Phister as Captain Scipio." Hiding under the pseudonym Procul, Kierkegaard praised the acting skills of his Copenhagen acquaintance Phister, who had played Scipio in the comic opera *Ludovic* in 1846. What Kierkegaard singled out for special attention was Phister's ability to act drunk and not drunk simultaneously. "It would surely require a comedian of considerable stature just to conceive such a problem correctly," he wrote, "not to speak of solving it, a tipsiness so perfectly kept secret that the clue, the betrayal, is just his attempt to conceal it" (*Crisis*, 122). By conceiving and then executing such a movement on stage Phister becomes in Kierkegaard's conception a reflective comedian, and this of course is what Kierkegaard himself has done in his 1847 confession. "The performance of a reflective comedian, who is conscious of every insignificant minutia, constitutes a demand that he be given back again with the same precision what he has with such precision presented," Kierkegaard wrote as Procul (111). We must reflect back the reflective genius of such a comedian and this is what Kierkegaard himself has done in the writing of that autobiographical confession, only now he is presenting to us what Phister has presented to him.

The repetition itself is significant as are all repetitions in Kierkegaard because the pseudonyms elevate repetition to a psychological and religious concept. Distinguished from recollection, the simple movement backward, repetition is a dialectic of a backward movement that allows an individual who is paralyzed by despair or confusion to move forward in time toward an existential becoming. Repetition adds something new and can allow an individual progress toward an intimacy with God, a god it must be noted who shares with Kierkegaard a fascination with the dialectic. "The dialectic of repetition is easy, for that which is repeated has been," Constantine Constantius explains in *Repetition* (149), the book explicitly concerned with the problems of repetition (and a book split into two parts, the second a repetition of the first), a book authored by a pseudonym with a repetitious name who is not only a repetition of Kierkegaard but who also repeats himself in the text in the creation of yet another pseudonym. The problem of the repetition is serious, but the treatment is comic. "He who wills repetition" matures in seriousness, Constantine tells us, but at the same time it is obvious that Kierkegaard, who has willed this repetition, is maturing in the comic (*Repetition*, 132).

The 1848 essay on Phister repeats the 1847 essay on the secret and happy relationship with laughter, revealing it to be a repetition of Phister's 1846 performance. We move backward then forward over the secret/betrayal paradox, and if we then understand Kierkegaard as a reflective comedian, we must respond to him in kind, as Kierkegaard has responded to Phister. Reading Kierkegaard as repetition, we repeat his pattern of repetition and mature in seriousness. We are being forced to become reflective comedians. Kierkegaard repeats Phister but in the process of moving backward moves forward beyond Phister, and how this is so we discover when we move backward into Kierkegaard's own texts to allow our interpretation to move forward. "The humorous, present throughout Christianity, is expressed in a fundamental principle which declares that the truth is hidden in the mystery, . . . which teaches not only that the truth is found in the mystery . . . but that it is in fact *hidden* in the mystery" (*Journals*, 2:252). This is the first appearance of the paradox, in 1837, and what our movement backward in time reveals is a connection to Christianity. Phister is repeating a fundamental principle present throughout Christianity, though of this he has no knowledge; Kierkegaard describes him simply as an inspired stage comic. But Kierkegaard on the other hand has this secret knowledge, and therefore his repetition of Phister allows him to find a way of animating the principle and of moving beyond Phister to become a Christian humorist, or a humorous Christian, for the exact nature of this relationship is still vague, a new secret in the new revelation.

We are now freed to move forward, to the *Training in Christianity* written in 1850, where the humorous principle present throughout Christianity is revealed. There writing under the pseudonym Anti-Climacus, Kierkegaard describes contradiction as (1) the life of Christ, both man and god, and (2) the unity of jest and earnest. The first contradiction is not one Kierkegaard can repeat; the second therefore is the Christian repetition. "A communication which is the unity of jest and earnest is such a sign of contradiction. It is by no means a direct communication, it is impossible for him who receives it to tell *directly* which it is, because the communication does not *directly* communicate either jest or earnest" (*Training*, 125). The effect, however, is of "the highest earnestness" because it makes "the receiver independently active."

With each repetition we learn more and more of the secret, until Kierkegaard's method of composition is revealed. A pattern of irony and repetition set up by Kierkegaard teaches us irony and repetition and Christianity, allows us to dance through the texts, circling the repeating paradox, the secret/betrayal, which is alternately named humor, irony, comedy, laughter, jest/earnest, and which is alternately identified with the stage and the church. The fundamental step in this dance is the turn, backward or forward, though each repetition is a kind of maturity for us as it has been for Kierkegaard. We are moving across the dance floor of philosophy, art, religion. "Three cheers for the dance in the vortex of the infinite," Constantine's repetition exclaims near the end of his repetition (*Repetition*, 222). And in the preface to the *Philosophical Fragments* Johannes Climacus explains, "I have disciplined myself and keep myself under discipline, in order that I may be able to execute a sort of nimble dancing in the service of Thought, so far as possible also to the honor of God, and for my own satisfaction." But other kinds of dancing disgust him, especially the Hegelian, which he compares to "an acrobatic clown in the current circus season, every moment performing these everlasting dog-tricks of flopping over and over, until it flops over the man himself" (5–7). Hegel's serious dance is revealed as slapstick, while Kierkegaard's comic dance approaches the highest seriousness. Climacus's partner is "the thought of Death."

This is a dialectical two-step that can lead us into any aspect of Kierkegaard's thought, but we are concerned here with the secret and happy relationship with laughter. And for this subject we are close to a resting place. In 1849, one year after the essay on Phister and one year before *Training in Christianity*, Kierkegaard wrote, "I am a martyr of laughter and my life has been designed for that; I understand myself so completely as such that it is as if I now understand myself for the first time." This statement is followed by its dialectical inversion, "To be able to become just that, I am the wittiest of all, possessing a superlative sense of comedy" (*Journals*, 6: 119). The 1849 journal entry repeats the 1847 autobiographical footnote, but there are now no overtones of irony. Kierkegaard has matured in seriousness, and we are moving toward clarity. In 1854, one year before his death, he wrote, "My entire existence is really the deepest irony" (2: 277).

II

WE ARE not meant to see *through* this irony but we are meant to understand the irony for what it is, a secret and happy relationship with laughter that is at the very center of Kierkegaard's life and work. Kierkegaard is a reflective comedian, a Christian humorist, a master of irony, a martyr of laughter, a clown; and his writing, especially his pseudonymous authorship, is a clown's work, within which is a complex and extensive meditation on the meanings of laughter, humor, irony, ridicule, and the comic. It is the most elaborate study of the subject in modern European intellectual history, and for the most part it has been ignored or downplayed by Kierkegaard's critics, for they have been after the serious content. In the twentieth century two diverse groups of critics have claimed Kierkegaard—orthodox Christian theologians who study his religious tracts written under his own name, and existential philosophers who study his pseudonymous stories and essays. Kierkegaard's irony or at least his interest in irony is often noted and sometimes discussed, but only very rarely do critics understand how that irony is directed by Kierkegaard against them.

> Most people have no idea of what it means to enter into a character role . . . have no idea of the difference between saying to another person: I shall assume this or that guise, and then standing directly opposite him and carefully doing everything to carry through the character-role. I have attempted this with irony. I told a man that I am always somewhat ironical. What happened? We understood each other—I had revealed myself. But the very moment I stepped

into character, he was bewildered. At that moment all direct communication was cut off; my whole appearance, vis-
age, and speech were nothing but question marks. Aha, you
are being ironical, he said. He of course expected me to answer *yes* or *no*—that is, to communicate directly. But the
moment I stepped into character I tried to be completely
true to it. Now, however, it was impossible for him to be
sure whether or not it was irony—precisely this was the
irony of it. (*Journals*, 2: 270–71)

It is difficult to deal with the kind of taunting contained in this
passage and others like it throughout the journals and autobiographical essays. The secret of irony is revealed but is then discovered to have maintained its secret. Kierkegaard adds, "it
pleases God to want to be incognito" (2: 271). We are playing
hide and seek with the master. "Generally speaking, there is no
safer hiding place for inwardness than behind mirror glass,"
Kierkegaard tells us. "And this can be done if in your association with anyone you deftly and agilely practice reflecting correctly, just as a mirror does, and changing your phenomenal de-
portment in relation to his, so that no one manages to converse
with you but only to converse with himself—although he thinks
that he is talking to you" (*Journals*, 2: 269). So confident is
Kierkegaard that he can hide that he is willing to tell us how he
is doing it. Either "pull the silk curtain (irony's) of quips and
bantering," he wrote, or "put mirror glass in the windows" so
that "curiosity and envy and partisan sympathy see only their
own mugs" (2: 269). For over a hundred years the curious, the
envious, and the sympathetic have been peering through a curtain of irony at Kierkegaard's mirror glass, and what have they
seen is what he told them they would see, their own mugs. The
theologians and the philosophers have been so fascinated by
their own reflections that they have not noticed a mirror at all or
that a curtain of irony has obscured their view. The journal entry of 1847 reminds us that we are in a labyrinth of mirrors and
of mockery.

The Point of View for My Work as an Author followed in

1848. Subtitled *A Report to History*, it is a small masterpiece of mirrors and mockery, for if the 1847 journal taunts the would-be critic that he will only see himself in Kierkegaard's mirrors, the 1848 autobiography shows us Kierkegaard stepping out from behind the mirrors to reveal himself; but he now appears as the critic of Kierkegaard, mocking and subverting the critical process of interpretation. Kierkegaard must be understood fundamentally as a religious writer and not as a poet, Kierkegaard tells us, but the essay concludes in an unscientific postscript by a poet who demonstrates to us that Kierkegaard has really been a poet of philosophy all along. *The Point of View*, which contains praise of the *Concluding Unscientific Postscript*, thereby negates the either/or of the two points of view, indicating that both are far too limited, yet virtually all Kierkegaard scholarship divides neatly between these two alternatives. We are mirroring Kierkegaard then and repeating him, but Kierkegaard is mirroring and anticipating us. (Of course, this first critic of Kierkegaard, the author of *The Point of View*, is a Kierkegaard ironist. Thus what we are presented with is only what Kierkegaard himself wanted us to know or to believe, not the hidden truths of his inwardness. But even if *The Point of View* is an elaborate deception, there are truths enough revealed, truths about the processes of deception.)

Moving backward into Kierkegaard's texts we discover more of our critical responses mirrored into the work. In 1837 he wrote, "I can imagine someone's wanting to make a theatrical presentation of the fallaciousness of the age; but when he himself sits among the spectators he sees that no one, after all, takes it to heart except to detect the fallacy in his neighbor; he makes one more attempt and stages this terrible scene in the theatre, and people laugh at it saying Isn't it terrible how most people can see the faults of others and not their own" (*Journals*, 3 : 714). There are mirrors within mirrors here, but although Kierkegaard stages this terrible scene in what is, after all, his own theatrical presentation of the fallaciousness of the age, the audience does not understand how thoroughly it is implicated, never sees that the audience in the passage is the audience reading the passage. When we should see ourselves in the mirror glass we see only a neighbor, and when we think we see Kierkegaard in the glass we see only ourselves. Moving forward in Kierkegaard's texts we return to *Training in Christianity*—a sign of contradiction Anti-Climacus tells us calls attention to itself. "There is something which makes it impossible for one to desist from looking—and lo! while one looks, one sees as in a mirror, one gets to see oneself, or He, the sign of contradiction." It is now Christ, the god-man, who appears in the mirror. "A contradiction placed directly in front of a man—if only one can get him to look upon it—is a mirror; while he is judging, what dwells within him must be revealed" (126). More of the secret is revealed, and we can now understand that it is not hide and seek with Kierkegaard that we are playing but hide and seek with ourselves. The mockery and the mirrors are meant to bring us to self-recognition and then to Christ. This is the unity of jest and earnest. Kierkegaard's name for this is "double reflection," and it is meant to describe the appropriate critical response to ironic indirect communication. Double reflection is also allied to repetition, for it is the movement backward and forward in philosophic space as repetition is the movement backward and forward in historic time. According to Johannes Climacus: "The reflection of inwardness gives to the subjective thinker a double reflection. In thinking, he thinks the universal; but as existing in this thought and as assimilating it in his inwardness, he becomes more and more subjectively isolated" (*Concluding Unscientific Postscript*, 68).

We are back in the labyrinth of mirrors and of mockery one hundred years after Henry Fielding. Kierkegaard has as many affinities to Fielding and the comic tradition as he does to Sartre or to Karl Barth, and it is time for the ironists and mockers to step forward and recognize the reflections of their own mugs in the mirror glass. There may be no way of evading Kierkegaard's mockery, no way of saying something about Kierkegaard that he has not already anticipated, but there is a way of understanding the mockery and understanding the importance of the mockery by focusing on the tricks of the glass themselves and the curtain of quips and bantering that hangs in front of it. There is also a difference between Kierkegaard's confessions that he is a poet or a religious writer and his confessions that he is an ironist or comic, for the confessions of seriousness are presented or undercut by irony while the confessions of irony are presented in all seriousness. Thus, to return to *The Point of View*, the most complex autobiographical confession, within the mutually exclusive either/or of religious writer/poet is a both/and, an interpretation of Kierkegaard as a master of irony and then as an object of ridicule, the positions sketchily presented in the journals. As I mock I must also be mocked, Kierkegaard argues, and the truth of this is demonstrated by *The Point of View* itself, for in this mock autobiography Kierkegaard is simultaneously mocking himself and his critics-to-be.

We are back again to Fielding and to similar movements along the current of laughter in *Joseph Andrews* and *Tom Jones*. Both Fielding and Kierkegaard write using a sequence of personas and pseudonyms with comically improbable names; both construct intricate symmetries and oppositions with mirrors; both alternate between jest and earnest; both hide behind the mirror glass; both use the mirror for comic and for religious purposes. There is at least one significant difference: the narrators of *Joseph Andrews and Tom Jones* move on a current of laughter within their fictions, but Kierkegaard claims that he himself moves on the current of laughter not in fiction but in fact. Kierkegaard's work is concerned with the life of the subjective existing individual, and thus what Kierkegaard does in the labyrinth of the comic with the mirrors and the quips and bantering is to explore it himself, with the life of the only subjective existing individual he has under his control, his own. In repeating Fielding, Kierkegaard then goes beyond him. The clown is real. The line of influence between Fielding and Kierkegaard goes through Sterne to Schlegel and to the Schlegelian concept of romantic irony, but the exact path of transmission is less important than the result. The comic is made a matter of ethics, of existence, not of aesthetics and of art.

In this respect Kierkegaard owes as much to Sterne as to

Fielding—Sterne had similarly alternated between religious tract and comic fiction, and had combined the roles of preacher and jester in the persona of Parson Yorick, who was both a character within *Tristram Shandy* and a name by which Sterne himself came to be known. Several key elements of Kierkegaard's philosophic clown show repeat themes from *Tristram Shandy*: the notion of repetition as a movement backward and forward in time; the comparison of writing to the dance; the idea that a life recounted in print will make a better impression than the life lived in the world.

If Kierkegaard anticipated that his critics and biographers would claim him as religious writer or as a kind of poet, he also predicted that no group of ironists or tricksters would claim him at all. "There is as little social unity in a coterie of ironists as there is truly honesty among a band of thieves," he wrote in *The Concept of Irony* (266). The statement repeats Falstaff's speech in *I Henry IV* after Hal has tricked the master trickster at Gad's Hill. "A plague upon it when thieves cannot be true to one another" (2.2.30), Falstaff complains as the current of mockery reverses against him, and what the Shakespearean ironist and thief applies to his fellow thieves, Kierkegaard applies to the larger fellowship of ironists in his study of the life of Socrates and the mistakes of Schlegelian irony. Elsewhere Kierkegaard indicates that an ironist is also a master thief because he is a living deception to everyone he meets, but here in *The Concept* what is deceptive is the statement itself, since by repeating Falstaff's speech on the lack of unity among ironists Kierkegaard affirms a unity between himself and Falstaff. "He who does not understand irony and has no ear for its whisperings lacks *eo ipso* what might be called the absolute beginning of the personal life" (*Concept*, 339).

The same must be said for anyone who would understand Kierkegaard. "The only person I can say I envy is he, when he comes, whom I call my reader, who in peace and quiet will be able to sit and purely intellectually enjoy the immensely comic drama I have allowed Copenhagen to perform just by living here," Kierkegaard wrote in 1848 (*Journals*, 6:79). Kierkegaard

has had a number of sensitive readers who have seen the irony—
but that Kierkegaard has been the author of an immensely comic
drama has been more difficult to discern. These readers have described with some care the functions of irony and humor as they
are presented by the pseudonyms, but the processes have always
seemed secondary to them, a kind of comic relief to the obses-
sions with suffering and despair that also characterize his writing. And a few critics have described ways in which Kierkegaard
is trickster or humorist in his pseudonymous authorship.[1] None
has attempted to claim that he is clown in both his life and his
work, or that clown, comedian, fool, is the best way to understand the man who is also religious writer and philosophical
poet. That Kierkegaard's life and work is a labyrinth is the thesis
of Josiah Thompson's *The Lonely Labyrinth, Kierkegaard's
Pseudonymous Works*, but for Thompson the labyrinth is the
creation of a psychologically disturbed agoraphobic who can
find no way out of his wanderings, no end to the repetitions of
guilt, despair, and confinement within consciousness. It is certainly not a comic place, yet to make this interpretation Thompson has had to ignore the comic aspects. "The more one suffers,
the more I believe has one a sense for the comic," Quidam
writes in *Stages on Life's Way* (231), and in the *Concluding Unscientific Postscript*, Johannes Climacus explains, "Existence itself, the act of existing, is both pathetic and comic in the same
degree" (84). For Fielding too the world was not simply comic,
but comic and pathetic in the same degree, although his critics
have played up the comic while Kierkegaard's, the pathetic.

Like existence itself, Kierkegaard's works are pathetic and
comic in the same degree—the religious authorship is balanced
by the pseudonymous authorship. But because the pseudonyms
are mirror reflections of Kierkegaard, their authorship is itself
pathetic and comic in the same degree, alternating between discussions and demonstrations of pathos and despair and discus-

---

1. Gregor Malantschuk discusses Kierkegaard as a humorist in *Kierkegaard's Thought*, 90. Josiah Thompson calls Kierkegaard a "maieutic trickster" in his *Kierkegaard* (New York: Knopf, 1973), 184.

sions and demonstrations of the comic. Quidam is not the only
pseudonym who moves easily from one point of view to the
other, and most are fascinated by the meanings of the comic, of
irony, humor, mockery, ridicule, laughter. There are extensive
commentaries on these meanings and arguments between the
pseudonyms throughout the authorship. What complicates the
reading of these passages is that there are very similar statements in Kierkegaard's journals and autobiographical essays,
and many of these suggest that Kierkegaard understands himself
as a comic figure. The pseudonyms are simply elaborating a biography of the author. But in *The Point of View* Kierkegaard
presents the opposite point of view, that he has acted out special
poses in Copenhagen in order to facilitate a proper reading of
his work. The life is an illustration of the work.

This kind of fooling never stops, but it is a kind of fooling we
can now identify. What the medieval or Renaissance fool was,
Kierkegaard is, a figure who is a mixture of fact and fiction and
who lives, according to Bakhtin, in the spaces between life and
art (*Rabelais*, 7). He is the same character off stage as on. Kierkegaard is such a harlequin many centuries after the harlequin
has disappeared from the streets of European towns and cities, a
century after harlequin has finally disappeared from German
comic drama. His clown drama is the pseudonymous authorship; his clown life is the self-consciously scripted performance
he played out for his contemporaries in Copenhagen and the
performance that has played out for us in the pages of his autobiographical essays and journals since his death. When Kierkegaard's biographers examine his life from the standpoint of the
real they are led into medical diagnoses of illness and abnor-
mality, but were they only to approach his life from the standpoint of the history of the comic, they would see harlequin. In
the unfinished *Johannes Climacus or De omnibus dubitandum
est* Kierkegaard wrote about "a historic person . . . so poetical
that his every word, his every gesture" would be "pure poetry, so
that he would, therefore, need no metamorphosis to go on the
stage but could go straight there from the street just as he is, and
without the slightest embarrassment" (124). This book too is

another thinly veiled autobiographical fragment never published during the author's lifetime. That the pseudonymous authorship is a puppet theatre is by now a well-established point of view about Kierkegaard. I am suggesting that Kierkegaard too, or at least the Kierkegaard that is presented to us, is another of these theatrical fictions. The real Kierkegaard hides forever from us in his inwardness; but the theatrical performance that we are left with, which is all we have, must not be pushed aside. "An actor in his personal existence is perhaps in our time the only usable figure who is not used," Kierkegaard wrote (*Journals*, 1 : 58).[2]

The medieval or Renaissance fool talks about more subjects than his fooling, although he is always fooling with the subjects he does talk about, and the same is true of Kierkegaard, whose subjects include: the meanings of suffering and despair, the search for love and pleasure, the mistakes of the Hegelian philosophy, the mistakes of the Schlegelian philosophy, the promise of religion, the significance of human existence. The pseudonymous authorship can be seen as a repetition of Erasmus's *Praise of Folly*, which it resembles in both structure as well as subject matter. As we make that connection, we begin to see the history of the fool, of harlequin, in Kierkegaard's mirror, and there is more. Kierkegaard is becoming by a trick of the mirror glass his own coterie of ironists: Socrates, the master of irony; Christ, the object of ridicule; Stultitia; Falstaff; Fielding; and from Kierkegaard's own time, Phister of the Copenhagen theatre, and Beckmann and Grobecker of the Berlin Königstäter Theatre. Along with these reflective comedians, Kierkegaard also repeats other critics of the comic, most notably the standard critical works on the comic, on irony and humor from his own time—Schiller on play and comedy, Schlegel on irony, Richter on irony and humor, and Hegel on comedy and drama. We are presented with an extremely complex pattern of repetitions and of mirrored reflections from the history of comic fiction and drama, comic

2. For a more thorough consideration of Kierkegaard's interest in acting, actors, and the theatre, see Malantschuk, *Kierkegaard's Thought*.

theory, and comic existence. Kierkegaard the fool out of time in nineteenth-century Copenhagen is the fool of all time, ancient, medieval, modern, pagan, Christian; he is the mocker and the mocked, the real fool, the fictional fool, the theoretical fool; and he is both himself and fragmented into a series of pseudo-nyms who recapitulate the psychological development of the fool. In the long history of clown acts this is a virtuoso perfor-mance. That the fool undergoes a constant metamorphosis is one of the central points in *The Praise of Folly*, but in repeating Erasmus, Kierkegaard goes significantly beyond him. "If there is anything I have studied from the ground up, and pursued into its farthest ramifications, it is the comic," Johannes Climacus explains in the *Concluding Unscientific Postscript* (431). The same may be said of Kierkegaard.

III

"AS AN historical figure," Enid Welsford writes about the fool, "he does not confine his activities to the theatre but makes every-day life comic at the moment and on the spot. The Fool, in fact, is an amphibian equally at home in the world of reality and the world of imagination" (*The Fool*, xii). And according to Wil-liam Willeford, the fool is the confrontation of the fictional with the real. Both Welsford and Willeford go on to detail at some length the characteristics of this fool—it is an inventory of per-sonality that Kierkegaard fits almost perfectly. There is the mat-ter of the fool's dress, meant to call attention to itself, and the stick he carries as a sceptre. Kierkegaard walks the streets of Copenhagen in old-fashioned clothes, carries an umbrella whether it is raining or not, and is lampooned for the uneven length of his trousers. There is the matter of the fool's orienta-tion to the world, his failure to marry, the confusion of his sex-uality. Kierkegaard's extended courtship of Regine Olsen and then his fearful retreat from marriage was the event in his life that he wrote about most obsessively; the nature of his sexuality has become one of the arguments among his biographers. There is the matter of the fool's introversion and his role on the boundaries of the normal. Kierkegaard's introversion, his inwardness, is what he will protect from us at all costs; on the boundaries of Copenhagen society, he watches as an eccentric outsider. There is the matter of the fool's purpose, his special ability to speak the truth within the jest, to transvalue and to invert, and so to bring an audience to a new understanding of the truth. This is the role Kierkegaard self-consciously adopts for himself. There is the matter of the fool's paradoxical speech, which alternates between jest and earnest, meaning and meaninglessness, the worthless and the valuable. This is the language of Kierkegaard's texts. There is even the fool's special interest in his own disguises, the ways in which he calls attention to his masks as masks and asks us to see through the disguises. This is the manner in which Kierkegaard presented the pseudonymous authorship to Copenhagen—what appeared under Hilarius Bookbinder, Johannes Climacus, and the other names, the city knew Kierkegaard had published. One major characteristic Kierkegaard lacks—a partner. Most fools live in pairs, one as wit, one as butt, and without this other Kierkegaard is forced to improvise. He acts both parts himself, master of irony and martyr of laughter, moving on the current of laughter.

In *Rabelais and His World* Bakhtin argues that clowns and fools "are characteristic of the medieval culture of humor. They were the constant, accredited representatives of the carnival spirit in everyday life and out of carnival season" (8). In Bakhtin's history of the comic there is a gradual destruction of this medieval culture of humor with the rise of capitalism, a loss of the people's humor, and in the romantic period a return to carnival, but only to false carnival, individualistic, alienated humor. "In its Romantic form the mask is torn away from the oneness of the folk carnival concept. . . . [N]ow the mask hides something, keeps a secret, deceives. . . . The Romantic mask loses almost entirely its regenerating and renewing element and acquires a somber hue" (40). Certainly for Kierkegaard the mask hides, keeps a secret, deceives, but at the same time Kierkegaard designed the mask to be regenerating and renewing. For Bakhtin the medieval fool animates the spirit of grotesque realism, the style most clear in Rabelais. "One of the main attributes of the medieval clown was precisely the transfer of every high ceremonial gesture or ritual to the material sphere" (20). The romantic clown does not do this—but in his own way Kierkegaard does transfer the high ceremonial gesture to the material sphere. Kierkegaard's continual attacks on Hegel for his system, for forgetting the subjective existing individual in the material sphere, illustrate precisely Bakhtin's notion of the medieval clown, without of course the Rabelaisian emphases on sexual and excretory functions. For Kierkegaard what was most important was not any contact with the material sphere but contact with the material sphere that would lead to the more vital contact with the spiritual. It is not Rabelais to whom he must be compared but Rabelais's spiritual mother and father, Erasmus. It is the role of holy fool Kierkegaard aspires to, not Gargantua. Here, if anywhere, are the limits of Kierkegaard's appropriation of the comic and the clown—the holy fool does not include the profane fool. While the Christian church tolerated both in the Feast of Fools tradition during the Middle Ages, Kierkegaard will not, or can-not. Cut off from all biological functions, the Kierkegaardian fool is entirely philosophical, psychological, theological.

"Christianity is waiting for a comic poet *a la* Cervantes, who will create a counterpart of Don Quixote out of the essentially Christian," Kierkegaard wrote in his journal (2:274). Such a person, the simple Christian, will be derided by an age that has lost contact with true Christian values. There are other entries in the journal that concern the religious function of the fool. "There certainly was humor in the Middle Ages, too," he wrote, "but it was within a totality, within the Church, and was partly about the world, partly about itself" (2:258). And in *The Concept of Irony* he wrote, "What the Christian talks so much about during agitated seasons, namely, to become a fool in the world, this the ironist realizes in his own fashion—except that he feels no martyrdom but the highest poetic enjoyment" (298). These are two stages of fooling quite distinct from each other that Kierkegaard was to expand upon in his pseudonymous authorship.

Irony, the role as ironist, was Kierkegaard's beginning. *The Concept of Irony* was his first major work and in defense of it, Kierkegaard argues, "As philosophy begins with doubt, so also that life which may be called worthy of man begins with irony" (349). The book is a study of the life of Socrates as it is described by Xenophon, Plato, and Aristophanes, then as it is appropriated by Schlegel and the German romantics for their own concept of romantic irony. What fascinated Kierkegaard was the manner in which Socrates had protected his own inwardness and simultaneously had attempted to lead Athens to truth. "One may say of Socrates that just as he journeyed through life constantly between caricature and ideal, so he continues to wander between them after his death" (51). To write about the real Socrates, Kierkegaard explained, was like "trying to depict an elf wearing a hat that makes him invisible" (50). In his journal, he wrote: "In what did Socrates' irony really lie? In expressions and turns of speech, etc? No, such trivialities, even his virtuosity in talking ironically, such things do not make a Socrates. No, his whole existence is and was irony" (2:278).

Because Socrates was this early inspiration, the beginnings of Kierkegaard's life "worthy of man," Kierkegaard lived a life in constant reference to Socrates, designing biographical traps for the unwary critic that make trying to write about the real Kierkegaard like trying to write about an elf wearing a hat that makes himself invisible, except that this time the elf is telling us that he is wearing the hat. Something is added in Kierkegaard's repetition of Socrates that enlarges the fool's role and brings it forward in history. Kierkegaard's journals, we now understand, are not always accurate, even though he wrote them apparently only for himself. The claims in them that his books were losing money are false. Nevertheless, we can establish the fundamental outlines of the life, whose basic events are simple enough: the father who had cursed God, and had come to believe that God would have his special revenge on him by having him outlive all

his children; the courtship with Regine that could not be con-
summated; the attack on Kierkegaard by the *Corsair*; the attack
by Kierkegaard on the Danish state church (of which his brother
was a major figure) for loss of Christian principles; the near riot
at his graveside when that church buried him. He lived to be
only forty-two and was apparently sickly for most of his life. His
favorite activity was walking the streets and engaging fellow
citizens in Socratic discourse.

But if the life appears simple enough, almost too simple,
Kierkegaard's elaborations and interpretations of that life are
not. Of these, *The Point of View* is the most complex—there we
see how Kierkegaard's repetition of Socrates becomes his repetition of Christ. "Authorship is and ought to be a serious calling
implying an appropriate mode of personal existence," he wrote
(44). The notion that "one need not inquire about the commu-
nicator, but only about the communication" was the mistake of
the age (45). We are asked to believe that Kierkegaard acted a
kind of harlequin drama before Copenhagen as a writer of aesthetic or pseudonymous literature, that he acted the idler or wit
so that he would appear to have no serious interests, and that as
the writer of religious tracts he acted the part of the object of
ridicule with no serious interests. All of this is anticipated in
The Concept of Irony, of which Kierkegaard's life is the repetition. "Either the ironist identifies himself with the nuisance he
wishes to attack, or he enters into a relation of opposition to it,
but in such a way, of course, that he is always conscious that his
appearance is the opposite of what he himself subscribes to, and
that he experiences a satisfaction in this disparity" (266). Both
poses are deceptions. With the end of the pseudonymous authorship in 1846, at the time of the publication of the *Concluding Unscientific Postscript*, Kierkegaard ends the pose as master
of irony and wit and makes himself the object of ridicule. The
repetition of Socrates becomes the repetition of Christ. In his
journal he wrote: "It is frequently said that if Christ came to the
world now he would once again be crucified. This is not entirely
true. The world has changed. . . . Christ would be ridiculed,
treated as a mad man, but as a mad man at whom one laughs"

(6:133). Thus we have the full sequence: Socrates; Christ; and with the martyrdom of Kierkegaard, the authorship is transfigured, the pseudonyms disappear, and all that remains are the serious religious tracts that serve to make the religious meaning of the clown show obvious to all. Thus *The Point of View* insists Kierkegaard is to be understood fundamentally as a religious writer, but also as a poet, for the life of the religious writer is itself a fiction.

The Point of View does not speak of martyrdom and does not make comparisons to Christ—these are reserved for the less public journal. Ridicule in *The Point of View* is described as a mask, a deception, but only in the journal does one see that what it masks is an incredible kind of pride, and pride of course is the traditional object of ridicule. But in Kierkegaard all of this is inverted—ridicule is necessary for the pride to come into being. The fool is able to transvalue the comic itself. Also kept from us in *The Point of View* and revealed in later journal entries is that Kierkegaard acted out yet another comic pose following the *Corsair* incident, court fool to the Danish king, Christian VIII. Such a description of himself in *The Point of View* would have destroyed the neat dialectical symmetries of that work.

Following the martyrdom of laughter, Kierkegaard explains in his journal, he needed to find another relationship toward the comic, and this he acted out in all secrecy with the king in 1846 and 1847. We have this transcription of a meeting.

> I have often reflected on what a king should be. In the first place, he very well could be ugly. In the next place he should be deaf and blind, or at least pretend to be, for it simplified many difficulties: a foolish or inopportune remark, just because it is said to the king, acquires a kind of significance, which is brushed aside best by an "I beg your pardon," signifying that the king did not hear it. Finally a king must not say much but have an aphorism he uses on every occasion and which as a consequence says nothing. He laughed and said: A delightful description of a king. Then I said: "Yes, it

is true, and one thing more, a king must see to it that he is
sick occasionally so that he arouses sympathy," whereupon
he burst out with a strange interjection of almost joy and
jubilation: Ah, that is why you talk about being in poor
health. You want to make yourself interesting. (*Journals*,
6:94)

Welsford explains in her book on the fool that "as late as the
eighteenth century the professors of German Universities could
augment their incomes by playing the fool at court" (*The Fool*,
7). There is precedent then for Kierkegaard's behavior, although
the echoes are of Shakespearean fool–king discourse. In fact,
the advice Kierkegaard tells us he delivered to Christian VIII is a
precise repetition of the advice Henry IV gives Prince Hal in *I
Henry IV*, when Hal has announced he will become the dutiful
son. I have kept myself hidden from the people in order to gain
power, Henry tells him, but Henry is the villain of the piece and
the question then becomes, Does Kierkegaard mean this advice
to the king of Denmark seriously? The king laughs and sees a
connection to Kierkegaard's life: that Kierkegaard who suggests
he fake illness must be faking his own illness, and indeed the
journal entries from the period confirm that Kierkegaard has
been faking illness to limit his contacts with the king. However,
at the same time Kierkegaard is offering the king this advice to
make himself aloof and inaccessible, he is offering the precise
opposite point in his essay "The Crisis in the Life of an Actress."
There as the pseudonym Inter et Inter he dismisses public figures
who seek to hide from the public and praises "the unselfish servants of the truth" who interact with the people. "They have
never played hide and seek with the masses in order to play the
game of bedazzlement by exhibiting themselves on rare occasions as the subjects of stunned amazement. They have on the
contrary always shown themselves regularly, in everyday clothes,
lived with the common man, chatted in the streets and byways,
and renounced all prestige" (*Crisis*, 82). Inter et Inter describes
another aspect of Kierkegaard's life, his pose of the common
man talking with the common man. Half of the truth is exposed

to the king, the other half kept hidden, while in the published essay on the life of the actress the other half of the truth is revealed to the public.

According to Kierkegaard's biographers he was a political conservative and supporter of the king and his party. But if that was the case why does he give the king only half the truth? The king is not an ironist. The Shakespearean fool speaks in riddles that hide the truth but the Kierkegaardean fool speaks in clarity that hides the riddle. We don't know if Christian VIII ever passed beyond the stage of innocent amusement but we do know that Kierkegaard came away enlightened by the discourse. "Generally speaking," he wrote, "Christian VIII has provided me with many psychological observations. Perhaps a psychologist ought to pay special attention to kings, especially absolute kings, for the more free a man is . . . the more there is to know in the man" (*Journals*, 6:97). Christian VIII was no absolute king, but a historical anachronism without real power. Kierkegaard is being ironic, and in the process he is also inverting the traditional fool-king relationship. It is the fool who now benefits.

IV

As KIERKEGAARD undergoes a fool's metamorphosis—ancient pagan, ancient biblical, medieval-Renaissance—he produces a fool literature, the pseudonymous authorship, fragmenting himself into a series of mirror reflections that are another progression, psychological rather than historical. The pseudonyms have their own secret and happy relationships with laughter and the varieties of the comic, and from the beginning the pseudonymous authorship appears to have been a project closely tied to laughter and the comic. Early journals consider "A study of the significance of *fools* in the Middle Ages: how to a large degree fools were, if you please, the chorus of the world's tragedies which were performed in the Middle Ages," (2:248) and "a suitable subject for a dissertation: concerning the concept of satire among the ancients, the reciprocal relation of the various Roman satirists to each other" (5:107). But it is the subject di-

vided psychologically rather than historically that Kierkegaard
finally turns to. "It would be interesting to follow the development of human nature . . . by showing what one laughs at on the
different age levels," he wrote in 1837, four years before starting
the project. Along with showing the related development of how
one responds to comedy and to tragedy at different ages and
how one understands the relationship between comedy and
tragedy, such a study would "contribute to the work I believe
ought to be written—namely the history of the human soul"
(4:280). The pseudonymous authorship is this history.

"You are a laughing lot, and I myself am a friend of laughter,"
the aesthetic young man tells a group of fellow pseudonyms in
"The Banquet," the repetition of Plato's *Symposium* that makes
up part of *Stages on Life's Way*. "When I began by wanting to
talk about the comic side of love, you perhaps expected to have
a laugh," he tells them, "and yet perhaps you are not laughing.
The effect was a different one, and yet it proves precisely that I
have talked about the comic. If nobody laughs at my speech—
very well, dear boon companions, then laugh a little at me, it
will not surprise me" (60). He is answered by Constantine Constantius, who corrects the young man's understanding of the relationship between love and the comic with his own understanding of the relationship, which is equally limited. This is a
typical moment of Kierkegaardean fooling and it does show the
extent to which the pseudonyms share Kierkegaard's secret. In
the young man's speech the failure of the audience to laugh
proves that the subject is comic, and then the audience is presented with two alternatives, either to laugh with the young man
or at him. It apparently matters very little to him. *Stages on
Life's Way* appeared in 1845, one year before Kierkegaard
claimed he was to offer Copenhagen the precise same alternatives with respect to himself. The aesthetic young man is shal-
low; Kierkegaard is not. Kierkegaard repeats the young man's
movement along the current of laughter but involves himself in a
way that the young man cannot. The repetition is a movement
forward.

There is also hidden in this speech by the young man a joke on Kant's definition of the comic, the standard definition of the period, that the comic is the sudden disappointment of expectation and the result laughter. All this the young man neatly stands on its head, for what is expected is laughter, and the disappointment of this expectation cannot therefore be laughter. The aesthetic young man knows his Kant, however, and insists that all of this thereby proves his speech *is* comic. The interchange between the young man and Constantine is itself a repetition of a similar argument in *Either/Or* between the same young man and Judge Wilhelm. When the young man mocks at everything he is scolded by the judge for misusing laughter, but there the young man is not given an opportunity to respond. The repetition also marks a maturity for the young man since in *Either/Or* he has insisted that he always have the laugh on his side, but in "The Banquet" he is just as willing to be the object of mockery. When offered any gift by the gods, the young man replies in *Either/Or*, "I choose this one thing, that I may always have the laugh on my side," and when the gods respond by laughing, the young man decides that his wish has been granted (41–42). The opposite, of course, is what the reader is expected to conclude.

The young man may put the most value on laughter but virtually all of the pseudonyms are similarly convinced that laughter and the comic are essential to their existence. Quidam's statement about the connection between suffering and the comic, already discussed, is another such theory, as is Johannes Climacus's argument that existence is equally comic and pathetic. But although Quidam does suffer and therefore should know, Quidam is the pseudonymous invention of Frater Taciturnus, who does not suffer and who therefore should not know. The Frater, of course, is the pseudonymous creation of Kierkegaard, who does suffer and who therefore should know. We should laugh with Quidam, at the Frater, and with Kierkegaard, achieving a complex dialectical laugh. And Climacus's argument derives from Kant, from Kant's definition of existence as neces-

sarily incongruous and of the comic as the response to incongruity. Thus Johannes Climacus offers us the opportunity of laughing with Kant, while the young man offers us the possibility of
laughing at him.

The ways in which the pseudonyms laugh and thereby come
to understand laughter and the comic depend of course on the
stage along life's way in which they are fixated. There are three
stages and two intermediate zones, at least according to Johannes Climacus: the aesthetic, the ironic, the ethical, the humorous, and the religious. Climacus claims to be a humorist, and
what he explains in detail is first the difference between the humorist and the ironist, then the difference between the humorist
and the religious individual who must masquerade as a humorist to protect his inwardness. Combining Climacus's theories
with other explanations by Quidam and Frater Taciturnus, then
with demonstrations by the aesthetic young man, by Constantine Constantius, and the others, we can come up with the following system: An aesthete laughs in total mockery, then despairs of his attitude and becomes an ironist. He now mocks the
limited viewpoint of his earlier stage of existence and learns to
use mockery as Socrates uses it. When he understands the limited viewpoint of this attitude he despairs and becomes the ethical individual, a Judge Wilhelm, and now he is very careful to
use his laughter for clear ethical principles. When he understands the limited viewpoint of this attitude he despairs and becomes a humorist, a position different from an ironist because
he now includes himself and his present position within the
mockery. He is now more loving and sympathetic, more clearsighted. Finally, when he understands the limited viewpoint of
this attitude he despairs and becomes a religious man. Mockery
is not a characteristic of religious man except that religious man
must find a way of protecting his inwardness, must adopt an incognito, and so he masquerades as a humorist. In a similar manner the ethical man uses irony as his incognito. The pseudonyms
are masters of the masquerade, and therefore we are told that
there is no way we can tell when we meet someone who appears
to be a humorist whether he is in fact only a humorist or really a

religious man, no way to tell when we meet someone who appears to be an ironist if he is in fact only an ironist or in fact an ethical man. It is this part of Kierkegaard's system—humor and irony, and their use by the pseudonyms as masks—that has received the most critical attention.

"By showing what one laughs at on the different age levels," the project considered in the 1837 journal entry, Kierkegaard constructs a "history of the human soul." In *Repetition*, Constantine Constantius repeats and expands Kierkegaard's notion while sitting in Berlin's Königstäter Theatre and attempting himself to achieve a repetition. "Anyone wanting to make a pathological study of laughter at various social and temperamental levels ought not to neglect the opportunity offered by the performance of a farce" (159), he explains. All serious forms of art, even "comedy," provide signals to the audience that dictate a certain kind of response, but farce does not. Neither can the "critic" provide help. "For a cultured person, seeing a farce is similar to playing the lottery" (159), as the individual is set free to discover his individuality. The content of farce is the absolutely general, the abstract, acted out by talented comedians, and the effect on the audience is to free the absolutely unique, the individual. The dichotomies of German idealism, universal/individual, are thereby set in motion toward synthesis. In his repetition of Kierkegaard, Constantine makes the project of the pseudonymous authorship much clearer: the pseudonymous authorship is, if not exactly farce, then at least very similar to farce, the absolutely general acted out by talented comedians; and the effect on us, the audience, is to free us in our individual unique responses. Left without any clear directions about how to respond, we laugh only to discover that the talented comedians who act out this farce in front of us are laughing too. We are the repetition of Constantine, sitting in the theatre watching the laughter at different social levels. On the stage of the Königstäter Theatre are Berlin's two great comics: Beckmann ("an incognito in whom dwells the lunatic demon of comedy" [164]) and Grobecker (who has "a lyrical understanding with laughter" [165]). Unlike Phister, the "reflective comedian," Beckmann and Grobecker are unreflective geniuses who are simply taken over by the force of laughter. The reflective genius is Constantine in the audience. However, Beckmann and Grobecker prove to be just as valuable: sitting in the Königstäter Theatre, Constantine is bathed, virtually baptised in the laughter they let loose. When the orchestra finishes its prelude, "and then begins that second orchestra, which does not obey the conductor's baton but follows an inner drive, that second orchestra, the nature sound in the gallery" (165). This is laughter. "Before me the vast space of the theatre changed into the belly of the whale in which Jonah sat; the noise in the gallery was like the motion of the monster's viscera" (166). The laughter takes control of Constantine. "When I had watched Beckman and let myself be convulsed with laughter, when I sank back in exhaustion and let myself be carried away on the current of jubilation and hilarity and then climbed out of the pool and returned to myself again," then, Constantine explains, he sees a young woman in the audience whom he understands will be a figure of salvation (167). The theatre provides a religious experience.

We who repeat Constantine in our own experience in Kierkegaard's farce should find a similar religious salvation from the pseudonymous authorship. Within *Repetition* the episode of the farce is paralleled to the Book of Job. What Job provides the young man, Constantine's repetition, is what the farce provides Constantine—an understanding of man's fate and man's freedom. "That the theatre actually was for the pagans what the church is for us is apparent also in the fact that the theatre had no admission charge; that it should cost something to go to the theatre was just as unthinkable to the pagans as it would be for us to pay admission to go to church" (*Journals*, 1 : 56). What we approach in Kierkegaard's farcical theatre is contact with the universal. Reviewing Scribe's comedy *The First Love*, the aesthetic young man of *Either/Or* explains, "When the curtain falls, then everything is forgotten, only nothing remains, and that is the only thing one gets to see; and the only thing one gets to hear is laughter, which like a sound in nature, does not issue from a single human being, but is the language of a world force, and this force is irony" (271). He repeats Kierkegaard in *The Concept of Irony*, describing the "cleansing baptism of irony that redeems the soul" and a "bath of regeneration and rejuvenation" indispensable to personal life (339). As the language of a world force the sound for the aesthete is Hegelian, while for Kierkegaard it is religious, Christian. Inter et Inter, in "The Crisis in the Life of an Actress," adds later, "It is usually said that a comedian must be able to make the audience laugh, but it might better be said that he must first and foremost be able absolutely to soothe, and then the laughter will follow of itself" (76). Kierkegaard's pseudonyms can not agree precisely on function, given the different stages they occupy on life's way, but they are all aware that they are in touch with something powerful and significant for their own psychic or religious well-being. If we laugh with or at any of these pseudonyms the same opportunity is afforded to us.

V

THIS COMPLEX philosophic study of the comic is "transcendental buffoonery." The term is Friedrich Schlegel's, and it occurs in one of the fragments he wrote to describe romantic irony. "Internally: the mood that surveys everything and rises infinitely above all limitations, even above its own art, virtue, or genius; externally, in its execution: the mimic style of an averagely gifted Italian *buffo*" (*Lucinde and the Fragments*, 148). A good part of Kierkegaard's pseudonymous authorship is an attack on Schlegel and his concept of romantic irony. The aesthetic stage is a parody of the Schlegelian point of view, just as the ethical is a parody of the Kantian categorical imperative and of Hegel's own ponderous criticisms of the Schlegelian point of view; but although Kierkegaard had major disagreements with Schlegel and with other German critics of art and aesthetics, he nevertheless is dependent on the tradition.

Between the publication of Kant's *Critique of Judgment* in 1790 and Marx's *The Eighteenth Brumaire of Louis Bonaparte* in 1852, the problem of the comic in relationship to art, ethics, politics and culture was a subject of intense interest within German philosophy. Kierkegaard's work in the 1840s is a culmination of earlier work by Kant on laughter, Schiller on play, Schlegel on irony, Richter on irony and humor, and Hegel on irony, comedy, and drama. Kant had made the comic important for philosophy by positing a fundamental incongruity between noumena and phenomena for human existence, and then by defining the comic as the perception of incongruity. Those who inherited the Kantian system made the obvious connections between the two points: Schiller devised play as the position of aesthetic distance that could reconcile finite and infinite and defined play as a lack of seriousness; Schlegel devised irony as the position of the poet and defined it as a hovering between the real and the ideal; Richter distinguished between humor and irony as separate attitudes between finite and infinite; and Hegel corrected what he saw as the mistakes of Schlegel and his fellow ironists, arguing that romantic irony loses all meaningful contact with the real and becomes simply a justification for the fantastic.

Kierkegaard took elements from all these philosophical works, devising a transcendental buffoonery with the critical works on transcendental buffoonery. It is a playing with play, an ironic treatment of irony, and joined to it is an equally important borrowing from the great Renaissance study of the subject, Erasmus's *Praise of Folly*.

In *The Praise of Folly* Stultitia goes through three stages of existence: she is first comic, foolish, enamored of pleasure-seeking, intoxication, sexuality, flattery, self-love; then she is satiric, wise, critical of everything she has praised, angry at the world and its folly; finally she is the wise fool, religious, the simple Christian praised by Paul in 1 and 2 Corinthians. These are, of course, the three stages of Kierkegaard's pseudonymous authorship: aesthetic, ethical, religious. Appended to *The Praise* is Erasmus's "Letter to Martin Dorp," which explains that the mock encomium has been written "under a laughable persona" (147) in order "to call the world back to true Christianity" (156). Erasmus argues that it has the same serious purpose as his explicitly serious works but it is nevertheless only a piece of foolishness that we do not have to take seriously. *The Praise* is not important. This is of course the apologia Kierkegaard writes for himself as *The Point of View for My Work as an Author*, which presents the exact same arguments: that the pseudonymous authorship has the same serious purpose but that it is indeed only written under laughable personas and not finally worth taking seriously. There are other repetitions of Erasmus within Kierkegaard's writing more generally. Stultitia talks about Erasmus, and the pseudonyms talk about Kierkegaard; Stultitia attacks systematizers who forget the individual and so do the pseudonyms—for Erasmus these are theologians, for Kierkegaard, Hegelians. Both Erasmus and Kierkegaard compare the world to a theatre and both discuss the false laughter of the mass as it is directed against a wise individual who dares to go against the mass.

"Live with your century, but do not be its creature," Schiller wrote in his *Letters on the Aesthetic Education of Man* in 1795, lecturing the would-be poet on his role. "Render to your contemporaries what they need, not what they praise" (54). Schiller challenged the ephebe to return to the past to "grow up to full maturity beneath the distant skies of Greece" in order to return to the present "as an alien figure" not to please the world but to "cleanse it" (51). What the poet will find is "beyond all time," and what he will bring is salvation. If this describes the way Kierkegaard moves backward in time, not only to Socrates in distant Greece but to Erasmus in distant Europe of the Renaissance, the way Kierkegaard chooses to move before his contemporaries comes also from Schiller. "The real artistic secret of the master consists in his *annihilating the material by means of the form*," Schiller wrote in the *Letters* (106). Certainly this is the intent of the aesthetic authorship, and perhaps also of the autobiographical fragments left behind that annihilate the possibility of biography. Schiller's interest in the comic is not great but what he does say on the subject in "On Naive and Sentimental Poetry" also reappears in Kierkegaard. Tragedy has the more important subject matter, Schiller argued, but comedy demands the more important poet because the content of tragedy is determined before the poet writes but the content of comedy is not—it must be entirely determined by the poet. The comic poet must rely on his freedom in the act of composition. And it is the possibility of freedom that concerns Kierkegaard, far more than the heavy hand of fate.

From Schlegel Kierkegaard took the concept of transcendental buffoonery, and with that the metaphor of the mirror. What the averagely gifted Italian buffo knows intuitively, the poet and philosopher must learn, Schlegel argued—the way to call attention to oneself and one's style, the way to break the illusions of reality and call reality into question. The circus clown is the unreflective comedian. When the reflective poet/philosopher learns the craft, the result is the fusion of all forms of literature, philosophy, and rhetoric, animated with "the pulsations of humor," and this, which is romantic poetry, can become like the epic "a mirror of the whole circumambient world, an image of the age." And "it can also . . . hover at the mid-point between the portrayed and the portrayer, free of all real and ideal self-interest, on the wings of poetic reflection, and can raise that reflection again and again to a higher power, can multiply it in an endless succession of mirrors" (*Lucinde and the Fragments*, 175). At the center of this infinity of reflections, the poet becomes invisible. Kierkegaard becomes invisible in the whirl of the pseudonymous reflections. "A human being should be like a work of art which, though openly exhibited and freely accessible, can nevertheless be enjoyed and understood only by those who bring feeling and study to it," Schleiermacher wrote in one of the *Athenaeum* fragments published anonymously, under Schlegel's general supervision (*Lucinde and the Fragments*, 213). Kierkegaard made himself into such a work of art.

Jean Paul Richter expanded on Schlegel in 1804 in his *School for Aesthetics*, distinguishing between harsh irony and sympathetic humor and then explaining four central characteristics of humor: its totality, its use of the annihilating or infinite idea, its subjectivity, and its sensuousness. All four were important to Kierkegaard's conceptions. Humor is total, Richter argued, because its object is not a single specific folly, but universal folly. It is therefore mild and tolerant of individuals. Humor is annihilating or infinite because from its perspective of detachment and perfect vision, it sees all the contradictions of real and ideal, finite and infinite, and thereby annihilates all. Humor is subjective because it sides with the individual, not with the universal. And finally, humor is sensuous because it is grounded in material existence. Calling it "a kind of psychic vertigo" and comparing it to the "feast of fools of the Middle Ages" when "an inner spiritual masquerade innocent of any impure purpose, reversed the worldly and spiritual," Richter complained that the present age was far too corrupt to allow such humor to reappear (*School for Aesthetics*, 94). But what Richter described Kierkegaard became. The humorist "introduces his personal circumstances upon the comic stage, although he does so only to annihilate it poetically. The humorist is both his own court jester or quartet of masked Italian comedians and at the same time their prince and director" (94). This is the pseudonymous authorship.

Finally there is Kierkegaard's use of Hegel. Kierkegaard's general borrowings from, abuses of, and ambivalent feelings toward Hegel have been the subject of many careful and extensive analyses. What is relevant to this study of the comic is the extent to which Kierkegaard found in Hegel's writings on aesthetics a way of doing what Schlegel had directed him to do, of turning his life into a work of art. What Kierkegaard called his aesthetic authorship, the pseudonymous literature, is designed in part as an answer to Hegel's aesthetic authorship. What Hegel neatly and dialectically separated into the sequence art, religion, philosophy, in his *Philosophy of Fine Art* published shortly after his death in the 1830s, Kierkegaard neatly conflated into a synthesis of art, religion, and philosophy in the writings of the pseudonyms. It is impossible to separate the three subjects. And what the pseudonyms constantly attack Hegel for is his lack of interest in the subjective existing individual—it is as if they are engaged in a massive project of rewriting Hegel. The Hegelian system as seen from the inside, by the subjective existing individual, reveals that Hegel simply got everything backward.

But in the construction of his own life as a work of art and in
the conception of his role as a dramatist of the system, Kierkegaard borrowed rather directly from Hegel. In *The Phenomenology of Spirit*, Hegel wrote:

> The pretensions of universal essentiality are uncovered in the
> self; it shows itself to be entangled in an actual existence,
> and drops the mask just because it wants to be something
> genuine. The self, appearing here in its significance as some-
> thing actual, plays with the mask which it once put on in
> order to act its part; but it as quickly breaks out again from
> this illusionary character and stands forth in its own naked-
> ness and ordinariness, which it shows to be not distinct from ·
> the genuine self, the actor, or from the spectator. (450)

It would be hard to find a better gloss on Kierkegaard's life as an
author. In *The Phenomenology of Spirit* acting is not something
that happens only in the theatre but something that happens in
everyday reality, the playing with masks that is imposed on every
individual who wrestles with the problem of existence. In *The
Philosophy of Fine Art* acting is restricted to the theatre, but the
elements discussed there—the nature of the dramatic character
on a stage, the relationship between the dramatic poet and his
actor, the value of performance, the actor's special skills—are
all appropriated by Kierkegaard in the drama he acts out for
Copenhagen. Drama is the highest manifestation of art, Hegel
argues in *The Philosophy of Fine Art*, because it is the synthesis
of form and content, subject and object, inner and outer, mental
and physical, epic and lyric. What it shows, like the epic, is external event, but what it reveals, like the lyric, is the stripping
away of externals and the subjective individual. At the center of
drama is the self-conscious individual who resolves on a course
of action and puts it into practice. The individual we see in drama
is thus always self-determining, and nothing about the life is accidental, trivial, or without meaning. The collision of this individual with others of a similar nature makes for the plot.

This is the basis for Kierkegaard's autobiographical frag-

ments, particularly *The Point of View*, as well as for the pseudonymous literature. Kierkegaard himself is this self-conscious,
self-determining individual who does nothing accidentally, who
resolves on a course of action and puts it into practice, who
needs collisions with others—the *Corsair* incident, the attack
on the Danish state church—to advance the plot. We see both
external event and the subjective individual within the event—
the life is epic/lyric, inner/outer, and, as *The Point of View*
makes explicitly clear, a synthesis of form and content. A mode
of living accompanies a mode of authorship.

A stage drama has three acts; its actions, Hegel wrote, are to
be concentrated on a few important motifs, and there is no need
therefore for frequent changes of scene. In Kierkegaard's life
there are three acts: master of irony, martyr of laughter, religious
hero; the motifs in his life are few, and the writings concentrate
on them. An author must never forget that the true power of the
drama is in the performance, that only when an audience sees a
living actuality, only when universal aims and actions can be
given life, can the drama work, can the individual and the abstract come together. The drama requires physical bodies, and
thus the poet must depend on the actor, who must suppress his
real self in order to communicate the universal pathos of the abstract. The performance demands talent, intelligence, reflection.
This is the basis for Kierkegaard's life drama acted in Copenhagen—the suppression of the real self in the demands of art.
Kierkegaard is both poet and actor of this script.

For Hegel comedy is the culmination of art, the final stage of
drama before it gives way to religion. Having destroyed the serious drama, comedy finally turns its mockery onto itself and
vanishes. Tragedy is universal truth victorious over the subjective individual, while comedy is the reverse, the victory of individual over system. Tragedy shows individuals bringing themselves to destruction while comedy shows individuals dissolving
everything in laughter, celebrating their victory. Hegel called it a
hale condition of soul, but was clearly much more interested in
tragedy. There is also a third genre for Hegel, "of less striking
importance," a harmonization of the tragic and the comic in

which a serious individual exists in a comic environment, and thus there is a happy ending, but although Hegel is elsewhere enthusiastic about dialectical syntheses, in this discussion in *The Philosophy of Fine Art* he is not (2:1202). The form did not interest him, in part because it was the kind of drama popular in his own time, in part because it ruined the neat symmetry of his argument about comedy. For Kierkegaard what mattered was this particular synthesis of the comic and the tragic that he divided into the tragicomic (the Hegelian concept) and the comitragic (the Kierkegaardian concept): the first was trivial, he admitted, but the second was the essential nature of human existence. He found it in Socrates, in irony, in humor, in his own life, and he reproduced it in the pseudonyms. "The relative difference which exists for the immediate consciousness between the comic and the tragic, vanishes in the doubly reflected consciousness where the difference becomes infinite, thereby positing their identity," Johannes Climacus explains in the *Concluding Unscientific Postscript* (82). This is what Hegel has not understood. When Kierkegaard believed the age had become comic—with the success of the *Corsair*—he made himself into the tragic individual martyred by the community's laughter. But when he believed that he was in fact a tragic individual doomed to despair and suffering he played the part of a comic wit and ironist.

Hegel and Schlegel (almost the names for a vaudeville team) were involved in bitter recriminations with each other over romantic irony and romantic poetry. The whole age was obsessed with distinguishing between classical and romantic. Kierkegaard effectively made of them all—Socrates, Christ, Erasmus, and Kant, Schiller, Schlegel, Richter, and Hegel—a grand synthesis. Repeating history, he made it into comitragic drama. "Finally the theatre becomes actuality and actuality comedy," he wrote (*Journals*, 5:83).

VI

"THE POWER to wield the weapon of the comic I regard as an indispensable legitimation for everyone who in our age is to have any authority in the world of the spirit," Johannes Climacus argues in the *Concluding Unscientific Postscript* (250). The problem for Johannes is that everyone laughs and the world becomes comic but few individuals laugh correctly or *understand* the comic. "The power to wield the weapon of the comic is the policeman's shield, the badge of authority, which every agent who in our time really is an agent must carry" (250–51). Later, in a long footnote, he explains, "the comical has become the tempter in our time." But if these laughers understood the comic, they would "lose their laughter" (462). Kierkegaard, who wields this weapon of the comic, gains authority in the world of the spirit and gains also a shield. But no one else understands the comic in this way. Two years after Climacus's explanation, Kierkegaard repeated Climacus in his journal.

> I have never been a Diogenes, have never bordered on cynicism; . . . I have been able to crack jokes with an individual over my thin legs—but when it is the rabble, the utterly brutish humanity, the rowdies, silly women, school children, and apprentices who abuse me: that is the meanness and lack of character of a people directed against one who truly merits something from his people. The most tiresome aspect is that I am the only one who has the right to joke, but on those terms I cannot and will not joke. And yet I need the refreshment of laughter so often. But then, alas, that the one who is clearly the wittiest in a little country is the only one who is not witty—but the riffraff and the fools are all witty and ironic. (6:10–11)

We are back again at a repetition of the 1847 confession with which we began, but now we can understand the sadness behind the laughter ("And yet I need the refreshment of laughter so often") of one who would laugh *against* the laughter of the others. Later, also in 1848, he wrote in his journal:

> Granted that eternity is too earnest a place for laughter . . .
> it seems that there must be an intermediary state where a

person is permitted to laugh outright. The person who with extreme effort and much self-sacrifice discovers the comic really has no opportunity to laugh himself out; he is too tense and concerned for that. Thus it seems an intermediary state ought to be assumed. And no doubt the pious pagans, for example, Socrates, would be found in this intermediary state. (2:272)

No doubt we will find Kierkegaard here too—this is, after all, the hovering-between state Schlegel defined as transcendental buffoonery—half-way between the real and the ideal, the finite and the infinite, between the concerns of a philosopher of existentialism and of a theologian of Christianity. Kierkegaard ascends to the place of infinite laughter. Granted one wish by the pagan gods, the aesthete of *Either/Or* asks to have the laugh on his side. Kierkegaard asks the same—at the very end of his pseudonymous authorship.

5

Vanity Fair: The History of Comedy

AT THE same time that Kierkegaard was publishing his involved studies of the comic in Copenhagen under a series of comical pseudonyms—what is called in Kierkegaard criticism his puppet theatre—Thackeray was involved in a comparable project in England. There is the same use of comical pseudonyms and, in *Vanity Fair* in particular, an intricate comic study of the comic acted out by characters who are identified at the beginning of the novel by the showman as puppets. Kierkegaard's puppets act out a psychology of laughter and the comic; Thackeray's act out a history of laughter and the comic. The philosopher comedian and the novelist comedian repeat each other in another significant respect, in their interest in the relationship between comedy and repetition. In 1843 Kierkegaard published *Repetition*, about the possibilities of repetition, and within the elaborate series of repetitions that make up the text the central events are the repetition of comic and tragic events, the performance of a farce, the reading of the Book of Job. In 1847–48 Thackeray published *Vanity Fair*, a large and very traditional kind of comic novel with multiple echoes of Fielding's *Tom Jones*. It too is about the meanings of repetition, and all of the central events are an elaborate series of repetitions between the life of Becky Sharp, which is comic, and the life of Amelia

Sedley, which is melodramatic. Thackeray repeats Kierkegaard. It is highly unlikely that either knew of the other's existence.

The interest in repetition and in comic/tragic repetition in particular appears to have been shared by others as well. Marx makes a similar argument in *The Eighteenth Brumaire of Louis Bonaparte*, published in 1852, but he inverts the position held by Thackeray/Kierkegaard. For him everything happens twice in history, the first time as tragedy, the second as farce, and from that understanding he reads the history of 1848 to 1852 in France as the comic counterrevolution. These three books constitute a perfect repetition, *Repetition* being published four years before *Vanity Fair*, *The Eighteenth Brumaire of Louis Bonaparte* four years after. This chapter is about the central text in the sequence, the comic novel. It is, of course, a repetition of *Tom Jones* and, to a somewhat lesser extent, of *Joseph Andrews*; and therefore it is their *serious* repetition. The metaphor of the mirror, playfully applied by Fielding in both novels, and the allegory of comic history imposed by the narrator of *Tom Jones* upon the journey from country to city are now appropriated· by Thackeray and his showman narrator. Their purposes are more serious. The position taken by Fielding and his narrators is now countered. The attack in *Tom Jones* is on the Puritan destruction of comedy; and the great and glorious moment of comic celebration, the farce at Upton, is the Restoration. This history is now stood on its head by Thackeray and his showman, and the comedy and satire of the Restoration is revealed for the vile and corrupt era Becky Sharp demonstrates it to have been. Fielding got everything backward.

About Fielding, Thackeray wrote: "What generations he has taught to laugh wisely and fairly! What scholars he has formed and accustomed to the exercise of thoughtful humour and the manly play of wit! What courage he had! ("The English Humourists," 219). Fielding's accomplishment, as I have already argued, is more complex than this—he plays the wish to teach readers how to laugh wisely and fairly against the impossibilities of ever doing it. Thackeray misses the current of laughter in Fielding's texts, although his reference to Fielding's courage does indicate some awareness of the difficulties Fielding faced in those texts. About the novels Thackeray wrote, "The fashion and ornaments are, perhaps, of the architecture of that age, but the buildings remain strong and lofty, and of admirable proportions—masterpieces of genius and monuments of workman-like skill" ("The English Humourists," 210). And about *Tom Jones* in particular he wrote, "As a picture of manners, the novel . . . is indeed exquisite: as a work of construction, quite a wonder" (214). In *The* [London] *Times* (2 September 1840) he wrote, "As a work of art" *Tom Jones* is "the most astonishing production of human ingenuity" (see Wright, *Mask and Feast*, 71). In the century between Fielding and Thackeray there are a great many comic novels that turn reflexively onto the problems of the comic—*Humphrey Clinker, Tristram Shandy, Pride and Prejudice, Nightmare Abbey* paramount among them; but it was not until Thackeray wrote *Vanity Fair* that Fielding's project was taken up in a very specific and detailed way, and then developed in ways that go beyond either *Joseph Andrews* or *Tom Jones.*

Thackeray called *Vanity Fair* a comic history. Most obviously the novel is the story of everyday life in England during the time of Napoleon and the years that followed; chronicled in a detached and often mocking style, it is a comedy of English history. But the novel is also the story of comedy itself and its life in England from the Restoration to Thackeray's own time, a history of English comedy. In the comedy of history, the characters are men and women representative of their class and age who act out English cultural history in a story about disintegrating aristocrats, upwardly mobile merchants, and ruined speculators. In the history of comedy, the central characters are genres representative of their class and age who act out English literary history in a story about Becky Sharp as comedy, Amelia Sedley as her opposite, sentimental melodrama, and the narrator as their combination, genial humor. The literary history has a dialectical precision that the cultural history lacks, but the themes of both are similar: vanity, stupidity, and capricious individualism. The two histories are closely related; the life of forms reflects the forms of life in this story that makes mirroring its central image.

Vanity Fair has been studied carefully as a comedy of history, but it has not received similar attention as a history of comedy; and critics of the comedy in the novel have not recognized the extent to which Thackeray is also a critic of comedy in the novel. Thackeray wrote both comic criticism and comic fiction, of course, but *Vanity Fair* is a more complex form, criticism as fiction. The narrator who mediates between comic and sentimental styles also mediates between critical and fictional forms. Thackeray turned the mirror of comedy back onto itself, making comedy into the subject of comedy, just as he turned it onto himself as author in the illustration in *Vanity Fair* that shows a harlequin revealing Thackeray's face behind the mask. "The world is a looking-glass and gives back to every man the reflection of his own face" (19). The novel turns back onto its comic, sentimental, and humorous styles, but while the narrator gives equal attention to Becky Sharp's comic style and Amelia Sedley's sentimental style, Becky's is far more important to him, for it is against her pure comedy that he struggles to create his own mixed comedy. Both Thackeray and the narrator identify themselves as harlequins.

The narrator writes comedy at the same time that he writes about comedy, and his story is designed to show his readers that comedy and the criticism of comedy are only opposite aspects of the same activity, the mirrored images of comedy. The narrator addresses his readers as "brother wearers of motley" (180) and thereby unmasks them as harlequins, just as within the novel he unmasks Becky Sharp, Dobbin, and himself as harlequins. The novel hints it is Thackeray who is to be unmasked as the harlequin author, but it is left to the readers to recognize the clue presented in the illustration that accompanies the written text. They are thus encouraged to mirror Thackeray and to join into the complicated relationship of mutual unmasking in which readers, author, narrator, and characters are revealed as harlequins and as unmaskers of harlequins. The narrator unmasks Becky Sharp as a harlequin who unmasks other clowns and puppets and also as a laugher who interprets the laughter of others. When she hears a character's "laugh ringing on the stair," the narrator explains that she "knew quite well how to interpret his hilarity" (621). He wants his readers to be able to do the same. Comedy and the criticism of comedy are joined in this novel for all the kinds of harlequins joined by the novel. Being a harlequin means being a critic of harlequin in this story that has on its title page an illustration of a harlequin looking into a mirror. Whatever the novel's other subjects, it is a comedy about comedy, a critical fiction that belongs as much to the tradition of English comic theory as to the tradition of English comic literature. Thackeray made the literature into the novel's subject and made the theory into his narrative technique. What resulted is a unique contribution to both, a metacomic story in which authors and texts become aspects of character and action, and principles of theory become novelistic styles and structures.

Three years after completing the novel Thackeray told a London audience that he had examined the comic plays and novels of the past, but in the lectures he gave that were later published as "The English Humourists of the Eighteenth Century," he spoke instead "of the men and of their lives, rather than of their books" in order to show "harlequin without his mask" ("The English Humourists," 3). Laughter was not the harlequin's only interest, Thackeray explained, and the very finest was the humorist who combined ridicule with tenderness, a weekday preacher: "And as his business is to mark other people's lives . . . we moralise upon *his* life when he has gone—and yesterday's preacher becomes the text for to-day's sermon" (4). The comments also describe *Vanity Fair*, the story of men and of their lives written to show the harlequin without his mask, whose narrator, a weekday preacher, first marks the lives of the other characters and then enters the novel to become the text of his own sermon. The novel is many times more complex than Thackeray's later lectures and can not be simply reduced to them, but there are important similarities between his two studies of the harlequin without his mask. They are histories of nearly identical material. One is relatively straightforward history; the other is fiction that must be unmasked as history. "What do we look for in studying the history of the past age?" Thackeray asked in one of his lectures ("The English Humorists," 88). If it is to learn about great men or ordinary times then history is much less truthful than fiction, which can show the manners, movement, dress, pleasures, laughter and ridicules of an age. He was repeating Fielding without acknowledgment, but while the point can justify a comic novel like *Joseph Andrews*, it can only serve to invalidate the kind of factual history Thackeray was committed to presenting in his lectures and which he dressed up as much as he could with anecdotes into lives of the comic saints. It does explain *Vanity Fair*, however, the comic fiction that tells the truth of comedy's history. No treatment could be more appropriate for the subject.

II

THE NOVEL moves through literary and cultural history at the same time, and although actual battles and political events may be more easily recognized, the literary aspects are just as important. When Becky travels to Queen's Crawley early in the novel to become a governess, the narrator compares the event to Sam Weller's travels by stage across the same landscape. Becky's whole life is a story of such literary correspondences. She starts out as a young Moll Flanders, is put in the care of a Dickensian school for girls, and then becomes a governess in a parody of the castle of Udolpho, where she meets two brothers very similar to those in Sheridan's *School for Scandal*, and she writes letters like Pamela. Her adventures begin as in Fielding's *Tom Jones*, climax as in Wycherley's *Country Wife* or Congreve's *Way of the World*, and conclude as in Shakespeare's *II Henry IV* with the rejection of Falstaff (but Becky's survival skills are much superior to his and she endures like the very best of the comic rogues and tricksters in literature). It is not surprising that as governess she teaches her young charges Fielding, Smollett, Voltaire, and French drama—the Smollett for his "history," since her history recapitulates theirs though not in strict chronological order. (Thackeray was not as precise as Joyce was later to be in the

"Oxen of the Sun" chapter of *Ulysses*.) Even Amelia Sedley's
story borrows from earlier comedy, taking from *Emma* the episode of the piano that arrives anonymously and is attributed to
the wrong source.

Becky's story is more than a repetition of incident from earlier
comedy, and in all essential respects her life is the history of English comedy, her character the basic quality of comedy as genre,
at least as Thackeray saw it. She rises and falls (repeatedly and
therefore erotically, for the structure of the plot reflects the values of her being) just as comedy rises and falls. Witty, charming,
brilliant, she entertains society and wins favor; but insufficiently
respectful of moral codes, she overreaches and falls. The rake
she has married turns Puritan and casts her out, forcing her to
return to the low life from which she has come, and although
she rises again it is with much greater difficulty because of her
reputation. Thackeray takes this life of comedy from its bawdy
Elizabethan origins to its success in the Restoration and its disgrace in the eighteenth and nineteenth centuries; and when the
narrator appears in the comic coda to the story at Pumpernickel,
he is the representative of genial humor come to replace Becky
as the subject of the history. The narrator's part is played by
Thackeray, who ironically was one of the last genial humorists in
English literature, though he could hardly have known or predicted that in 1848. History was to add meaning to his history.
When Thackeray's history is ended Becky is not altogether van-
quished, and the narrator watches her closely. The future chapters of comedy are yet to be written.

Tough, satirical, pleasure-loving, intelligent, devoid of feeling,
Becky is described as a "consummate comedian" (498) with the
"keenest sense of humour" (299). She laughs at and mimics
most of the other characters, ridiculing their pretensions and
lampooning their eccentricities even when she plays up to them.
She can laugh at anything: at misfortune, when a much needed
inheritance turns out to be a pittance; at danger, when her husband is about to go into battle. It is "no laughing matter," he
tells her but she does not understand, and the narrator explains,
"It was only when her vivacity and sense of humour got the

better of this sprightly creature (as they would do under most circumstances of life indeed), that she would break out with her satire" (285). This comic sense is her distinguishing characteristic. Like the spirit of comedy, she is strong and confident in adversity. "While there is life, there is hope," she tells Rawdon, "and I intend to make a man of you yet" (363). She assures him that she is never defeated or without a plan for long, and while Rawdon is a part of her plan he is a major beneficiary of her pure spirit of life. Like comedy, "Becky's aim in life" is "to be, and to be thought, a respectable woman" (460), but like comedy she reveals her true disreputable nature in performance, when she acts in a charade that also has Rawdon cast as a cuckold before the people she has been trying to charm into accepting her. And like comedy she is brought down when the rakes and fops who have been entertained are replaced by moralists and Puritans who are only scandalized.

She is Thackeray's genealogy of comedy. Born in poverty to a French mother with musical talent and an alcoholic English father with drawing talent, she spends her childhood making the bohemians laugh and fetching their gin, becoming in the process a wild vixen with a strong sense of ridicule. When she is orphaned, polite society in the form of Miss Pinkerton's School tries to reform her, but she sees through its hypocrisies and turns on it "with a horrid sarcastic demoniacal laughter" (23). The middle class, in the form of the Sedley family, wants to have little to do with her, although there are some sentimental attachments felt by overly sentimental Amelia, and some vague temptations felt by Amelia's repressed brother Jos. The country aristocracy, in the form of the Crawleys, decayed and crawling, is much more taken with her and by her until she marries into the family and tries for too close an alliance. She moves into London society where her "wit, cleverness, and flippancy made her speedily the vogue . . . among a certain class" (361), and then she begins her flirtation with Lord Steyne. She is the comic out of control. Writing about Becky Sharp, Thackeray assesses the comic spirit and its history in England. In its period of excess, comedy was clearly immoral, unpleasant, and vain—faults he cannot easily forgive. Becky destroys Rawdon when he no longer serves her vanity, dismisses her son because children bore her, and attacks the genuine sweetness of Lady Jane. Thus she becomes vulnerable to attack. "To be a wicked woman—a heartless mother, a false wife?" Lady Jane cries. "She has deceived her husband, as she has deceived everybody; her soul is black with vanity, worldliness, and all sorts of crime. I tremble when I touch her" (531).

Becky Sharp is a character of great richness and psychological complexity, but she is fundamentally the muse of comedy. In his lectures on the English humorists, Thackeray described the comic muse as a bright, alluring, and dangerous woman, "merry and shameless," a "wild and dishevelled Laïs, with eyes bright with wit and wine," who had come to England from France with Charles II at the Restoration, and had sat in his lap, laughed in his face, and "when she showed her bold cheeks at her chariot-window, had some of the noblest and most famous people of the land bowing round her wheel" (54–55). Becky Sharp, of course, makes her own notable appearances at carriage window, and comes to the attention of a king, never identified by name, but taken to be George IV because the action takes place in the 1820s. When the novel is read as a history of comedy, the royal personage becomes Charles II. The Puritans finally began to hoot this comic muse, Thackeray wrote in his lectures, and when Collier attacked "that godless reckless Jezebel" (54), the men who had taken up with her were forced to turn her out in order to defend her reputation. "But the jade was indefensible, and it is pretty certain her servants knew it" (55). In *Vanity Fair* the narrator includes the scene that shows Becky's servants making a similar recognition. "That miserable rouged, tawdry, sparkling, hollow-hearted comedy of the Restoration" fled at the time of Steele, Thackeray noted when he returned to the same history yet again in his 1852 lecture "Charity and Humour," and "like the wicked spirit in the Fairy-books, shrank, as Steele let the daylight in, and shrieked, and shuddered, and vanished" (277). Thackeray saved Becky from such a horrible and historically inaccurate fate, but the life of comedy she represents does go into significant decline after Rawdon does finally let the daylight in. His characterization is very similar to Thackeray's later biography of Steele, which explains that the handsome and dashing captain lived in constant want of money and constant fear of the bailiffs after he married, but not before. Rawdon is forced to repeat his history.

And while Rawdon is based on Steele, Becky is based on Swift and Congreve, the only humorists of the eighteenth century whom Thackeray despised. Thackeray's biographies of these men in 1851 show how he had earlier made the abstraction of the comic muse actual. Swift scorned and insulted individuals of no use to him and played up to the rest, who only saw his bright sarcasm and thought "he had no object in view but the indulgence of his humour, and that he was the most reckless simple creature in the world"; but all the time he was abusing them behind their backs ("The English Humourists," 9). Swift lacked respect for marriage, children, and the clergy, and although he had a genius for the truth, he spent it in ridicule. Thackeray called his *Drapier's Letters* "masterpieces of dreadful humour" (29), argued that the last book of Gulliver was too horrible to read, and concluded that "his laugh jars on one's ear after seven score years" (46). What he wrote about Congreve was little better. He was a pagan and a sinner who devoted himself to youth, pleasure, and strength, and when these gave out he was left ruined and lonely because the "banquet of wit" without love "palls very soon" (59). His plays were like the ruins at Pompeii, and Thackeray, walking among them, observed the rotting skull of harlequin. The individuals at these pagan feasts must have been "the very worst company in the world" (58). Becky Sharp has these attributes of Swift and Congreve—even her letters included in the text are masterpieces of dreadful humor. A combination of the sharp satirist and the comic sinner, she relives their history.

In Thackeray's lectures comedy took a happy moral turn with Addison, Steele, and the other humorists of the eighteenth century, all of whom he described in nearly identical terms as the kindliest of laughers and the most moral of authors. Their lives became the basis for Thackeray's portrait of the narrator just as their work had served as the basis for his own development as a writer. It may even have provided the model of the comic genealogy that Thackeray was to elaborate into his novel. Truth fathered good sense who fathered wit who married mirth and produced the child humor, Addison wrote in his 10 April 1711 *Spectator* paper; but against this genial male line there was a corrupt female line. Falsehood mothered nonsense who gave birth to son frenzy who married the daughter of folly known as laughter who gave birth to the monstrous infant false humor (no. 35; 1:145−48). *Vanity Fair* is the genealogy of the female false humor, born of laughter and frenzy, as told by the genial male true humor, born of wit and mirth.

III

STRUCTURALLY Becky Sharp's life is only half of *Vanity Fair*; the other half is Amelia Sedley's life, which personifies the genre of pathetic or sentimental melodrama. Her life is both a direct reflection and a contrast to Becky's, for they experience similar events but respond to them in opposite ways. They are tied to each other in intimate and inverse ways: when one blossoms the other languishes (although Amelia's statement to Becky early in the novel "I shall always be your friend, and love you as a sister—indeed I will" [24] proves to be a typically sentimental exaggeration). They are extremes of genre as well as of character. Amelia, born of middle class prosperity, protected from any real knowledge of the world, and educated in the polite but useless arts, can only do one thing well, luxuriate in her own suffering and helplessness. She has sweetness, light, and morality on her side, but she is hardly an attractive alternative to comedy, and few characters in the novel find her either attractive or interesting. For the narrator neither the pure comic nor its opposite, the pure sentimental, will do, and he mediates both in his own mixed style, alternately laughing and crying. Within the story

Dobbin—the clown with the yellow face, lisp, and large hands and feet, who can laugh and cry in equal measure—also mediates the extremes in this way.

This precise mirroring and dialectical mediating is the central structural device of the novel, but it does not reflect the history of comedy, which hardly had this kind of perfect symmetry with its sister genres. It reflects the history of comic theory. "To explain the nature of laughter and tears, is to account for the condition of human life;" Hazlitt wrote in his "Lectures on the English Comic Writers" in 1819, "for it is in a manner compounded of the two! It is a tragedy or a comedy—sad or merry, as it happens" (5). There is a serious middle ground between them, he argued (7), while cautioning against the life of laughter or the life of tears. "An excess of levity is as impertinent as an excess of gravity" (27). "People who are always laughing at length laugh on the wrong side of their faces; for they cannot get others to laugh with them" (27). Thackeray's lectures follow in the form of Hazlitt's, and his novel follows a significant part of their content. Hazlitt's lectures were one of the standard critical works on comedy in the first half of the nineteenth century, and while Thackeray did not always accept the lectures, his novel shows their strong influence. "We laugh, when children, at the sudden removing of a paste-board mask: we laugh, when grown up, more gravely at the tearing off the mask of deceit" (8). Hazlitt's statement reappears as action in *Vanity Fair*. Comedy "holds the mirror up to nature" (149), he wrote, also without acknowledging Fielding; but he also explained that "like the mirrors which have been added to the sides of one of our theatres, it reflects the images of grace, of gaiety, and pleasure double, and completes the perspective of human life" (70). This notion, also in Fielding, is important for *Vanity Fair*. Becky and Amelia are the kinds of mirrored reflections of character suggested by Hazlitt's description. One is an excess of levity, the other of gravity; and the narrator occupies the serious middle ground between them, accounting for the conditions of human life by explaining the nature of laughter and tears. Although the narrator and Dobbin have manners compounded of the two, most of the other characters are neatly divided between excess laughers (Becky, Sir Pitt, Rawdon, Miss Crawley, Lord Steyne, George Osborne, his son George, and, before it is ruined, the Sedley family, except for Amelia) and excess weepers (Amelia, Lady Crawley, Pitt the younger, his wife Jane, Jane's mother, the Sedley family after it is ruined). The ability to laugh at oneself is a characteristic of the finest of humor characters in literature, Hazlitt wrote (22). Both the narrator and Dobbin laugh at themselves.

But Thackeray did not simply follow Hazlitt. Just as Amelia as Becky's reflection is also her opposite, so Thackeray as Hazlitt's reflection is also his opposite. Were the history of comedy to be conceived as a woman, Hazlitt suggested, she would be a "high court lady" and not a literary prostitute" (152). Restoration comedy was her greatest achievement and Congreve and Wycherley her greatest writers until Collier and Steele destroyed the form. Wycherley's plays reflected the manners of the age and held them up to scorn; thus they were "worth ten volumes of sermons" (78), while Steele's plays, which were written in order to reform morals rather than to reflect manners, did neither. The fault was Collier's, whose attack "did much mischief: it produced those *do-me-good*, lack-a-daisical, whining, make-believe comedies in the next age . . . which are enough to set one to sleep" (90). Thackeray simply turned this on its head, first in *Vanity Fair*, the comic inversion of Hazlitt and thus a "comic" history, then in his lectures where he argued that Steele was a weekday preacher.

Thackeray took his history from Macaulay who had revived Collier's attack in 1841, six years before *Vanity Fair*. Macaulay granted Congreve considerable skill as a writer but argued that Restoration comedy ridiculed the good and glorified the bad, and that it was "a disgrace to our language and our national character" ("Leigh Hunt," 354). The plays needed to be preserved as authentic history, but they were too close to the present age to be read safely. "The comic poet was the mouthpiece of the most deeply corrupted part of a corrupted society" (367). Thackeray, who was also to argue that parts of Swift could not be safely read, accepted Macaulay's version of the history of comedy and combined it in *Vanity Fair* with Hazlitt's history of eighteenth-century sentimentality, eliminating in the process humorists like Steele from the classification. Becky represents Macaulay's history as Amelia does Hazlitt's; and as the narrator mediates their extremes of character, Thackeray mediates their extremes of history.

One year before *Vanity Fair*, Hunt defined humor as "incongruities of character and circumstance" (12) in which "all extremes meet" (8). "The more the incongruities the better," he wrote, "and the more strikingly they differ yet harmonize, the more amusing the result" (*Wit and Humour*, 12). Thackeray's comic novel shows how the incongruities of comic theory differ yet harmonize, and thereby it makes humor from the criticism of humor: from Hazlitt and Macaulay on its history, from Walpole and the genial humorists on its character, and from Hobbes and Shaftesbury on its laughter. Walpole wrote in the second half of the eighteenth century that "*this world is a comedy to those that think, a tragedy to those that feel*" (*Correspondence*, 23:166), while others, including Addison, had argued that sympathy was an important part of comedy, the style properly called humor. In Thackeray's own time writers and critics were more inclined to accept the mixture of comedy and feeling, and Thackeray defined himself as such a humorist. But in *Vanity Fair* (where there is the character of Sir Walpole Crawley, the first baronet) both positions are presented as correct—the novel shows how they differ but harmonize. The world is a comedy to Becky Sharp, who thinks a great deal and feels hardly at all. She credits her success to her "brains" (410), and the narrator explains that after the chaos of Waterloo "no man in the British army . . . could be more cool or collected in the presence of doubts and difficulties" (288). Amelia feels a great deal and thinks hardly at all, so little that she appears pathologically unable to recognize her own best interests. The narrator does both, showing how thinking and feeling harmonize, and while he has the advantage because he tells the story, the story Thackeray has given him to tell illustrates a position he considers objection-

able. It is as if Thackeray had forced a genial humorist to tell a
story as conceived by a wit; the results, according to Hunt's definition of humor, should have been droll, at least to the harlequin
and critic of harlequin sensitive enough to detect the humor
turning back against the critics of humor.

The greatest incongruity in the comic theory of Thackeray's
own time was in the explanation of laughter. Just before the
Restoration period Hobbes had argued that laughter was sudden glory felt at the sufferings and infirmities of others, and just
after the Restoration period Shaftesbury had argued that laughter was geniality, good will, and sympathy at the faults and
weaknesses of others. The two positions were impossible to reconcile, and by the early nineteenth century neither was a wholly
adequate explanation. Coleridge simply accepted both, distinguishing in his lectures on comic literature between the purely
laughable, which is opposed to the moral sense ("Distinctions,"
275), and humor, which combines the two in "an acknowledge-
ment of the hollowness and farce of the world" (278). In *Vanity
Fair*, the narrator describes life as a "farce of sentiment" (223),
and while he combines comedy and morality, Becky Sharp does
not. But although he is by temperament a Shaftesburian laugher,
the story he has been given by Thackeray to tell is primarily
about Hobbesian laughers. The early chapters of the novel support Hobbes, and Becky is the victim of such laughter long before she is its creator. The Sedleys feed her a hot pepper and
laugh at her distress, and although she wants to choke them she
passes if off as harmless fun. Later she watches Mr. Sedley make
fun of his son Jos's size, while the narrator notes the son is thinking about patricide. The pattern of comic abuse is common
within the family and its circle, and at the Vauxhall dinner party
it starts up again when Jos drinks an entire punch bowl. He
laughs in drunkenness, but when he returns home his valet laughs
in scorn, and then later both George Osborne and Dobbin laugh
at his distress. When Jos fails to visit Becky the following day to
make a marriage proposal, Osborne laughs at her too, earning
her instant distrust. The narrator is not immune from all this
either, and to the extent that he joins in with his mock horror at

the powers of the punch bowl, he joins the company of laughers. His laughter, of course, is more genial, supporting Shaftesbury, but he has no power to influence Becky herself, unlike the characters who become her tutors within the story. The Crawleys are worse than the Sedleys, especially Sir Pitt who laughs "he he" and "haw haw" (the latter of which also identifies the laughter of the entire Crawley family, including Rawdon and Bute's son James) at family, neighbors, servants, and at Becky herself in his drunken carousings with the butler. She hates the abuse just as she has hated it from Osborne, and she is later able to have her revenge on all of those who have laughed at her when she surpasses them all in laughter. At the height of her glory later in the novel, when the celebrated wit Mr. Wagg tries again to make her the butt of jokes, she has swift revenge and eliminates him from polite society. The same fate awaits her, for the same reason. Many characters enjoy laughing at others in superiority, but none enjoys being the object of laughter. Becky then is only a reflection of her society, a victim of history and its Hobbesian laughter, which she cannot escape. Her comedy typifies a society that is willing to be cruel and abusive, and that wants to be entertained in this fashion. The genial narrator can hold himself out as a more humane alternative, but he cannot deny the truth of her history.

"How much lies in Laughter: the cipher-key, wherewith we decipher the whole man!" Carlyle wrote in *Sartor Resartus*, a decade before *Vanity Fair* (24). This statement from Carlyle's fictional editor becomes for Thackeray's narrator a central truth, a cipher key not only of character but of plot. The intensity and frequency of Becky's laughter increases as she rises in society and learns what society wants from her, and just before her fall at the moment of her greatest position she is described by the narrator again and again as laughing. When Rawdon comes home unexpectedly after his arrest, he hears her laughing with Lord Steyne, who attempts to laugh as Rawdon strikes him. Cast out, Becky discovers her own servants laughing at her, then runs to Pitt to explain that Steyne was really laughing at another matter. Lord Steyne's laugh, of course, is suitably horrible— "when he laughed, two white buck-teeth protruded themselves and glistened savagely in the midst of the grin" (366). Laughter is even important in Amelia's story, for she has failed to appreciate Dobbin because her husband and son have ridiculed his imperfections, "and their jeers and laughter perhaps led poor little Emmy astray as to his worth" (602). Dobbin's laughter, of course, is of a very different kind from the others', even if he has at one point joined in the laughter against Jos Sedley. His "tender laugh of benevolence" is in sharp contrast to the comic abuse he has been subjected to throughout the novel, and he tries to avoid offense by laughing out of sight of his objects.

Comic criticism and theory is usually considered to be derivative of comic literature, but with *Vanity Fair* the opposite is true. Laughter is the cipher key for character and plot; laughter theory is the cipher key for the novel as a whole. The books and lives of the English comic writers provided Thackeray with subject; the books of the English comic critics provided him with technique. "O brother wearers of motley!" the narrator exclaims. "Are there not moments when one grows sick of grinning and tumbling, and the jingling of cap and bells? This, dear friends and companions, is my amiable object—to walk with you through the Fair . . . and that we should all come home after the flare, and the noise, and the gaiety, and be perfectly miserable in private" (180–81). While his address is to the readers, it should also be clear that the narrator's friends and companions in motley are the comic writers and comic critics he has made his subjects and his guides. Walking through their common history with them has been his aim, along with his wish to retire with them afterward when their time at the fair is over. The readers of the novel have been invited to go along and contemplate the grinning, tumbling, and jingling, and then to see the realities behind the harlequins. The walk is designed as a comic education.

IV

IN HIS lectures Thackeray wrote that "pleasure is always warring against self-restraint. . . . A man in life, a humourist, in writing about life, sways over to one principle or the other, and laughs with the reverence for right and the love of truth in his heart, or laughs at these from the other side. Didn't I tell you that dancing was a serious business to Harlequin" ("The English Humorists," 55). This is the most important contrast about the comic in *Vanity Fair*, where it takes the form of the two principal harlequins, Becky Sharp and the narrator. Thackeray makes the distinction very clearly in his statement, but in his novel, which demonstrates how all extremes about comedy meet, this distinction is another incongruity that can be seen to differ and to harmonize. The readers of the novel who have accompanied the narrator on his walk through the fair and have gained their dress of motley in the process must finally judge the similarities and differences of these two harlequins for themselves. Thackeray sets the novel up to encourage their active judgment. The narrator writes his story from the mirrorings of Becky and Amelia, but Thackeray writes his critique of the comic from the mirrorings of Becky and the narrator. Becky, like the narrator, is an artist invited to "make a grand historical picture of the scene" (37), and like the narrator she is a prose writer with considerable skill to influence an audience. Her letters, or satires, as the narrator once calls them, stand in the text in contrast to the narrator's own satire. These she either writes in her own name or ghostwrites for Rawdon, putting her words in another's mouth. The narrator does the same, writing both for himself and for other characters. Some of her letters are descriptive, as the early one to Amelia from Queen's Crawley that makes her life there into a story and that contrasts sharply to the narrator's story of her life there, which it repeats in part. Other letters are manipulative, particularly the letters she writes for Rawdon to Miss Crawley and to his brother, and her own letter to Briggs. All are successful in achieving at least partial reconciliation between writer and reader.

The narrator guides the readers by judging the style of these letters, and on occasion by comparing Becky's behavior to his own. He does his best to be impartial. Thus when Becky plays up to Miss Crawley the narrator admits he would do the same given the opportunity. But while he includes himself in the general survey of vanity, Becky holds all the other characters in scorn and thinks highly only of herself. And Becky is much more of a hypocrite, playing up to a character while abusing the individual behind his back—behavior of which Thackeray accused Swift; while the narrator is more detached, rarely praising or blaming in this way, but always watching. When Becky approaches the narrator's style, he praises her. "Miss Sharp's account" of the younger Pitt's behavior "was not a caricature" (84), he admits, and it is only when Becky is involved in what she writes about that she distorts the truth—when, for example, she does not reveal her romance with or marriage to Rawdon. But then the narrator teasingly delays providing this same information.

He is much more upset with her use of laughter. "Rebecca is a droll funny creature, to be sure," he comments after she has abused Sir Pitt in a letter, and her descriptions are "very smart, doubtless, and show a great knowledge of the world" (80), but she does not use laughter correctly. When characters are good one should love them; when they are silly, one should "laugh at them confidently in the reader's sleeve" (81); and when they are wicked one should abuse them in the strongest terms. The narrator then tries to separate himself from her ridicule of Sir Pitt. "Otherwise you might fancy it was I who was sneering at the practice of devotion, which Miss Sharp finds so ridiculous; that it was I who laughed so good-humouredly at the reeling old Silenus of a baronet—whereas the laughter comes from one who has no reverence except for prosperity, and no eye for anything beyond success" (81). It is against such godless egoists as Becky that laughter must be turned, he argues, against the faithless, the hopeless, and the charityless, against the quacks and fools, for it is "to combat and expose . . . no doubt, that Laughter was made" (81). But the narrator is only mouthing comic theory here, and the statement is confused. Not only is Becky described as laughing good humoredly but the narrator is endorsing exactly what she has done in turning back laughter against the faithless, hopeless, and charityless Sir Pitt and his laughter. In addition, the narrator does sneer at devotion in the novel, particularly the variety practiced by the reeling old baronet and described by Becky in her letter, the hypocritical and drunken devotion that deserves no reverence and gets none, from Becky or from the narrator. The narrator turns his laughter against religious characters, against religious tracts like *Thrump's Legacy* and *The Blind Washerwoman of Moorfields*, and against such proper and serious figures as the dowager countess of Southdown. Becky lampoons her to Rawdon, whose "explosions of laughter were as loud as usual," and then to Lord Steyne, who had "many a laugh over the story" (406), and the narrator claims "for the first time in her life" the countess has been made amusing. But he has already made her amusing for his readers, describing her "with a large black head-piece of bugles and feathers, which waved on her ladyship's head like an undertaker's tray" (403), and thus the narrator deserves the credit he has mistakenly given to Becky. She may lie from excess vanity but he lies from its mirror opposite, excess humility. If there is a middle position between these two excesses in the novel it must be supplied by the readers.

The narrator may perhaps be forgiven more easily for his faults, but his comic style is not so very different from hers. It is simply that Becky laughs all the time and the narrator does not; instead, he alternates between the comic and the sentimental, and mixes the comic with the serious by including in otherwise straightforward narrative such characters as the Reverend Felix Rabbits, the father of thirteen; Mr. Smirk, the celebrated ladies' doctor; and a whole series of cheeses, including the dowager duchess of Stilton, the duc de la Gruyere, and the comte de Brie. When the narrator enters the story it is not as a cheese but as a bread, in the tiny German state of Pumpernickel where all the characters belong in farce: from the petty English and French factions of the state to its own ludicrous history, from Tapeworm to his Transparency the Duke and his Transparent family. Having written the history of comedy, the narrator is finally able to write the comedy of history, which comes at the end of the novel as farce seen by a bystander. Becky's story was satire as seen by the heroine, and it is finally this that is the crucial difference between the two comic styles. His novel has no heroes. The comedy of vanity ends as the comedy of humility, its own mirror image, and the narrator does finally become the reflection of Becky. We are led to see the ways in which the harlequin of pleasure and the harlequin of self-restraint and compassion mirror each other, differ and harmonize; but we are also led to judge the narrator as morally preferable. The errors of the humble, even the excessively humble, are not as serious as the errors of the vain. The narrator has found a way of writing moral comedy and Becky Sharp has not.

Out of these mirrorings, the narrator has written a history of comedy, then a comedy of history; and out of the story of Becky Sharp as comedy and Amelia Sedley as sentimentality, he has found a way of mediating between them to create his own comic style. The mirror, held up to Fielding, has inverted him.

6

The Ordeal of Richard Feverel: The Labyrinth Again

"MAN IS the laughing animal," George Meredith wrote in *Sandra Belloni* in 1864, "and at the end of an infinite search, the philosopher finds himself clinging to laughter as the best of human fruit, purely human, and sane, and comforting" (215). At the end of his own search almost half a century later, Meredith lived out his prophecy. We have Virginia Woolf's testimony that when the old man had gone stone deaf at Box Hill, "all the time this highly wrought, artificial conversation, with its crystallised phrases and its high-piled metaphors, moved and tossed on a current of laughter. His laugh curled round his sentences as if he himself enjoyed their humorous exaggeration. The master of language was splashing and diving into his elements of words" (245–46). Describing Meredith in a scene that is simultaneously comic and serious, Woolf describes for the moment like Meredith in highly wrought artificial prose. It is comic that the novelist cannot hear his own language, comic too that he cannot hear the replies that are made to him, comic yet again that he does not care; but this is a sobering moment. As his mental and physical capacities fail him, the philosopher clings to what has most sustained him, laughter and language. The torrent of words that has been directed previously into texts now floats freely around him. Woolf returns them to the page—a "current of laughter" and a "laugh curled round his sentences"—recovering Meredith's prose style: the imps of laughter that curl around Sir Willoughby Patterne in *The Egoist*, the "electric chain of laughter" that circles through a dinner party in *The Ordeal of Richard Feverel*, seizing everyone in its path.

Meredith moved and tossed on a current of laughter for his entire creative life, writing comedy and writing about comedy, studying laughter and provoking it, from 1854 when he complained, "Shall Clown for ever rest unsung by Bard?" in the early poem "Motley" (*Poems*, 2:758) to the posthumously published and unfinished novel, *Celt and Saxon*. "Humor," Meredith wrote in that novel, "in its intense strain has a seat somewhere about the mouth of tragedy, giving it the enigmatical faint wry pull at a corner visible at times upon the dreadful mask" (57). The celebrated essay "The Idea of Comedy and the Uses of the Comic Spirit" was first delivered in 1877, at the mid-point of his long search into the current of laughter, but it is only the most visible and explicit study of the subject we have from him. Meredith wrote poems about the idea of comedy, and short stories, novels, and one unpublished play about the uses and abuses of the comic spirit. Clowns, wits, and satirists are among the central characters of these stories, and their narrators discuss the nature of comedy and the meaning of laughter as they alternately watch the laughter of these characters and provoke laughter from their readers, use comic forms and structures and then question their significance. Almost every novel contains some discussion of these interrelated subjects, and in some it is extensive: *The Ordeal of Richard Feverel*, *Sandra Belloni*, *The Egoist*, *The Tragic Comedians*, *Diana of the Crossways*, *One of Our Conquerors*. "I do not know that the fly in amber is of any particular use, but the comic idea enclosed in a comedy makes it more generally perceptible and portable, and that is an advantage," Meredith wrote in "The Idea of Comedy" (56). For Meredith's major novels, the advantage is real: the comic idea is contrasted to the comedy, and it is that which propels Meredith through a continual study and reevaluation of the comic idea, the comic spirit, the comic muse, and the comic imps; the relationship between comedy and laughter; the differences between comedy, humor, and satire; the contrasts between the masks of comedy and tragedy; the meanings of all these concepts both as life attitudes and as generic styles. The poet who complained in 1854 that the clown was in danger of remaining unsung by bard spent the rest of his life making sure that no such oversight could ever be found again. What Woolf saw, near the end, was that it would only be his death that could stop this obsessive singing.

Comedy, Meredith suggested in *The Egoist*, was the result of the control of the comic spirit over the imps of laughter. But Meredith himself had a much more difficult time controlling these imps who were always escaping his grasp and returning to mock his failures, much as they mocked the confident mocker of the novel, Sir Willoughby. No explanation satisfied Meredith for very long, but he tried them all. Borrowing from other writers and critics who had explored the labyrinth of the comic before him, he sounded sometimes like Molière, sometimes like Baudelaire, sometimes like Nietzsche; he wrote sometimes in the manner of comedy, sometimes in the manner of humor, sometimes in the manner of satire; and he imitated Old Comedy, New Comedy, Restoration comedy, Molière, Fielding, and Thackeray. The notion that an Apollonian comic spirit controls a Dionysiac collection of laughing imps and thereby creates comedy is an elegant schema borrowed directly or indirectly from Nietzsche's essay "The Birth of Tragedy," published in German seven years before the Meredith novel. What Meredith's lifetime of struggle in the current of laughter suggests is that no control is ever really possible.

This chapter is concerned with Meredith's first major struggle, *The Ordeal of Richard Feverel*, in part because it is well known to students of the nineteenth-century English novel who may not know novels like *Sandra Belloni*; in part because Meredith's first exploration of the labyrinth of the comic became programmatic of his life's work, following the call for the bard in "Motley"; and in part because *Richard Feverel* is an intricate reworking of Fielding's exploration of the labyrinth of the comic, *Tom Jones*. Woolf suggested in her commentary on *Richard Feverel* that "the first novel is always apt to be an unguarded one," and that because the author will display "his gifts without knowing how to dispose of them to the best advantage," the critic will have a relatively easy starting point (*The Second Common Reader*, 247). It is for that reason, too, that this discussion of Meredith deals with the early novel.

The gifts Meredith displays in *Richard Feverel* are considerable, as are his borrowings. The novel is a precise and intricate mirror inversion of Fielding's labyrinth of mirrors, *Tom Jones*: a repetition, elaboration, reversal, and condensation of the comic epic and a mockery of Fielding's mockery of mockery. Meredith's novel also contains extensive critical discussions of laughter and comedy, based on the standard Aristotelian distinction between the excessively gay buffoon and the excessively grave boor, but this too is now mirrored into a second opposition (borrowed from Baudelaire's essay "The Essence of Laughter," published four years before *Richard Feverel*) between the angelic laughter of the innocent and the diabolical laughter of the experienced. Combining symmetries from Aristotle and Baudelaire, Meredith imposes an anatomy of laughter onto Fielding's symmetrical text and from that produces what is in neither the fiction nor the theory, a direct connection between the styles of laughter and the styles of comic literature from Aristophanes to the mid-nineteenth century.

By a trick of mirrors the reflection of Fielding's comic epic becomes a reflection of the evolution of comic forms. The novel, of course, was published in the same year as Darwin's *The Origin of Species*, the analysis of the evolution of living forms; but as a history of comic forms it also mirrors and inverts Thackeray's *Vanity Fair*, published a decade before, which is itself a mirroring and reflection of Fielding's *Tom Jones*. Thackeray's narrator grasped Fielding's comic mirror and turned it directly on harlequin, writing into the allegory of the life of Becky Sharp a history of comedy from the Restoration to the mid-nineteenth century, inserting himself directly into the action toward the end of the story at Pumpernickel as the genial and amiable humorist Thackeray, come to replace the sharp satiric and immoral tradition of Miss Sharp. Grasping Thackeray's mirror, Meredith reflects and inverts this reflection of Fielding, beginning his history not with the Restoration but with the Homeric laughter of Adrian Harley and with the Bakewell Comedy written to mimic Aristophanes. In contrast to Thackeray, he makes himself into the humorless Sir Austin Feverel; sends the figure of genial and amiable humor, Austin Wentworth (Sir Austin's mirror reflection), out of the action of the novel to do good deeds around the world, and in his absence shows the comic spirit going to ruin in England; and ends his history with the disappearance of his comic narrator altogether and the total negation of both comedy and amiability.

What Schlegel described at the end of the eighteenth century as romantic irony, the "endless succession of mirrors," and what Kierkegaard in the 1840s elaborated into "double reflection" and the disappearance of the author that results from it, Meredith made into the basis of his fiction. Thus the fate of the narrator at the end of the novel. *The Ordeal of Richard Feverel* then does not simply reflect *Tom Jones* or Baudelaire's essay on laughter but catches up in the flashings of its mirrors a tradition of comic literature and a tradition of comic theory. Beyond Thackeray and the German romantic ironists, other imitations and repetitions and inversions are mirrored into the text. The novel begins to sound like a parody of Gothic romance in the style of Austen's *Northanger Abbey*, complete with ghosts and a curse at the old abbey; but by the end it has become the mirror inversion of this form, a serious Gothic, complete with a duet of mad screams between Lucy, dying of brain fever, and Richard, whose mind is going blank. Similarly, the novel mocks tales of knighthood in the manner of Cervantes' *Don Quixote*, for under their influence Richard goes off on his project of rescuing fallen women, only to fall himself; but this mockery is opposed by its mirror inversion, a serious presentation of Austin Wentworth as a modern knight capable of rescuing the downtrodden of the earth, and maybe even the Feverel family, almost in the manner of the *Amadis de Gaul*. Other passages of the novel repeat and mock Shakespeare, Molière, Congreve, and Steele, at the same time that they are mirrored reflections of the plot of *Tom Jones*. The principal theoretical statements about comedy and laughter written in English in the decade before the novel are also echoed and applied to the story: Thackeray's argument from "Charity and Humour" in 1852, Hunt's essay "On the Combination of Grave and Gay" in 1854, anonymous essays from *Chambers' Edinburgh Journal* (in 1847 "Anatomy of Laughter," and in 1852 "The Philosophy of Laughter"), the long series of anonymous essays on "Eutrapelia" that appeared in 1856 and 1857 in the *New Monthly Magazine*, and Carlyle's pronouncements on humour from the 1820s. It is not simply that Meredith's novel, like these various essays, is interested in the problems of the comic and therefore raises similar kinds of questions—there are highly specific repetitions of parts of all of these works in the Meredith novel that must be seen as simultaneously comic and about the comic, a fictionalization of theory.

The Ordeal of Richard Feverel, like *Tom Jones*, is a virtuoso performance executed in mirrors in the labyrinth of the comic. Like *Tom Jones*, it is made up of bits and pieces of the comic tradition, which it sometimes reflects and sometimes inverts, and like *Vanity Fair*, it arranges these bits and pieces into a chronological order; but to the extent that it inverts these two novels and therefore negates them, it also smashes the tradition of comic fiction from Fielding and Cervantes to Austen and Thackeray to bits. There are echoes also of Peacock, of Maturin, of Herbert Spencer in the serious and scientific Sir Austin: the novel that is a reflection of Fielding's comic epic is also a reflection of the history of comedy from Aristophanes to Meredith, and of English prose styles of the nineteenth century, both comic and serious, romantic and horrific. It is also a reflection of the principal arguments in English and in some European comic theory from Meredith's own time. Fielding's comic epic has mirrored into an epic about the comic. We are returned again to the labyrinth of the comic, but where the narrator of *Tom Jones* found few clear answers and instead playful excitement in the shifting currents of laughter and the ability finally to hold the oppositions of mirth and decency in some sort of momentary synthesis, the narrator of *Richard Feverel* finds illumination and danger. He does understand, and at least for us he does make the shape and significance of the labyrinth clear, but he also disappears into the recesses of the maze at one of the sudden turnings of the plot, and we are left to work our way out without him, guided only by what he has taught us and by the letter from Lady Blandish to Austin Wentworth. But by the end of the novel we know that letters cannot always be trusted. The narrator of *Vanity Fair* also found answers to the labyrinth of the comic, only to become as vain as the other subjects of his history. Attempting to avoid this monster, pride, that lurks in the labyrinth, Meredith's narrator disappears into the mirrored reflections of romantic irony. Comedy will end by destroying itself after it has destroyed all other forms of literature, Hegel predicted in his lectures on aesthetics, published in the 1830s. A generation later, Meredith also made Hegel's prediction come true.

II

THE COMPLEX relationship begins with Fielding's *Tom Jones*, the source for the structure of the plot and the character types. The general correspondence between *Tom Jones* and *Richard Feverel* has been noted by other critics, and a number of the major resemblances have been examined with some care. In 1968, P. D. Edwards compared Raynham Abbey to Paradise Hall, Richard's family and education to Tom's, the major events of Richard's life to Tom's; and then he examined the more fundamental resemblances between the texts, the issues of philosophy and religion on the nature of man and the functions of education. *Tom Jones* "is the comedy of nature triumphant over education," while *Richard Feverel* "is the tragedy of education triumphant over nature" ("Education and Nature," 24). More recently, Judith Wilt has compared the narrators in Meredith and Fielding, arguing that Meredith inherits the convention of the civilized reader from Fielding, which becomes one of the major reasons for his novel writing. It may only be a minor addition to point out that Meredith uses Fielding's own device, the

mirror, against Fielding's own labyrinth of mirrors; but there
has as yet been no examination of the ways in which Meredith
seizes this device from Fielding to repeat Fielding's journey into
the labyrinth in an attempt to control the current of laughter
and mockery and thus to see the labyrinth clearly, and in so doing to rewrite the history of comedy. Fielding, of course, boasted
of his ability to turn the ridicule against the ridiculer, to shift the
current of laughter, and the narrators of *Joseph Andrews* and
Tom Jones both demonstrate this skill, although at times there is
no doubt that Fielding himself is also turning the current of
laughter against them. At the end of *Joseph Andrews* the narrator disables Joseph as a fictional character, explaining that
Joseph's life is now too boring and besides he has no interest in
ever returning to print, an attempt to prevent another author
from picking up the current of laughter and turning it against
Fielding as Fielding had done to Richardson and Cibber. Meredith took up the challenge and the project, turning the current
of mockery back against Fielding as Fielding had turned it back
against Swift and raillers in general; but Meredith selected the
greater and more complex text, *Tom Jones*, mocking the master
of the mockery of mockery.

Richard's eyes meet Bella Mount's eyes in a glass in her apartment and he finally sees what she represents, passion and sexuality. He lets go of her at once. The mirror scene mirrors the mirror scene in *Tom Jones* when Tom's eyes meet Sophia's eyes in a
glass at Lady Bellaston's apartments and, as Martin Battestin
has argued, they see their ideal selves, and Sophia's emblematic
meaning as pure beauty is revealed. Richard should be looking
at Lucy—the scene has somehow been played with the wrong
woman—and thus, when he does meet Lucy walking in the
park, he manages to keep her from seeing him at all. Having already played Fielding's mirror recognition scene, although in an
inverted form, he plays yet a different sort of inversion of the
scene. Fielding's mirrors are working again but the reflections
are producing an inverted text. In *Tom Jones* it was the female
characters who peered compulsively into mirrors; in *Richard
Feverel* both male and female characters are caught up in the

reflections. Richard and Bella are mirrored by the love scene between Richard and Lucy earlier in the novel, which in turn is mirrored by a scene between their mirror inversions, Sir Austin and Lady Blandish. Rowing on the water—"pure mirrors to the upper glory" (107)—Richard meets Lucy on the bank of a stream reading the burnt fragments of his sentimental poetry. He sees her as the reflection of this ideal and not at all as the reflection of his own vanity, which the reader certainly is encouraged to see. This is mirrored after Sir Austin has kept Richard at Bellingham to force a separation with Lucy, and the father reads a letter from Lady Blandish reporting on her interview with Lucy. When he reads a long postscript about comic literature and Lady Blandish's lack of humor and her difficulty reading Falstaff and Quixote, Sir Austin twice throws "a look into the glass in the act of passing it" (175). Here the narrator's language, "luminous glances at the broad Reflector which the world of Fact . . . holds up to us to see ourselves in when we will" (176), reflects back to his earlier description of Lucy mirrored in the water. Sir Austin realizes that he too lacks a sense of humor—the mirror that has shown Richard Lucy's best self now shows Sir Austin his worst self—and the narrator explains that his lack of an ability to laugh cuts him off from compassion; it is his greatest flaw. But in a minute the reflection in the mirror is gone, and he does harden his heart against Lucy: "he had no glass before him . . . and he had rather forgotten the letter of Lady Blandish" (176). Significantly, the mirror is still working for the reader but now in a different way: Sir Austin lacks a sense of humor and therefore lacks compassion, but Lady Blandish, who lacks a sense of humor, does not lack compassion. Later, when Richard has married Lucy in spite of Sir Austin's interventions, Sir Austin feels himself humiliated and without a sense of humor; he also fears ridicule. The mirror of Lady Blandish's letter becomes the mirror of Lady Blandish's eyes. "You feel yourself strangely diminishing in those sweet mirrors, till at last they drop on you complacently level" (284). Sir Austin is also mirrored in his dyspeptic brother Hippias, who looks into a mirror when Adrian has told him that he is swelling to Gargantuan proportions; but although Richard and Adrian laugh, Hippias sees nothing and only resents the ridicule. There are other more minor incidents of mirrorings: Mrs. Berry looks into a mirror after the wedding breakfast as Adrian enters her rooms; Adrian later says that Mrs. Grandison is mirrored in her children. And at the end of the novel, when Richard tells Lucy that he is about to leave again to fight a duel, the narrator reminds us that he must "shatter the image she held of him" (425). But she is apparently dependent on that image, because when it shatters she dies of brain fever; and Richard is apparently dependent on that image too, for when it shatters he shatters too. His mind goes blank. What shatters at the end of the story, of course, is Fielding's labyrinth of mirrors, for the story is over and Meredith is finally freed from his images.

Meredith's mirrorings of Fielding are intricate and extensive, although when we first become aware of a major mirrored episode it appears relatively straightforward: Richard is caught poaching by Farmer Blaize and whipped for it. There is a comparable episode early in *Tom Jones*, but Richard arranges for Tom Bakewell to fire the farmer's ricks, and when Tom is apprehended after the arson Richard refuses to come forward and admit his guilt, even though Tom will not "peach" on the original poacher. We are now in an inversion of the episode in *Tom Jones*, for there Tom will not implicate Black George even though the servant has been responsible. Meredith thus has mirrored Jones into Richard and into Tom Bakewell, just as Black George has been inversely mirrored into both Richard and Tom Bakewell. The situation is additionally complicated because both Richard and Bakewell have mirrored inversions: Richard with Ripton Thompson, who is also involved; Tom Bakewell with Tom Blaize, who will shortly be introduced as the farmer's son. We are suddenly thrust into a labyrinth of reflections. "This Tom beats that Tom" (223), the narrator will later write in another episode, and it is as if he is deliberately trying to confuse us. In fact, there is a play with language that is not present in *Tom Jones*, because Meredith has the narrator's language mirror the actions of the characters: fevered Richard Feverel arranges for a rick to be fired by Tom Bakewell, which results in a blaze at Farmer Blaize's. The incident is much more serious than the comparable incident in *Tom Jones*, but the narrator's language is much more mocking. Style inverts content. It also makes content: Tom Bakewell is a mirroring of Tom Rakewell from Hogarth's *A Rake's Progress*.

Language mirrors language in the novel. We are presented with characters with mirrored names like Mrs. Doria-Forey and Great Aunt Grantley, and with characters whose names mirror each other like Tom Bakewell and Tom Blaize, or Adrian (Rady), and Brader, and Lady Blandish. Sir Austin is mirrored by Austin Wentworth, by his brother Algernon, by Adrian Harley (who also mirrors Austin Wentworth); Blandish is mirrored by Berry and by Bella. We move into a multiplying maze of mirrored language and it is comic. When we finally learn that Bessy Berry's maiden name was Andrews, the joke is at once Meredith's on Fielding, but Bessy explains that Berry said to her "you was 'A,' and now you's 'B' so you're my A.B. he says . . . the bad man with his jokes" (340). Adrian turns Mrs. Doria-Forey into Mrs. Doria Battledoria (250), while Bella turns Ripton into "Ripson, Pipson, Nipson" (361), and Adrian turns dewberry into "yewberry, blueberry, glueberry" (203). "He trifles with Vice!" (126), Ripton Thompson's father exclaims when his son is discovered to be reading pornography—to the extent that language mirrors itself it becomes comic and denies the seriousness of its subject.

If the narrator and his characters sometimes talk in mirrored language about mirrored subjects, Meredith is at the same time mirroring Fielding's text in opposing directions, sometimes multiplying characters, sometimes reducing them. Squire Western fragments into both Farmer Blaize and Sir Miles Papworth, while Allworthy and his two nephews are reduced to Sir Austin and his single son. Ripton tries out for the part of Blifil, but Sir Austin rejects him as unsuitable, and he spends relatively little time with Richard when they are growing up. Tom has two tutors, Thwackum and Square, while Richard has only one, Adrian. Austin Wentworth should be his second tutor and is

shown in the story of the arson as a major influence, but then
Sir Austin rejects him as unsuitable because he has married
his mother's housemaid, and Austin spends relatively little
time at Raynham as well. Tom's relationships with Allworthy,
Thwackum, and Square are, however, mirrored by Richard's
relationships with Sir Austin, Austin, and Adrian, but with
the same kind of multiple fragmentation as in the Tom–Black
George transposition into Richard–Tom Bakewell. Sir Austin
combines Allworthy's humorlessness with Thwackum's moral
severity and attitude to the world, while Austin mirrors Allworthy's goodness and Square's view of the world and ability to
laugh; and Adrian mirrors Thwackum's cynicism and Square's
hypocrisy, and at the same time he inverts Square's ability to
laugh, from the Shaftesburian model to the Peacockian. With
other characters in the novel the mirrorings are reduced in complexity. Molly Seagrim reappears as Molly Davenport, the servant girl who allows Adrian (Square) to buy her sexual favors,
but this Molly has no involvement with Richard sexually. Mrs.
Waters reappears as Lady Blandish, the older mother substitute
with sexual desires for the son, but this time there is no involvement with Richard sexually. Only Lady Bellaston, who is reborn
and renamed as Bella Mount, has the sexual relationship—now
she is Richard's own age rather than an older woman, and she
now has a comic name in the tradition of a Lady Booby or a
Fanny, and is contrasted to a mirror inversion, with a mirrored
name, Lady Judith Felle.

The relationship between Richard and Bella is emblematic of
the ways in which Meredith both simplifies and complicates the
reflections from Fielding. Bella moves in the scene from being a
perfect mirror inversion of Lady Bellaston to being a perfect
mirror inversion of Richard, for Meredith not only makes her
Richard's own age but he makes her just slightly older than 21
and Richard just slightly younger than 21, a fact he reveals as
they approach the mirror in her apartment. Then the events of
her seduction are mirrored by the events of Mountfalcon's failed
seduction of Lucy, just as Tom's seduction by Lady Bellaston is
mirrored by Lord Fellamar's failed seduction and rape of Sophia,

but what in Fielding is limited to the main outlines of the two mirrored episodes is made over by Meredith into a meticulous mirroring of minor details. Bella seduces Richard after singing a ballad to him, while Lucy has Mountfalcon read history to her unborn son; Bella appeals to Richard's vanity by telling him he lacks vanity, while Mountfalcon does the same to Lucy; Bella laughs wildly and catches Richard up in the power of her diabolical humor, while Mountfalcon, when accused by Lucy of laughing at her, somberly denies it. We then move back into simplifications and complications of Fielding: Lady Bellaston writes Tom letters after the seduction, while Richard writes Bella a single letter with the same sort of sexual content. But this letter is used by Meredith in the manner of the single letter Tom has written to Lady Bellaston, the insincere proposal of marriage, which Lady Bellaston turns over to Sophia's aunt with the intention that it be used to drive Sophia from Tom. Richard's letter is stolen by Brader from Bella's table and turned over to Mountfalcon so that he can drive Lucy from Richard, but he will not— it is too low a trick. Instead he sits calmly in the dark room reading to Lucy in sharp contrast to Lord Fellamar's attempted rape, and is interrupted in this activity by the sudden and comic arrival of Mrs. Berry, who mirrors the arrival of Western in the nick of time in *Tom Jones*. But while Sophia is rescued by a single protester when she really needs help, Lucy is rescued by two when she does not. There is a ring at one door and a knock at another, from Berry and from Tom Bakewell, and then Tom delivers a double knock. These mirrorings work down to the most miniscule details of plot: there are two letters waiting for Richard when he returns from Europe.

By the end of the novel this play of reflected images is intense, even dazzling, as they reduce, multiply, combine and recombine. *Tom Jones* has begun as a comedy and then grown increasingly serious until Tom is imprisoned in his fight with Mr. Fitzpatrick and is informed in jail of his apparent incest with his mother; it then reverses itself suddenly and becomes comedy again with a series of recognition scenes and a happy ending. *Richard Feverel* has also begun as comedy and then grown increasingly serious until Richard abandons Lucy and the child he does not know about; similarly, it suddenly reverses itself into comedy as Austin Wentworth reenters the story in the manner of a Molière raisoneur and starts tidying up the loose ends. Sir Austin welcomes Lucy and the baby to Raynham Abbey and Richard agrees to come home. But then the novel suddenly reverses itself again into tragedy. In the fine details of the final scenes of action the mirror plays more tricks. Tom injures Fitzpatrick in an impromptu fight, and, falsely accused of having started it, he is thrown in jail. The episode of course inverts then repeats Tom's first meeting with Fitzpatrick in the inn at Upton when Fitzpatrick falsely attacks Tom for being in bed with Mrs. Waters, whom Fitzpatrick mistakes for his wife. The episode is now inverted again by Meredith. Richard Feverel is injured by Lord Mountfalcon in a duel that is formal and prearranged, and although he does recover, Lucy goes mad and dies of a brain fever from all the stress and Richard's mind goes blank. The novel ends.

Onto this inversion of the Tom-Fitzpatrick fight, Meredith mirrors at least two other episodes from the Fielding novel: the challenge to a duel delivered by Fellamar's man to Squire Western, which is made so insulting that Western should be forced to accept, and the trick of the unexpected death, which is mirrored and repeated twice in the first part of *Tom Jones*. Western is so insensitive that he misses the insult entirely and no duel is arranged; Lord Mountfalcon, on the other hand, is forced into the duel he does not want because Richard is so insulting—he tells Ripton exactly this. Captain Blifil contemplates the prospect of Allworthy's death and dies himself; then we are asked to contemplate Allworthy's deathbed scene, and instead Brigid Allworthy Blifil dies away from our attention. These deaths seem comic and just since in both cases the allworthy man lives and the unpleasant character is eliminated; but in the Meredith novel it is the allworthy and entirely innocent Lucy who dies and Richard who is allowed to live, although he is not allowed to live very well—the mirror keeps mocking. We now see the dark side of Fielding's comic labyrinth.

Meredith mirrors both himself and Fielding into this narrative space as well. In a curious way the two men meet in the labyrinth that is made up of their joint skills. Meredith is fragmented in the mirrors of his own text: into Sir Austin, who repeats the story of his abandonment by his wife; into Richard, who repeats the story of the critical destruction of his poetry; into Adrian, who repeats his love of mockery; even into Bella, who shares with him a father who is a tailor. Fielding is similarly fragmented: when he was eighteen he attempted to elope with a young girl but was stopped by her uncles, the episode inverted into the story of Richard and Lucy. Later Fielding married his own housemaid, the episode inverted in the story of Austin marrying his mother's housemaid. The novel is as much based on the ordeals of Fielding's life as on the ordeals of Meredith's. Meredith similarly combines Fielding's fiction with his criticism, making Lucy a Catholic on the model of Sophia, who is only mistaken for the lover of the Pretender by an ignorant innkeeper, and making her a dairymaid on the model of Fielding's argument in the *Covent Garden Journal* that "there is very little difference between the education of many a squire's daughter, and that of his dairy maid, who is most likely her principal companion; nay, the little difference which there is, is, I am afraid, not in the favour of the former" (no. 56, 221). Adrian calls Lucy the papish dairymaid. Her name mirrors luck, the quality she represents and the quality Sir Austin rejects, but nevertheless the quality Fielding praises again and again as fortune. Virtually everything can be reflected back in some direction to Fielding.

Caught in all this is the narrator, who in many respects is a perfect mirror repetition of the narrator of *Tom Jones*, like him combining comic styles with serious styles and vacillating wildly between a great many masks and poses as he bounces against the reflecting walls of the labyrinth. The narrator of *Tom Jones* mocks himself and so does the narrator of *Richard Feverel*, but the Meredith narrator can also mock his ties to the Fielding narrator. Just as Richard is doomed to repeat the mistakes of the father and relive the curse on the house of Feverel, so is the narrator doomed to repeat the steps of his fictional father and relive the curse on the house of comic fiction, which is Fielding's house. Richard lives his fate because he is taken up by the pride and passion of the Feverels, but the narrator avoids this in his self mockeries. And if Richard is the serious mirror to the narrator's fate, Hippias, allegorized as the nineteenth century, is his comic mirror. As Hippias is shown "expended in his gaze" (146) to great aunt Grantley, allegorized as the eighteenth century, so is Meredith's nineteenth-century narrator allegorized to Fielding's eighteenth. Lady Caroline Grandison is another comic mirror of the Meredith narrator, with her ludicrous attachment to the fictional Grandison family of Richardson's eighteenth-century novel, a characterization that simultaneously mocks the narrator's own ties to Fielding and repeats the kind of mockery Fielding was best at, the gibe at Richardson. Meredith also turns this technique of mockery directly onto Fielding when Bessy Berry's maiden name is revealed to have been Andrews.

Meredith's narrator, of course, disappears before the end of his story, while Fielding's finally achieves a synthesis of mirth and decency. There are significant differences between the two by the end of their stories. Fielding's insists on the importance of making distinctions and urges his readers on to greater and greater tasks of discerning the good from the bad, the false from the true. Meredith's narrator insists on the same, but his chapter "A Fine Distinction" turns out to be not a fine distinction at all, only that the Bantam can make an idiotic and patently false distinction between taking an oath on a Bible or without it. By the last third of the novel, all the oppositions that Meredith's narrator has presented are negated by the characters themselves, who appear to go out of their way to show up the narrator. The narrator has told us that Sir Austin hates women, but the women in the novel begin to perceive that he has a heart of a woman, and Bella, the archetype of the kind of woman he fears, dresses herself up as a man. That model of sexual propriety, Bessy Berry, climbs into bed with Lucy, making unmistakable sexual overtures; later she tells Richard she is as good as Richard's mother, which is somewhat ambiguous praise, but when she sees the mother she mistakes her for Bella. Lady Blandish has feelings

toward Richard that are identical to those of Richard's mother
and of Bella. Richard sees Bella and is reminded of his father,
sees her again and is reminded of Lucy and his mother. Adrian
sees Lady Judith as another Lady Blandish and Lord Mountfalcon as another Farmer Blaize; and then Lady Judith turns
out to be related to the Feverel family. By the end of the novel
Sir Austin resembles Mrs. Berry, and Lucy resembles Claire.
Richard and Mrs. Doria-Forey have been joined in their knowledge of the events of Claire's death, and Lady Blandish and Mrs.
Doria-Forey in their attempts to rescue Richard for Lucy. Everyone is implicated in the disaster of the novel's ending. There are
no more fine distinctions to be made, at least by the characters.

In *Tom Jones*, the narrator's continual requests to his readers
to make distinctions is contrasted once, by Sophia's insistence to
Tom near the end of the novel that he not make one fine distinction between the character of men and the character of women:
they are the same. In *Richard Feverel*, the narrator's early requests to his readers to make distinctions is finally obliterated
by the insistence of all of his characters that distinctions cannot
be made at all. Everything is everything. All styles are present in
the one comic epic, only as different layers of the text: Old Testament parable and new scientific treatise, story of knighthood
and mockery of knighthood, gothic horror and parody of gothic
horror, Shakespearean romance and parody of Shakespearean
romance, attack on pornography and imitation of pornography.
Ripton meets the smiling and pornographic Miss Random in
print, but Richard meets the laughing and pornographic Miss
Mount in the flesh. In the prologue to Plautus's *Amphitrio* Mercury asks the audience if it is frowning because he has said the
play will be tragedy. I am a god, he explains, "I'll convert this
same play from tragedy to comedy, if you like, and never change
a line" (9–11). The narrator of Richard Feverel is adept at this
subtle manipulation of the labyrinth of mirrors—with the same
lines, the story is simultaneously all major forms and styles of
literature. Mercury explains, "I shall mix things up: let it be
tragi-comedy" (11); and Meredith's narrator, after him, does

something similar, except that it is a more Polonian genre, a gothicopastoralromance, and its opposite as well.

III

ONTO THE elegant mirrored symmetries of Fielding's text Meredith imposes a second symmetry, an anatomy of laughter, derived in part from the standard Aristotelian opposition of the buffoon who laughs too much, the boor who laughs too little, and the wit who laughs just right—the mean between them. Meredith joins this with a second opposition derived primarily from Baudelaire's essay "On the Essence of Laughter," of the innocent who laughs angelically and the rest of us, who after the fall from grace laugh diabolically. There is at least one minor essay in the same period that describes angelic laughter and that may also have been a source. Layering one symmetry, the combination of Aristotle and Baudelaire, onto the other, the architectonic of Fielding, Meredith multiplies the complexities of the labyrinth and in the reflections of the mirrors within mirrors produces at least two additional layers of text: a history of comic literature from Aristophanes to the nineteenth century and a survey of the major prose styles of the nineteenth century. The dexterity with mirrors is impressive, for it is Fielding's text that, looked at from a slightly different perspective, metamorphoses into all of comic literature; then, from a slightly different angle again, into nineteenth-century literature.

In *Tom Jones*, Tom is at first the buffoon in contrast to Blifil, the boor, but by the end of the novel Tom is the mean between the extremes represented in a sequence of minor variations: the drunken mirth of Western/the humorless sobriety of Allworthy, the constant ridicule of Lady Bellaston/the constant fear of ridicule of Sophia, the excessive humor of Partridge/the excessive sentimentality of Mrs. Miller. Richard is surrounded by the mirror reflections of these pairs—Farmer Blaize/Sir Austin, Bella/Lucy, Adrian/Mrs. Berry—but Richard never moves into a middle point between extremes. Meredith also simplifies the

pairings, reducing them to two, Sir Austin/Adrian, the two men
who direct Richard's life, and Lucy/Bella, the two women who
lead Richard away from them. The other laughers are still present in the text, but there are now only four who are given this
kind of major role in the plot. The opposition between Richard's
father, Sir Austin, who broods humorlessly over the action like
the god of the Old Testament and who thinks man is a "self-
acting machine" (120), and Richard's cousin and tutor, Adrian,
who laughs constantly through the action like a pagan god and
who thinks man is an animal and boys are like monkeys, is
the same kind of Aristotelian distinction present in *Tom Jones*,
and then mirrored into a number of variants. The opposition
between Richard's bride, Lucy, who laughs angelically with
Richard and thereby leads him into love, and Richard's se-
ductress, Bella, who laughs diabolically with Richard and
thereby leads him into sex, is a qualitatively different distinction, not present in either Aristotle or Fielding. "Laughter is the
expression of a double, or contradictory, feeling," Baudelaire
wrote in 1855 (317). "The angelic and the diabolic elements
function in parallel" (316). Combining Aristotle and Baudelaire, Meredith made these two contrasting pairs into significant
mirror inversions of each other and a much more meaningful set
of contrasts than that present in *Tom Jones*. The extremes of Sir
Austin and Adrian represent perversions of the intellect; the extremes of Bella and Lucy represent perversions of the body.
Richard's soul is thus determined between them. While Adrian's
laughter leads Richard into cynicism and the denial of morality,
Sir Austin's humorlessness leads him into a system so rigidly
moral that it denies life. Bella's laughter leads Richard into pure
passion, Lucy's into pure love, and these two are extremes comparable to those of father and tutor, the one entirely good but
also childlike, the other entirely bad but also adult. The medieval ordeal by water and by fire is made into Richard's ordeal by
Lucy (water) and by Bella (fire).

    In "The Idea of Comedy" in 1877, Meredith characterized
the plight of the comic poet "beset with foes to right and left,"
the laughter haters to one side, the excessive laughers to the

other (4). The English middle class, which was this comic poet's best hope, was further drawn off into extremes of humor with its sentimental and loving laughter, and into satire with its harsh and bitter laughter. "The comic poet is the narrow field, or enclosed square, of the society he depicts" (46). Such an enclosed square is the grid Meredith imposed upon his first major exploration of the plight of the comic poet, *Richard Feverel*, eighteen years earlier. Richard should be the comic poet between these extremes, but his own sentimental poetry is burned before he can learn any other styles, and his ability to live in the mean is hurt because he has no model. Austin Wentworth and Bessy Berry are representatives of this mean (and mirror images of each other), but the one is expelled from Raynham because he marries his mother's housemaid and the other because she sees Sir Austin weeping over the infant Richard. While their presence in the novel indicates that a comic mean is possible, their absence from their proper place as influences over Richard's life indicates that achieving such a comic mean is beset with danger. A comic poet cannot come into being without a model. A Meredith must have a Fielding. In the enclosed square marked off by the extremes Richard can only vacillate wildly—the center cannot hold and sheer anarchy descends, until he is finally exhausted by the ordeal and his mind goes blank. The narrator who has been his mirror reflection and the narrative possibility for the comic mean disappears altogether. He also becomes a blank. "You follow one extreme, and we the other," Adrian tells the Doria-Forey family. "I don't say that a middle course exists. The History of Mankind shows our painful efforts to find one, but they have invariably resolved themselves into asceticism, or laxity, acting and reacting" (276). At another point in the novel, the narrator explains, "There was no middle course for Richard's comrades" (93).

Of the four extremes around Richard, Adrian is the one who has received the most critical attention. Judith Wilt calls him a *ficelle* after Henry James's description of Henrietta Stackpole in *The Portrait of a Lady*; he is our guide and representative in the novel. Beer calls him "comedy's representative in the book"

(*Meredith*, 16). Both agree with other commentators that he is
not to be trusted. To adopt the metaphor of the comic labyrinth,
one would simply see him as Ariadne, but he is a distortion of
her much as his name mirrors and distorts hers. Characterized
by the narrator as "delightfully sarcastic: perhaps a little too un-
scrupulous in his moral tone" (25), he is a man who takes
nothing seriously except the pleasure of taking nothing seriously—and eating. Life to him is a "Supreme Ironic Procession,
with Laughter of Gods in the background. Why not Laughter of
Mortals also? Adrian had his laugh in his comfortable corner"
(24). The narrator also tells us that he is "afflicted . . . with
many peculiarities of the professional joker" (203). According to
Wilt, he is the comic fallen into the sin of pride, for though he
can always see clearly, he never acts well. The arson is only opportunity for a Bakewell Comedy; Heavy Benson's spying on
Richard and Lucy is only opportunity for a wonderfully comic
beating. In contrast to Adrian is Sir Austin, who values Adrian
because he can sometimes make him laugh. But because he is
"cognizant of that total absence of the humorous in himself (the
want that most shut him out from his fellows)" (176), he never
understands the nature of Adrian's laughter, or, for that matter,
of any character's laughter. He lives in fear of ridicule, but what
is much worse, in a lack of self-knowledge about everything except his lack of a sense of humor. "For a good wind of laughter
had relieved him of much of the blight of self-deception, and
oddness, and extravagance; had given a healthier view of our at-
mosphere of life: but he had it not" (176). Adrian controls
laughter too well; Sir Austin too poorly. When he has almost
convinced Richard to give up Lucy, he "thought proper in his
wisdom to water the dryness of his sermon with a little jocose-
ness, on the subject of young men fancying themselves in love"
(167), but Richard only thinks his father is making him into an
object of ridicule and the argument is lost. This, in turn, is mirrored in the scene when Richard departs for London by train
with Uncle Hippias and Sir Austin watches from a distance as
his grave and sober son suddenly breaks into violent laughter.

The laugh troubles Sir Austin, although its meaning is innocent enough, and later when he learns that Richard has met Lucy at the station in London, he misinterprets this laughter to be a sign of his son's ridicule of him. The laugh comes to haunt him, "that this hideous laugh would not be silenced" (285). When Lady Blandish asks Sir Austin not to close off his heart to his son, all Sir Austin can hear is "Richard's laugh, taken up by horrid re-verberations, as it were through the lengths of the Lower Halls" (287). From this all the final catastrophes of the novel derive.

In the first part of the novel, during the so-called Bakewell Comedy, Austin Wentworth is able to position Richard as the mean between the extremes of father and tutor. When Austin and Adrian debate a proper course of action, the tutor argues that the arson is to be exploited for its comic possibilities. "All wisdom is mournful," he explains, " 'Tis therefore coz that the wise do love the Comic Muse" (59), but Austin's position is "Work first, and joke afterwards" (61). We are being offered a balanced view for the first time. Both Austin and Adrian inter-vene in the action and both interventions cause Richard to laugh, but now the contrast is mirrored between healthy laugh-ter and guilty laughter, a true/false position. When Austin lec-tures Richard on his pride and on his duty and then describes Tom Bakewell in prison, Richard begins to laugh. "Visions of a grinning lout . . . afflicted him with the strangest sensations of disgust and comicality, mixed up with pity and remorse." As he continues to laugh "an embracing humour" and a feeling of sympathy take hold of him. "He laughed at him, and wept over him. He prized him, while he shrank from him. It was a genial strife of the Angel in him with constituents less divine: but the Angel was uppermost and led the van: extinguishing loathing: humanizing laughter: transfigured Pride" (66). The contrast is with the kind of laughter that Adrian's intervention produces after he has bribed a witness to recant testimony and Farmer Blaize's case is destroyed. Blaize asks Richard "what he thought of England's peasantry after the sample they had there. Richard would have preferred not to laugh, but his dignity gave way to his sense of the ludicrous, and he let fly an irrepressible peal. The farmer was in no laughing mood" (75). Richard's guilt, which has been removed by Adrian's bribery, is reconfirmed by Richard's guilty laughter. Adrian's intervention negates Austin's intervention—it is the bribed witness that ends the Bakewell Comedy, and at the hearing before the local justice, Adrian laughs silently. "Very different for young Richard would it have been had Austin taken his right place in the Baronet's favour" (23).

Torn on the currents of laughter between these men, Richard is next ripped apart on the currents of laughter between women. When he meets Lucy by the stream and falls in love with her he is first caught up by her laughter. "Sounding harmonious bells of laughter in his ears," Lucy enters into a duet with Richard's adolescent gravity, and this "made them no longer feel strangers, and did the work of a month of intimacy." While this duet will be mirrored and inverted at the end of the novel in the duet of their mad ravings, here it is entirely joyful. "Better than sentiment Laughter opens the breast to Love," the narrator exclaims. "Hail the occasion propitious, O ye British young! and laugh." It is the laughter itself that enchants Richard. "These two laughed, and the souls of each cried out to the other, 'It is I,' 'It is I.'" And when the laughter is over Richard is in love. "They laughed and forgot the cause of their laughter" (114). Lucy can turn her laughter on others. At the Isle of Wight she turns it on Adrian, and it has a similar effect, winning him over ("Charming to the Wise Youth her pretty laughter sounded" [297]), but the significant mirror inversion of this scene is between Richard and Bella. When Richard meets Bella by the river and is caught up by her sexuality, once again laughter takes control of him. He watches her laugh, then observes as a laugh circles through a group of men and women, uniting them in sexual mockery, and he decides that his father has been wrong to believe that women lack a sense of humor. He tries to mimic Adrian's mockeries in his conversation with Bella, but she is the real master of the sexual laugh. In the weeks that follow he is taken over increasingly by her laughter—they walk the streets at midnight "and had great fits of laughter" (347). Bella laughs at society when it scorns her overt sexuality, inviting Richard to join in, then laughs at Richard as she seduces him. "First a smile changed Richard's face: then, laughing a melancholy laugh, he surrendered to her humour" (359)—just as he has done to Lucy and her laughter. Before the seduction, Bella's laugh has troubled him ("Your laugh sounds like madness. You must be unhappy" [358]), but after the seduction it becomes his own. "I laugh at myself like a devil," he tells Ripton, explaining that he can no longer continue his project of rescuing fallen women (355). "I notice he has a rather wild laugh—I don't exactly like his eyes," Mrs. Doria-Forey reports to Sir Austin (381).

Between these two extremes is Austin Wentworth's mirror reflection in the second half of the novel, Bessy Berry. "I'm for cryin' and laughin', one and the same," Mrs. Berry tells Lucy (375), but she is given little chance to practice such a mean. Instead she becomes the object of almost everyone's laughter because of the way she misuses language, and carries herself about the novel like a "cute" Dickens humor character. "Laugh away and show yer airs" (344), Mrs. Berry warns Richard after she has seen him repeatedly in the park with Bella and warned him of the dangers he faced, but Richard is too preoccupied with his own laughter to understand.

IV

LAUGHTER seduces Richard, enchants him, and leads him into love, into mockery, into confusion, into the fear of ridicule; and he is always its victim, never its master. Seized by "a demon of laughter" (207) at the train station with Uncle Hippias, Richard laughs uncontrollably. A serpent of laughter winds through the plot of the novel, controlling characters and situations and squeezing the life out of Richard. It may be let loose into the labyrinth by our Ariadne, Adrian, who opens his mouth" to shake out a coil of laughter" (160), but once free it is a force

unto itself—the monster in the heart of the labyrinth, the thread
we must follow that does not lead us out but only tangles us in a
web that is the narrow field and enclosed square of the novel.
The "electric chain of laughter" that circles through the party of
the beau monde in London does not stop there (327). Thinking
of Richard's marriage to Lucy, Sir Austin writes, "The Serpent
laughs below" (335), but it is Bella who then appears as the true
serpent of laughter. "Various as the Serpent of old Nile" (353),
she laughs with diabolical pleasure and tells Richard, "if you
could know what a net I'm in" (363). On her breast she wears as
an ornament an anchor—symbol of water and hope and thus of
her opposite, Lucy, "coiled with a rope of hair" (357). Lucy, in
contrast, finds that Bessy Berry's ring with which she has been
wed "has coiled itself round her dream of delight, and takes her
in its clutch like a horrid serpent" (253). The ring that John
Todhunter shoves onto Claire's finger seals her death, and later,
when Richard reads Claire's diary, he discovers that the last
thing Claire remembers as she dies is the sound of Richard's
laughter reverberating happily in her mind. The scene mirrors
Sir Austin's memory of Richard's laughter, and here makes
Richard realize that she has taken seriously what he has said in a
mocking way—that he would rather die than endure such a
marriage.

The electric chain of laughter is in its turn mirrored in a
lengthy description of the "electric circle" of the novel, with
which the hero, who carries the battery, makes everyone else
"caper and grimace at his will," but "though our capers be never
so comical, he laughs not" (197). The circle of laughter is finally
not comic; the circle of comedy is not laughable. The electric
chain of laughter is in its turn also mirrored when his mother
gives him advice later in the novel. Don't offend your father, she
urges, and "another chain was cast about him" (345). When
Bella seduces him, she first sets the carpet on fire accidentally
and as the fire circles her, Richard falls down on his hands and
knees to put it out; caught up in it, he becomes part of the circle
of fire around her. When he returns from Europe we are told

that he is surrounded by the circle of his family. This is not the magic circle of comedy but one of the circles in the inferno at the bottom of Dante's *Divine Comedy*. In the 21st and 22nd cantos, grinning demons prod each other with pitchforks—there is a clear connection between laughter and evil, and there is throughout medieval literature. The medieval French farce was a diablerie, a play acted by imps and devils, and played with four characters. Meredith's comic epic imposes this medieval content onto Fielding's eighteenth-century fable, just as it takes the medieval notion of an ordeal as a trial by fire and water and makes Richard undergo it in nineteenth-century form. Consumed in the circles of fire from Dante's hell, the fevered and fervored Feverel burns from the reflections of light in the labyrinth that is the history of comedy. Millimant commands a song to be performed in "The Way of the World," "And feeding, wastes in Self-Consuming Fires" (3.12). In that play, Mrs. Marwood plays incendiary, and Mrs. Fainall, like Richard, suffers from a peculiar education. Richard burns for all their sins as he mirrors, repeats, and inverts the comic tradition.

"We know the degree of refinement in men by the matter they will laugh at, and the ring of the laugh," Meredith wrote in 1877 in the "Essay on Comedy" (50). The echo is of Carlyle in *Sartor Resartus*: "How much lies in Laughter: the cipher-key, wherewith we decipher the whole man!" (25). The serpent of laughter that circles through *Richard Feverel*, constantly changing forms and rings, is animated by this project taken from Carlyle. The laughs themselves are taken or mirrored from the principal descriptions of laughter in the critical literature of the period. The novel mirrors comic theory as much as it mirrors comic literature; what circles and destroys Richard is what Meredith takes from the critics. In 1827, Carlyle wrote that humor was the product not of contempt, but of love, not of superficial distortion of natural forms, but of deep though playful sympathy with all forms of nature ("Jean Paul Richter"). The description becomes the basis for Richard's meeting with Lucy by the banks of the stream. Elaborating on Carlyle, Thackeray wrote in his lecture "Charity and Humour" in 1852 that humor "surprises you into compassion: you are laughing and disarmed, and suddenly forced into tears" (279). And in 1851 in his essay "The English Humourists of the Eighteenth Century," he wrote that "the humourous writer professes to awaken and direct your love, your pity, your kindness—your scorn for untruth, pretention, imposture—your tenderness for the weak, the poor, the oppressed, the unhappy" (4). The descriptions become the basis for Richard's laughter at Austin Wentworth's lecture on his responsibility to Tom Bakewell. In 1852, an anonymous essayist wrote on the "Philosophy of Laughter" in *Chambers' Edinburgh Journal* that "a woman has no natural grace more bewitching than a sweet laugh. It is like the sound of flutes on the water. It leaps from her heart in a clear, sparkling rill; and the heart that hears it feels as if bathed in the cool, exhilarating spring" (322). The description becomes the basis for Lucy's laughter. In 1854, Leigh Hunt wrote "On the Combination of the Grave and Gay," a fairly standard sort of plea that "no very great wit ever existed who had not an equal fund of gravity," while minor wits "discern only superficial difference of things" (562). Meredith's narrator appears to combine the strengths of Hunt's great wit with the weaknesses of his minor wit.

The major critical text for Meredith is Baudelaire's "On the Essence of Laughter, and, in General, on the Comic in the Plastic Arts," first published in 1855, then republished in 1857. Most well known today for its distinction between the absolute comic and the significative, between anarchic mockery and mockery with a clear object, the essay spends more time with a related distinction, angelic and diabolic laughter, and begins with a characterization of "*The Sage* [who] *laughs not save in fear and trembling*." Sir Austin, after all, is no simple Aristotelian boor— he is also the harsh god of the Old Testament. Baudelaire wrote: "The Sage . . . quickened with the spirit of Our Lord, he who has the divine formulary at his finger tips, does not abandon himself to laughter save in fear and trembling. The Sage trembles at the thought of having laughed; the Sage fears laughter" (312). From this Baudelaire concludes that "human laughter is intimately linked with the accident of an ancient Fall, of a debasement both physical and moral," or at least an orthodox Christian philosopher would come to such a conclusion. Although man lacks "all the seductive cunning of the serpent," it is "with his laughter" that he "soothes and charms his heart; for the phenomena engendered by the Fall will become the means of redemption" (313). All of this language reappears in Meredith: Sir Austin is the reflection of the sage, Bella of the serpent; the ancient fall is reflected in Richard's fall to Bella's laughter. But there is also the laughter of children, Baudelaire explains, "like the blossoming of a flower. It is the joy of receiving, the joy of breathing, the joy of contemplating, of living, of growing. It is a vegetable joy" (317)—and of course it is Lucy's childlike joy in the Meredith novel. "Imagine before us a soul absolutely pristine and fresh . . . from the hands of Nature," Baudelaire asks, but such an "angel" will not laugh until she finds knowledge (313). The only one of Meredith's principal laughers left out of this account is Adrian, but here too there are clear echoes. "The most comic animals are the most serious—monkeys, for example" (316), Baudelaire writes. "Boys are like monkeys," Adrian explains, "the gravest actors of farcical nonsense that the world possesses" (59). "You will find a certain unconscious pride at the core of the laugher's thought" (315), Baudelaire writes—it is of such pride that Adrian, more than any of the other laughers, suffers.

Baudelaire's essay influenced English criticism of comedy as early as 1856, when a long series of anonymous essays began appearing in *The New Monthly Magazine* on "Eutrapelia," the term taken by Isaac Barrow from the New Testament for his sermon on wit made at the end of the seventeenth century. "Is it wrong to laugh?" the English essayist asked in 1856. "Is an involuntary movement of our risible muscles a part of original sin? . . . Men are amply endowed with the faculty of laughter—the best men sometimes most amply. Are they to repress this inward tendency, smother this joyous disposition, mortify this hilarious inclination, as a matter of duty, and to the utmost of their power?" (108:365). The essay went on to include some power-

ful negative examples of this need to smother laughter. One
woman is described as "ready to choke herself with laughing"
(108:465). All of this is echoed in the Meredith novel, where
Adrian (Rady) is described as choking with laughter, and the
women around Sir Austin at the beginning of the novel are
shown to smother their silvery laughter. Laughter does appear
to be a part of original sin, but it is also a part of childish innocence. The questions that expand on "Is it wrong to laugh?" are
all thematic in the novel as well, and similar questions even
occur in the text. "Why is it you laugh so," Carola Grandison
asks Richard (171). "Why do you laugh, young man?" Mrs.
Berry asks Ripton after the wedding breakfast (262). His answer is "ha ha."

Only one major description of laughter remains unaccounted
for in this tracing of the labyrinth, the reverberating laughter
that so horrifies Sir Austin and haunts his estate. This comes to
Meredith from Maturin's *Melmoth the Wanderer*, praised as a
central text by Baudelaire in his essay. "Melmoth heard a laugh
that chilled his blood. . . . when he first recognized his supposed
demoniac character by the laugh with which he hailed the spec-
tacle of the blasted lovers. The echo of that laugh rung in
Melmoth's ears" (50). What Sir Austin hears in Richard's laugh,
we as readers finally hear in Bella's—she is the demoniac
character.

V

WE NEED to take a careful look at the narrow field of the enclosed grid that makes up this symmetrical anatomy of laughter,
because we are now in a position to see what Beer has characterized as the "baroque" design of the novel (*Meredith*, 30), and
Wilt the "Chinese-box-intricacy of its structure" (*Readable
People*, 18). I would argue that by imposing a symmetry constructed out of Fielding's comic text with a symmetry made up
out of comic theory, Meredith produced two additional symme-

tries: the history of comic literature from Aristophanes and the survey of nineteenth-century forms. Let me diagram the grid:

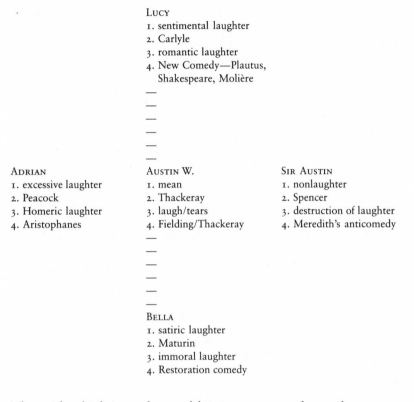

LUCY
1. sentimental laughter
2. Carlyle
3. romantic laughter
4. New Comedy—Plautus,
   Shakespeare, Molière

—
—
—
—
—

ADRIAN
1. excessive laughter
2. Peacock
3. Homeric laughter
4. Aristophanes

AUSTIN W.
1. mean
2. Thackeray
3. laugh/tears
4. Fielding/Thackeray

—
—
—

SIR AUSTIN
1. nonlaughter
2. Spencer
3. destruction of laughter
4. Meredith's anticomedy

BELLA
1. satiric laughter
2. Maturin
3. immoral laughter
4. Restoration comedy

The grid, which is made up of four extremes and one absence at the center, is in turn a grid of four layers. In addition, it is a reworking of Fielding's text. These four layers are numbered to simplify the explanation. We have been led first from Meredith's statement in "The Idea of Comedy" to perceive Richard as torn between two intersecting sets of extremes—this is layer one. Tracing the reflections of these laughs back into the critical literature, we have begun to identify each with a single nineteenth-century author—Lucy laughs as Carlyle would have her laugh, Bella as Maturin would have her laugh. I have not argued here a correlation between Adrian and Peacock because the connection has been made by other critics—most recently by Henkle—nor have I argued a correlation between Sir Austin and Herbert Spencer because that connection too has been made often in Meredith criticism. The principal symmetry of characters around Richard also represents nineteenth-century English prose, the choices Meredith had to select from in 1859.

What remains is to refract this mirroring into the inversion of this grid, into the *history* of laughter and comic forms from Aristophanes to the present, a chronology that is mirrored into the plot of the novel. The novel, as others have noted, is a mixture of comedy and tragedy, but it appears primarily as a comedy gone bad or a comedy with a tragic ending yoked by violence onto it. The structure is, however, mirrored and symmetrical in the manner of *Tom Jones*, and just as *Tom Jones* turns upon a center scene, the inn at Upton that is the middle of the middle section of the novel, so *Richard Feverel* turns on a center scene, "In Which the Last Act of a Comedy Takes the Place of the First." Comedy turns itself inside out at the center of the text, at which point we position the mirror, and the novel starts to play itself out backward. Preceded by the discussion of Time as "The Father of jokes, he is himself no joke: which it seems the business of men to discover" (241), the chapter begins with mention of Caesar crossing the Rubicon, a notion then capitalized as PHILOSOPHICAL GEOGRAPHY, and the announcement that "Richard Feverel was now crossing the River of his Ordeal" (242). The chapter ends with Richard's marriage to Lucy, the typical ending place for comedy, but when the next chapter begins, we understand that Lucy too has crossed her Rubicon into some mirror inversion of the genre of comedy, having "nobly preserved the mask imposed by Comedies, till the curtain has fallen, and now she weeps, streams with tears" (252). As Richard and Lucy cross the Rubicon, so do we. The novel that has been written like a long elaboration of stage comedy suddenly turns into something melodramatic and tragic. Explaining the special ordeal of the Feverel family to his son, Sir Austin provides more of this philosophical geography for us. "It is when you know them that Life is either a mockery to you, or, as some find it, a gift of blessedness" (165). At the center crossing point of the novel (which Lewis Carroll would later make into Alice's entry into the mirror world in the second part of her adventures, *Through the Looking Glass*), Richard is about to discover what he thinks is blessedness but will turn out to be mockery. The mockery that has sustained him as the hero of the comedy is about to turn against him and make him the object of the tragedy.

The novel that is divided this once at the center is then divided within each of its two sections into four. The first half of the story is first Bakewell Comedy, then New Comedy, and each of these parts is so named. There is no comparable naming in the mirror reflection of these two parts but they are just as distinct—we need only to follow the patterns of reflection. The second half of the story is first a mirror inversion of the New Comedy and then a mirror inversion of the Bakewell Comedy. Richard's marriage to Lucy is undone by Richard's seduction by Bella; the victory of lovers over blocking characters in the New Comedy is undone by the victory of the blocking characters over the lovers in Claire's forced marriage to John Todhunter. Similarly the Bakewell Comedy is mirrored in the final section of the novel: Richard's refusal to apologize to Farmer Blaize is mirrored by his refusal to apologize to Mountfalcon; his desire for revenge on the one is mirrored by his desire for revenge on the other. If we are asked to perceive that time, the father of jokes, is no joke, then we are also being asked by the narrator to perceive this pattern in the fabric of the novel. Just after Richard's eyes meet Bella's eyes in the mirror, Bella turns to the floor "divining the pattern of the carpet" (350). There is a pattern in the carpet of the novel as we have already seen—squares and circles, mirror inversions of each other. Circles around characters are matched in the enclosed square of the novel itself, but it is the large square that concerns us here, the four parts of the novel. We are offered an emblem for this relationship too, in a small moment in the novel when Ripton joins Adrian, Brader, and Richard for dinner at a hotel in London and they make a "square at the table" (318). Adrian and Brader are both parasites and therefore mirror reflections of each other, just as Richard and Ripton are mirror reflections of each other. But

Richard also mirrors and inverts Adrian—one is innocent, one experienced—in the same way that Ripton mirrors Brader. Richard and Brader mirror each other in their attitudes to Bella, while Adrian and Ripton mirror each other in their attitudes to food. If we are caught in a small tangle of reflections in this square at table, the reflections between the four parts of the larger enclosed square of the novel are almost infinite, or at least seem that way. Meredith has mirrored the three large sections of *Tom Jones*—country, road, city—into four: Bakewell, New, Anti-New, Anti-Bakewell (although it may be fairer to characterize the fourth part as a repetition and confirmation of Bakewell, but an Anti-comedy to all three earlier parts). The same is true for the small square at table: Brader and Richard are opposite in their attitude to Bella, while Ripton and Adrian the same in their attitude to food.

The four parts of the novel correlate precisely to the four extremes of laughter that determine Richard's fate. The major characters who take control of Richard's life also take control of the narrator's story of that life. Under the influence of Adrian, who laughs Homerically and acts like a pagan god, the narrator writes the Bakewell Comedy, as at least one critic, David R. Ewbank, has noted, in the style of Aristophanes—the old fool, Sir Austin, devises a scatterbrained scheme that backfires, because it is so new. Then under the influence of Lucy, who laughs angelically and acts like the heroine in romance, the narrator writes the new comedy in the styles of Plautus, Shakespeare, and Molière. Then under the influence of Bella, who laughs diabolically and acts like the heroine in comedy of manners, the narrator writes Restoration comedy in the styles of Wycherley and Congreve. Finally, under the influence of Sir Austin, who lacks a sense of humor and acts like Meredith himself when he was abandoned by his wife, the narrator writes first like Steele and the sentimentalists (Richard is in despair for his sins), then like Fielding (fortune will reverse itself), then like Thackeray (there must be large measures of sentimentality), and finally like Meredith (there is no comedy at all, only its failure). The final quarter of the novel unravels the first three. Comedy is destroyed and the narrator vanishes. The final pages are written by Lady Blandish, who lacks a sense of humor. Will this be the future of the novel? We are very close to what Joyce was to do much more visibly in *Ulysses*, and it is no wonder that his comic epic mirrors this in its own intricate ways (Bello-Bella from Bella-Sir Julius).

This is a system. It is a greater and far more complex system than that created as the System of Sir Austin and mocked by the narrator. The great compartmentalizer is mocked by the narrator who is an even greater compartmentalizer, but this system Meredith means very seriously, for Sir Austin's provides him with a way of making his mockery into an anatomy of laughter, a history of comedy, and a survey of nineteenth-century mocking and nonmocking literature. Whether or not Meredith believed in form, structure, and pattern is one of the major points of contention among his critics—that he would create a system to mock a system should be no surprise to anyone who understands the ways in which he spins the mirror. I have not argued for simple form here, but for the ways in which simple forms fragments into complex structure—in fact, into one of the most complex and symmetrical structures that any comic writer has created in English. To do this I have imposed a grid upon the novel, but although it may look like a gunsight drawn upon the text to destroy it or at least to reduce it to geometry, I hope that what I have done with the Cartesian plane is to use it to demonstrate the opposite, the richness and power of Meredith's creation.

The system is still more mirrored, and this basic grid of characters is reflected into a second:

Primary	Secondary
Lucy	Claire
Adrian—Austin—Sir Austin	Mrs. Doria-Forey—Bessy Berry—Lady Blandish
Bella	Lady Feverel

Lucy mirrors Claire; Sir Austin mirrors Lady Blandish; Bella mirrors Lady Feverel; Austin mirrors Mrs. Berry, and Adrian mirrors Mrs. Doria-Forey. They are all in some major respect repetitions and inversions of each other. (The grid of laughter is mirrored into a grid of tears, but to follow this reflection would take us in a totally noncomic direction outside the scope of this study, and maybe, like Richard, into madness.)

In *The Praise of Folly*, Stultitia complains about the philosophers who claim to know much but really know little. "But their arrogant scorn of the unwashed multitude is most notable when they bewilder uneducated people with their triangles, tetragons, and circles, and such mathematical figures, superimposing one on another to produce what looks like a labyrinth" (86). She is equally critical of "the sort of men who burn with an insatiable desire to build, replacing round structures with square and square with round. Nor is there an end to it, nor any limit, until they are reduced to such utter poverty that nothing at all is left—neither place to live nor food to eat" (61). In this fashion, Meredith has found a way to shape his own folly.

VI

THE NOVEL that takes as its subject Meredith's failed marriage into the family of Thomas Love Peacock makes as its subject Meredith's marriage into the great tradition of comedy and comic theory. Life, Mrs. Doria-Forey tells Richard just as he is about to get married, "is a game of cross-purposes" (245). Meredith is here also playing a game of cross-purposes with Peacock, not simply by making Adrian the representative of the Peacockian narrator and showing him up to be superficial and dangerous, for at the center of this labyrinth is Peacock's *Nightmare Abbey*. There Scythrop Glowry is torn between his love of Miss Marionetta Celestine O'Carroll, the orphaned niece of his uncle Hilary, and his love of Stella, the daughter of his father's close friend, Mr. Toobad. Uncle Hilary's merriment is "like a double-charged electric jar" (44), while Mr. Toobad's pessimism is matched only by the elder Glowry. In love with the daughters of both extremes, Scythrop is described to be "like a shuttlecock between two battledores" (95)—and desiring both, he ultimately gets neither. He considers suicide by pistol shot, and finally puts it off until it no longer matters. All of this Meredith rather neatly worked into his much more serious comedy—Stella becoming Bella, Marionetta becoming Lucy. Adrian in his best Peacockian style calls Claire the fair shuttlecockiana and her mother the battledoria. The narrator describes laughter by the Peacockian metaphor of electricity. The pistol at the end of *Richard Feverel* works. There are frequent references in *Nightmare Abbey* to Dante, to little blue devils, and to ghosts. Raynham Abbey suffers from the same comic scourges. One of the elder Glowry servants, one Diggory Deathshead, proves to be a laugher, and a seducer of servant girls, and is shortly dismissed from service. He becomes Adrian Harley. The abbey itself has four towers with their own special characteristics. It becomes the shape of the Meredith novel. Scythrop constructs a labyrinth in his tower while under the influence of German thought, in which anyone might disappear for extended periods of time—it is Stella's hiding place. It becomes the labyrinth of theory in which the Meredithian narrator finally disappears in *Richard Feverel*, never to be found again. Celebrating his abandonment by the Peacock family, Meredith rewrites a Peacock novel—it is now not nearly so much fun.

It is also, by a trick of mirrors, a rewrite of a Sterne novel, *Tristram Shandy*—Meredith's intent is to include as much English comic fiction as he can into his story about his rejection by Mother Peacock. Sir Austin, the great Meredithian systematizer, is a parody of Walter Shandy, the great and neurotic systematizer of Sterne's novel. Both construct elaborate plans for their sons' education, the Tristrapaedia and the System, which are designed to protect them against the snares of women and which are provoked by a fall. In Meredith's example, it is Sir Austin's abandonment by Lady Feverel; and in Sterne's, it is Aunt Dinah's impregnation by a coachman. Meredith's interest in the serpent, in the fall, and in the metaphor of electricity similarly echoes Sterne. His use of similar names—Tom Bakewell, Tom Blaize, Sir Austin, Austin, Adrian, and Algernon—appears to be taken from a device in Sterne: the multiplication of Tristram, Trim, Toby, and Tom.

Meredith's own folly becomes the opportunity for a detailed

inquiry into the nature of folly and into the ways other writers and critics have conceived of folly. The novel is one of the singular accomplishments in English letters, a conflation of comic theory and comic practice that, finally, avoids the folly of previous inquiries by studiously avoiding any final answer. But it is the questions asked that matter and the ways in which we are led to think about them. In the process the labyrinth of the comic becomes clear as a labyrinth, for the serpent of laughter is Ariadne's thread. But it can wrap around and tangle us if we are not careful. Perhaps knowing the nature of the danger and the shape of the place is enough, without ever penetrating to the center. Some horrible fate has overcome the narrator.

"How should you define Folly?" Adrian asks Hippias as he starts a parade of Richard's wedding cake around the befuddled man, creating yet another circle and teasing him into guessing the meaning of the symbol, cake. "I think," Hippias says, "I should define it, to be, a Slide." Adrian compliments him on the definition. "In other words, a piece of orange-peel; once on it, your life and limbs are in danger, and you are saved by miracle" (271). Hippias experiences a small slide a moment later when Adrian tells him the meaning of the cake, and his hand first "travelled half-way to his forehead, . . . and then fell" (272). "Ha!" shouts Hippias, "infamous joke!" "I'm not equal to this world of fools" (273). Adrian's question and Hippias's responses are worthy of Erasmus's *Praise of Folly*, and like *The Praise, Richard Feverel* is a meditation on the nature of folly and its opposite, mockery.

"I suppose we women do not really care for humour," Lady Blandish writes in a letter to Sir Austin. "You are right in saying we have none ourselves, and 'cackle' instead of laugh. It is true (of me at least) that 'Falstaff is only to us an incorrigible fat man.' I want to know what he *illustrates*. And Don Quixote—what end can be served in making a noble mind ridiculous?—I hear you say—practical! So it is" (175). These questions are like the question Adrian asks Hippias, but it is now we the readers of the novel who are mirrored into the story. Lady Blandish is the reader of two famous comic texts, showing herself to be confused, sharing her confusions with Sir Austin, the reader of her noncomic text, and with the reader of the novel, who is reading what still appears to be, at this point in the story, Meredith's own comic text. "What end can be served in making a noble mind ridiculous?" she asks, but immediately before Sir Austin has read her letter he has read one from Adrian on the same subject—Lucy, whose noble mind Adrian has made ridiculous. The narrator has already done the same to Sir Austin's noble mind, and, further, he is dangling clues in front of us that his comic creations do *illustrate* concepts more comic than "fat man" or fool. The questions implicitly posed by the text that Meredith could expect to be asked by his readers are explicitly positioned within the text, where they are never answered.

If there are answers, they too are to be found in the mirrors. Laughter bounces against the walls of the labyrinth, inverting, repeating, inverting again, just like everything else in the novel. We are now in a fun house of laughter. When Richard visits Farmer Blaize to offer an apology but discovers instead that the Bantam will make a fine distinction and negate his oath, Richard laughs and we are told the farmer is in no laughing mood. At their next meeting, when Richard wants to learn where Lucy has been sent, the farmer "laughed his fat sides into a chair" (182) and Richard is in no laughing mood. He looks at the mantle where he sees the pictures of the family, men "trying their best not to grin" and women "smiling an encouraging smile" (183). When the otherwise humorless Sir Austin is in a mood "for dignified fooling" Lady Blandish wants "serious converse" (101), but then a moment later "the lady became gay as the baronet grew earnest" (102). The father of jokes, time, is himself no joke. The narrator who has laughed and mocked throughout explains near the end: "I will not laugh at the Hero because he has not got his occasion. Meet him when he is, as it were, anointed by his occasion, and he is no laughing matter" (403). The mirroring is to the narrator's previous discussion of "the Laughing Dame," Venus, who has sent Richard scurrying through Europe away from his wife and child, simply for the pleasure of laughter, which in turn is a mirroring of Adrian

Harley's motivation in the Bakewell Comedy, when he sent Richard scurrying over the countryside simply for the pleasure of laughter. The mirroring is also of the narrator of *Tom Jones*, who makes a similar announcement at the start of the last book of his story.

Does the narrator of *Richard Feverel* mean it? Or is he simply caught up in the reflections and inversions? And how does it happen that a short time after making this assertion, he disappears altogether from the novel, suddenly and without a word of parting to us? The novel makes two contrasting points: that the Aristotelian mean is the only possible position for the comic poet; that no such position is possible. These are the two mirrored answers we must be satisfied with, for if the center is perfect balance and a perfect combination of the grave and the gay, it is also the center of the labyrinth, where Minos has confined the minotaur that devours everyone who comes upon him. But we know much more than we did before our narrator led us through the maze tinkering with it in his own fashion, and if our inquiry has always been mirrored into at least two contrasting perspectives, it should not be surprising that the answers at the end of the inquiry do the same. But the answers may be much less important than the inquiry itself, for Meredith has generated out of two of the oldest tropes in the history of comedy—the mean from Aristotle and the mirror from Cicero—the richest and most dazzling study of comedy written in the nineteenth century. In 1847, the anonymous essayist in *Chambers' Edinburgh Journal* wrote in "Anatomy of Laughter": "It is odd that among the multitude of our literary jokers, there is not one who has thought of considering what laughter is—who has inquired into the philosophy of his art. Surely this would be the best jest of all" (403). Thackeray may have been the first to respond to this complaint in *Vanity Fair*, which began appearing in 1847, but it was Meredith who was to give the more thorough answer in 1859. That answer was only his first: in *Sandra Belloni*, the next novel, he turned more directly onto *Vanity Fair* and started mocking Thackeray again. He didn't stop inquiring into the philosophy of his comic art until he stopped writing. He found a great many answers along the way, many contradictory, like his first major narrator, but for him as for this narrator it was the pleasure of being carried on the current of laughter that mattered, not any attempt to stop the movement and yell "Eureka."

7

The Scientific Discourse on Laughter:
Survival of the Wittiest

TWO SCIENTIFIC notions about the nature of man changed the direction of comic inquiry in the mid-nineteenth century: the physiological model of the human nervous system as a mechanism for the transformation and exchange of energy and the biological doctrine of evolution, natural selection, and survival of the fittest. Neither concept concerned comedy or laughter in any obvious way, yet each had a major effect on the development of new, uniquely modern attitudes toward laughter and comedy. Evolutionary biology and mechanistic physiology changed the ways men regarded human behavior and the assumptions they made about its causes and effects, and one result of this was a dramatic reevaluation of laughter as a human behavior and of the comic sense as a human attitude, which began with biologists, psychologists, and physiologists in the second half of the nineteenth century and which has continued well into the twentieth. Physiology explained how men laughed and showed laughing to be an important human activity; evolutionary biology explained why men laughed and argued that laughing was a significant factor in the survival of the species. The effect of all this on comic theory was a new emphasis on the value of laughter and a shift in concern from the causes to the effects of laughter. The "scientific" discourse on the comic had been dominated

by philosophers, by men like Hobbes and Locke, Kant and Hegel. In the mid-nineteenth century the discourse finally became
scientific in the modern sense of the term.

There are physiological theories of laughter before the nineteenth century—inventive notions in Joubert and Descartes, a
suggestion about biological health in Kant—and there are also
some careful phenomenological observations of the laughing
subject, in Boswell's account of Dr. Johnson's fits of mirth, for
example. But in the mid-nineteenth century scientists began to
take laughter seriously, to use their theories of physiology and
evolutionary biology as explanations for laughter as a behavior.
The first important critics—Darwin, Spencer, and Bain—were
British, and it is their work that initiates this new scientific inquiry into laughter and its relations to the comic. The discourse
dominated by literary critics, philosophers, and comic authors
themselves is here joined by scientists and social scientists, who
very self-consciously challenge the explanations offered by the
humanists. This chapter concerns this scientific discourse, focusing first on Darwin, Spencer, and Bain, and then on their
most important followers at the end of the century, both English
and American psychologists and social scientists, Dewey, Hall,
Sully, and McDougall. What these men write is much more
straightforward than the literary and philosophical explanations—they intend to simplify, not to add to the complexity of
issues. For them there is no labyrinth of the comic at all, but
nonetheless some of these critics do slip into labyrinthine mazes
that confirm literary rather than scientific models. Both Hall
and Sully, the respective founders of the American Psychological
Association and the British Psychological Society, write comic
essays about the comic that owe more to Meredith than to
psychology.

In 1860, one year after the publication of Darwin's *Origin of
Species* and of Meredith's *Ordeal of Richard Feverel*, Herbert
Spencer wrote a short essay on "The Physiology of Laughter"
for *Macmillan's Magazine*. There is no mention of Darwin or of
Meredith in the essay, but Spencer is clearly responding to both.
Following Darwin, Spencer argued that what appeared to be pur-

poseless behavior, laughter, was actually of important physiological benefit to the species, homo ridens. When an expectation
is suddenly disappointed, energy that has been built up in the
nervous system is no longer needed and this excess is harmlessly
expended in the muscular reflexes that constitute laughter. We
are bringing our body back into equilibrium. Following Meredith, Spencer demonstrated that a scientific humanist and a
great compartmentalizer could understand laughter and understand it better than the novelist who had made him a figure of
mockery and ridicule. As Meredith's critics have noted, Spencer's theories of education are the model for Sir Austin Feverel's
theories of education; as Spencer's critics have noted, he was the
great compartmentalizer and one of the principal scientific humanists of the mid-nineteenth century. In *Richard Feverel* Meredith's narrator makes a special point of the great compartmentalizer's tragic flaw, his inability to understand laughter. The
following year the great compartmentalizer responded. Meredith's mockery of the field in which Spencer claimed to be expert, education, is answered in Spencer's scientific discourse on
the field in which Meredith claimed to be expert, laughter.

The novelist's mockery of seriousness is mirrored by the scientist's serious study of laughter. Spencer turned the current of
laughter in this sense back upon Meredith, but he did it with the
kind of humorless certainty that characterizes Sir Austin Feverel.
Meredith is to be shown to have got the analysis of laughter
completely backward. We might subtitle Spencer's essay, "The
Revenge of Sir Austin Feverel." Everything Meredith argued in
the novel is inverted in the essay. In the novel Meredith studied
the effects of laughter on a variety of individuals, borrowing a
basic analysis from Aristotle and Baudelaire, among others,
without attribution; in the essay Spencer studied the effects of
laughter within the generalized individual, borrowing a basic
analysis from Kant and from the English physiologist William
Carpenter, also without attribution. For Meredith what was important was that all individuals laughed differently; for Spencer,
it was that all individuals laughed identically. Meredith argued
that laughter was a dangerous force, a demon, capable of de-

stroying individuals like Richard Feverel unless an equilibrium position could be maintained between excess and deficit; Spencer argued that laughter was a benevolent force that always produced an equilibrium within an individual by allowing for the overflow of excess energy. Meredith characterized the most excessive laugher in his novel, Adrian Harley, as a man who did nothing to burn off excess energy; Spencer explained in the essay that, by definition, laughter always burned off excess energy. Meredith couldn't have been more wrong. Following Carlyle, who had explained in *Sartor Resartus* that laughter was the cipher key for understanding the whole man, Meredith made laughter into a cipher key to personality and Spencer made it the cipher key to physiology. Meredith took laughter as external sign; Spencer took it as internal process prior to the sign.

Spencer's may be a humorless kind of refutation but it is nevertheless playful, and Spencer—who was also a principal Victorian theorist of play—was playing here with the playful novelist and showing Meredith that he could respond in kind. There is no mention of Meredith in the essay, because there is no mention of Spencer in the novel. And there are additional contrasts between the two texts. Spencer's essay was one of his earliest attempts to set forth the first principles of his "synthetic philosophy," a grand positivist system meant eventually to account for all human knowledge. It was to become his major life project. Meredith's novel was one of his earlier efforts to set forth the first principles of comedy and laughter, a constantly changing system of relationships that was to become a major part of his life project. Spencer's synthetic philosophy had as its basis a general universal law adapted from the theory of evolution, that all matter passes from "indefinite incoherent homogeneity to a definite coherent heterogeneity" (Sahakian, *History and Systems*, 367).

In Meredith's first major novel the opposite point is made, that matter passes from clear oppositions and distinctions into similarity and identity. Eventually the second law of thermodynamics, the concept of entropy, was to discredit the scientific humanist and demonstrate that the philosopher-novelist had the better intuitive grasp of evolution, but before that happened Darwin had hailed Spencer as a genius and borrowed key concepts from him. The sudden rise and fall of Spencer's reputation in his own lifetime, 1820–1903, is comparable to the rise of Meredith's reputation in his own lifetime, 1828–1909, and its subsequent fall afterward. Meredith wrote compulsively about comedy and laughter all his life, but what twentieth-century critics were to value most was his one explicit discussion of comedy, the essay of 1877. Spencer wrote compulsively about everything all of his life, but, ironically, after all the other grand syntheses had been discarded what has most endured is the one essay on laughter of 1860. For almost a hundred years after its publication virtually every scientific essay on laughter written in English has derived substantially from "The Physiology of Laughter." Meredith's essay has not fared nearly as well, although it has become one of the standard critical works referenced in essays written in the twentieth century about comedy. How much of this extensive similarity Meredith could have predicted in 1859 when he used both Spencer and himself as the basis for the character of Sir Austin Feverel it is impossible to say. It is one of the prophetic surprises of the novel.

II

THE SCIENTIFIC study of laughter that derives in part from Spencer ignores Meredith, while the literary study of comedy that follows Meredith ignores Spencer. What begins from a perfect mirror inversion in 1859 and 1860 has become in the repetitions of reflections more and more distant and distinct—in this case homogeneity has passed into heterogeneity in spite of the second law of thermodynamics. A hundred years after Meredith and Spencer began their discourse of mockeries on the nature of laughter there is virtually no common ground between the study of laughter in academic scientific psychology and the study of comedy in academic humanistic literary criticism. A psychologist graphing the arousal jags of an audience laughing at a comic film shares little with a literary critic studying the

comic novel on which the film is based. But we need to be reminded that the differences were not nearly so great in the nineteenth century. In *The Triumph of Wit: A Study of Victorian
Comic Theory*, Robert Martin explains that "the writers I have
concentrated on are those critics who were interested in comedy
as literature," and therefore "there is no mention of Darwin and
Spencer, who were chiefly interested in the physical aspects of
laughter" (viii). Martin has elevated a distinction into a difference; what he cannot see in this simplification of intellectual history is the extent to which writers like Darwin and Spencer are
engaging in debate with writers like Meredith. But it is primarily Anglo-American literary criticism that has kept itself
pure; and European critics—Bergson, Freud, more recently
Rene Girard—have moved more comfortably between laughter
and comedy. In "Perilous Balance: A Comic Hypothesis," published in 1972, Girard argues that "comedy is intellectual tickling," that comedy reproduces as its content the internal experience of being tickled—not only in that both make us laugh but
also in that both present us with the controlled loss of control,
one as story, one as physical experience (825). Girard echoes
Darwin, who suggested in *The Expression of Emotions in Man
and Animals*, published exactly one hundred years before in
1872, that "the imagination is sometimes said to be tickled by a
ludicrous idea; and this so-called tickling of the mind is curiously analogous with that of the body" (199). Darwin did not
elaborate; Girard, elaborating, makes no mention of Darwin,
and it is possible that he is unaware of the extent to which he is
merely following up the old suggestion.

We need to recognize the extent to which Darwin's and Spencer's project is similar to our own and to read their discourse
against the other great explorations of the labyrinth of the comic,
that of the English novelists from Fielding to Meredith and that
of the German (and Danish) philosophers from Kant to Marx.
This chapter is devoted to the tradition Darwin and Spencer initiated in the mid-nineteenth century—the special contribution
of Anglo-American psychology to the discourse on laughter and
comedy. While Meredith wrote text after text about laughter,

comedy, and their various interrelationships between 1859 and
the early years of the twentieth century, establishing himself as
the authority on the comic, evolutionary biologists, physiologists, and the first modern psychologists began to write about
laughter. While Meredith danced on the currents of laughter
celebrating its complexities in the tradition of Fielding, these
scientist-humanists sought to explain what had so long eluded
the novelists, critics, and philosophers—the nature of this force.
Writing in the tradition of British empiricism and armed with
what Darwin had taught them about the nature of animal behavior, they described laughter in great detail and considered
the ways in which such a behavior could assist in the survival of
the species. Challenged by the explanations of the comic in German philosophy and by the general stress on consciousness in
German structural psychology, they explained laughter as a behavior that could only be understood by Anglo-American functional psychology. What it was in the human consciousness was
far less important than what it did in the human body. It was not
the comic that mattered, therefore, but laughter. But in discuss-
ing laughter they often turned to the ludicrous, to the laughable,
and to the comic.

Between the mid-nineteenth century and the present, three
periods of this inquiry can be distinguished. The first, with which
this chapter is concerned, begins with Darwin, Spencer, and
Alexander Bain in the mid-nineteenth century and concludes
with James Sully and William McDougall in 1902 and 1903,
from the first physiological psychologists to the organization of
Anglo-American psychology as a distinct discipline. The second
period, from McDougall's first discussion of the comic in 1903
to his last in 1937, is rich in theoretical argument, somewhat
weaker in intellectual rigor. The third period, from the mid-
1930s to the present, is dominated by experiment rather than
observation and theory, and it is at this time that the psychology
of laughter becomes a much more alien discourse to philosophy
and literary criticism.

This first period, then, is almost exactly the time of Meredith's own study of laughter and the comic—from 1859, when

Alexander Bain published *The Emotions and the Will* and Darwin *The Origin of Species*, to the early years of the twentieth century, when Sully published *An Essay on Laughter* in partial imitation of Meredith's essay on comedy, which had been reprinted in 1897. Sully knew Meredith. There are really two moments in this period: (1) an argument between Bain, Spencer, and Darwin on laughter and the laughable, between 1859 and 1872; and (2) an argument between John Dewey and G. Stanley Hall on the relationship between laughter and the comic, between 1894 and 1897, and an exploration of the same relationship between Sully and McDougall from 1900 to 1903. The participants in this debate are all major figures in the development of modern psychology: Darwin (1809–1882), whose general theory of evolution and whose discussion of the expression of emotions had significant impact on Anglo-American functionalism; Spencer (1820–1903), whose *Principles of Psychology* (1855) was one of the standard textbooks in the second half of the nineteenth century; Bain (1818–1903), whose *Manual of Mental and Moral Science* (1868) was the other, an abridged version of *The Senses and the Intellect* (1855) and *The Emotions and the Will* (1859). Intellectual and emotional rivals, Bain and Spencer shared a belief in the importance of physiology for producing a new psychology and an assumption that the doctrine of association could explain the relationship between mental and physical behavior. They argued vigorously on the fine points, one of which was laughter.

G. Stanley Hall (1844–1924) was rivaled only by William James as the principal American psychologist at the end of the century. The first American Ph.D. in psychology (in 1878 at Harvard, under James), Hall was the founder of the *American Journal of Psychology* (1887) and of the American Psychological Association (1892). Later, as the president of Clark University, he was responsible for bringing Freud to the United States. John Dewey (1859–1952) was a student of Hall's at Johns Hopkins in the early 1880s and the author of the first American text on the subject, *Psychology* (1886). After its publication, however, Hall pronounced him incompetent and Dewey did not attend the organizational meetings of Hall's APA, even though he was a charter member. In 1894 Dewey took up the defense of James's theory of emotions, the so-called James-Lange theory, and in reconciling it with Darwin's discussion of the expression of emotions, he developed what he considered should be a Jamesian theory of laughter. Three years later Hall published his own rival explanation, disproving Dewey without ever mentioning his name. James Sully (1842–1923), Hall's counterpart in England, founded the British Psychological Society in 1901 and read the first paper before the society in 1902, on laughter. The author of the basic British textbook at the end of the century, *Outlines of Psychology* (1884) and of *The Human Mind: A Textbook of Psychology* (1892), Sully wrote a series of essays on laughter that was finally expanded into *An Essay on Laughter* in 1902. William McDougall (1871–1938), who was at the time on the faculty of the University College, London with Sully, was one of the members present when Sully read his paper on laughter before the first meeting of the society. When he reviewed Sully's massive essay in 1903 he presented his own rival explanation, one which he was to expand upon over and over until 1937, one year before his death. During the first part of the twentieth century he became the respected authority on emotions, and his *Introduction to Social Psychology* (1908) and *Outline of Psychology* (1923) went through many editions. Laughter is a part of that theory of emotions (see Klein, *A History of Scientific Psychology;* Robinson; Sahakian; Schultz).

None of this work between 1859 and 1903 is experimental, although all of it is based on scientific assumptions about human physiology and evolutionary biology. And none of it is done by men interested only in psychology or in a highly specialized study of men. They are all generalists with broad interests— Spencer, in his attempt to combine all human knowledge, the extreme. And only Dewey's and McDougall's essays are written in the style that twentieth-century psychologists would accept as scientific. Bain, who held the chair in Logic and Rhetoric at the University of Aberdeen, wrote about laughter in *The Emotions and the Will,* about the ludicrous in *A Manual of Rhetoric*

(1866), and although the emphases are different the essential content is the same. One is designed to help writers, the other to help thinkers. Darwin's discussion of laughter in *The Expression of Emotions in Man and Animals* has as many literary antecedents as scientific: like Fielding's "Essay on the Knowledge of the Characters of Men," it suggests a physiognomy of laughing faces; like Addison's essays on the comic, it distinguishes between true and false laughter. Hall began as a teacher of literature and rhetoric at Antioch College, and his essay is full of literary references. Sully's essay is as devoted to literature as it is to biology and physiology.

Although the discourse does not become purely scientific until the mid-1930s, there is a break between Sully and McDougall in 1902 and 1903 and the work that followed for another thirty years. Sully and McDougall firmly established the basic positions of Anglo-American psychology toward laughter and the comic: laughter was a survival instinct in the service of the species. What remained to be argued were the fine points of the *how*—in what ways did the laugh help us survive? Between 1903 and 1937 many answers were suggested, none of which ever gained the kind of acceptance that Sully's and McDougall's arguments had achieved. Most of this work has dated badly, unlike the earlier work between Bain and McDougall. The work done in the second half of the nineteenth century is produced by major figures—Hall is the weakest mind among them; the work done in the first three decades of the twentieth century, McDougall excepted, is not. A concept is becoming exhausted. But before it does finally disintegrate it supplies a powerful tool for the reinterpretation of laughter. If the important theoretical work on the comic in the first half of the nineteenth century is accomplished in German philosophy from Kant in 1790 to Marx in 1851, the important theoretical work on laughter in the second half of the nineteenth century is accomplished in Anglo-American psychology from Bain to McDougall. Spencer mirrors Meredith and sets off a half century of English functionalism that mirrors a half century of German structuralism. But if the German tradition had elevated irony, humor, the

comic, laughter, and comedy to the highest achievements of
man's spirit, of his art, and of his consciousness, the Anglo-
American tradition reduced laughter to a basic physiological response, an essential part of man's biological nature. Thus it can
be attacked for being reductive by critics who value consciousness, but it should not be misread as simplistic. The complexities of biological adaptation are simply the alternative to the
complexities of mental consciousness. The contribution is just
as great. If laughter assists in the survival of the species, then
anyone who would provoke it—comedian, clown, or comic
novelist—has a valuable scientific justification for the project.
And any literary critic who would examine the comic production works from a new assumption about the nature of comic
texts.

III

THERE IS no discussion of laughter in *The Origin of Species*,
but there is a challenge to anyone who would explain human
behavior. Only those behaviors or instincts that help an organism adapt to the conditions of life are preserved by the process
of natural selection, and maladaptive behaviors would disappear as those species exhibiting them were destroyed. Darwin
cautioned in 1859 that it would be difficult to decide exactly
what function many of the peculiarities of structure provided,
but he did expect that ultimately the theory of evolution could
account for them all. Darwin did not try to account for laughter
until *The Expression of Emotions* in 1872, perhaps because
Spencer had essentially done as much in his "Physiology of
Laughter" in 1860, which, although it does not mention Darwin, clearly demonstrates that laughter is a biological reflex that
assists man in adapting to the conditions of his life. Darwin's
discussion of laughter in 1872 is heavily dependent on Spencer's
essay.

But Darwin had another physiology of laughter from which
to choose, albeit a more primitive one—that of Alexander Bain,
whose explanation of laughter in *The Emotions and the Will*,

also published in 1859, was the first scientific account of the subject in English psychology in the nineteenth century. Spencer's essay, an indirect affirmation of Darwin and an indirect refutation of Meredith, was a direct refutation of Bain's theory, and thus an attack on the book in which the theory was contained, *The Emotions and the Will*, which, as the second volume of Bain's psychology text, was in direct competition with Spencer's own psychology text. That Spencer would select laughter as the topic with which to discredit Bain is in good measure determined by the essay's other function, to discredit Meredith. Bain's physiology is more primitive than Spencer's, but it deserves attention because it was the first and because it so clearly shows the ways in which English psychology took over key concepts from German aesthetics and made them more physical. Bain's theory, before it was presented as psychology, was presented as literary criticism in an anonymous review of Leigh Hunt's *Wit and Humour Selected from the English Poets*, which appeared in the *Westminster Review* in 1847. (Bain acknowledged authorship in a footnote to *The Emotions and the Will* when he revised the physiology and made it less German.)

The physiology derives from Kant's discussion of laughter in the *Critique of Judgment*, where Kant had argued that what begins as the play of ideas in the mind results in "the futherance of the vital bodily processes" (177). As the mind is caught up in the deceptions of a jest it is put through "a rapidly alternating tension and relaxation," which is then repeated by the body in the movements which are "beneficial to health" (179). If the joke depends on incongruity, the laughter that results "promotes the restoration of equilibrium" (177). The German theorists of the comic after Kant had little interest in this connection between mind and body, but in 1847 Bain took it over to write literary criticism. He immediately made it more physical. "The outburst of laughter is nature's provision for relieving an incompatibility of mental and bodily states, that would otherwise be painful in the extreme," Bain wrote ("Wit and Humour," 34). The perception of incongruities between mind *and* body rather than within the mind, as Kant would have it, would pull us in

opposite directions and produce the most terrible agony, rather
than, as Kant believed, simply relieve tension. There were two
possible happy resolutions for Bain, either that one feeling would
overcome the other, destroying the contradiction, or that "we
are agreeably relieved by laughter, which is a convulsive totter-
ing and relapse from the high and dignified to the vulgar and
easy" (37). In 1859, writing now an English psychology rather
than a Germanic literary criticism, Bain discarded the stress on
contradiction and simplified the physiological response. It is, he
argued, a release from the tension of grave and serious behavior.
"The best mode of giving the desired relief is to plunge the venerated object into a degrading conjunction, the sight of which
instantaneously liberates the mind and lets the emotions flow in
their own congenial channel" (*The Emotions and the Will*, 284).
In place of his earlier definition of incongruity, Bain substituted
the Hobbesian notion of degradation.

Spencer responded rather testily to all this in 1860 but also
brilliantly: he simply went back to Bain's sources—English
physiology and Kant's discussion in the *Critique*—and used
them more thoroughly and more intelligently. In the process he
wrote what has become one of the great nineteenth-century essays in the intellectual history of the comic and of laughter. "It is
an insufficient explanation," he wrote, that "laughter is a result
of the pleasure we take in escaping from the restraint of grave
feeling" ("Physiology of Laughter," 202). And again, "it cannot
be that the laughter . . . is due simply to the release from an
irksome attitude of mind: some other cause must be sought"
(203). Spencer sought the cause from English physiology but
combined it with Kant's discussion of laughter, achieving a synthesis of psychology and aesthetics more developed than that in
Kant. "You are sitting in a theatre, absorbed in the progress of
an interesting drama," Spencer wrote. "Some climax has been
reached." But suddenly a tame kid wanders onto the stage and
sniffs at the actors. "You cannot help joining in the roar which
greets this *contretemps*. Inexplicable as is this irresistible burst
on the hypothesis of a pleasure in escaping from mental restraint; or on the hypothesis of a pleasure from relative increase

of self-importance, when witnessing the humiliation of others," it can be explained by the "large mass of emotion" that has been produced in the spectators in anticipation of the normal events of the script. This emotion "suddenly checked in its flow" must find some other channel for discharge (203−4).

It is at this point that Spencer simply overwhelms Bain with the overflow of his knowledge of physiology. This blocked energy discharges along the three most habitual paths of motion in the body, as laughter: onto the nerves "with no direct connection with the bodily members," which would cause other ideas and emotions; onto the motor nerves, which would cause external movement; and onto the nerves connected to the viscera, which would cause internal stimulation to the stomach and the intestines (197−98). The source for this physiology is William Carpenter's *Principles of Comparative Physiology* (1854), which presents a detailed model of the relationship between the body's nervous system and muscular system along these lines. According to Carpenter, "the impressions made by external objects upon the afferent nerves" are first carried up the spinal cord to the cerebrum where they are transferred into sensations in the sensory ganglia, into ideas and emotions in the cerebrum itself, and into the intellectual operations of the will, in the body's motor nerves. "But if this *upward* course be anywhere interrupted," he noted, "the impression will then exert its power in a *transverse* direction, and a 'reflex' action will be the result" (691). Depending on where this interruption takes place, the reflex action takes place in one of three channels: excito-motor, sensori-motor, or ideo-motor.

Spencer made minor revisions in this scheme to account for laughter, trusting of course that Carpenter had got it all right. There is the same interrupted nerve energy, the same set of three channels for discharge, the same connection between mental and physical. Spencer's note about the beneficial motion for the stomach and intestines, however, comes directly from Kant, the source Bain had just discarded in 1859. Spencer went back to Kant for a more complete explanation of the mental aspect of laughter, outdoing Bain's 1847 literary criticism. Kant wrote in

1790 that *"laughter is an affection arising from the sudden transformation of a strained expectation into nothing"* (177). Spencer wrote in 1860 that "laughter naturally results only when consciousness is unawares transferred from great things to small—only when there is what we call a *descending* incongruity" (206). Refuting Bain's refutation of Kant, Spencer returned to the original text. Bain responded cautiously in 1865 in the second edition of *The Emotions and the Will*, admitting in a footnote that "the general principle" of Spencer's argument "is undeniable," but insisting that "he has been incautious in rejecting the fact of Degradation as the governing circumstance of the ludicrous" (253). Bain did not change his own physiology of release from restraint nor his attack on the incongruity theory, but he did add a discussion of genial and loving humor to his discussion of the laughter of degradation, thereby modifying his earlier insistence on Hobbes. And in the *Manual of Rhetoric* in 1866, he supplied students with models for writing both degrading comic prose and loving comic prose.

Darwin entered the argument between the two principal psychologists in 1872, graciously trying to avoid either position. "Many curious discussions have been written on the causes of laughter," he noted. "The subject is extremely complex" (*Expression of Emotions*, 198). Accepting neither Bain's theory of degradation nor Spencer's theory of descending incongruity, Darwin argued that laughter was primarily an expression of joy—the definition may be a reworking of Hegel's definition of the comic as the hale condition of soul. He praised Bain in a footnote for his "long and interesting discussion" (198), but then took over Spencer's physiology and simply elaborated on it. This endorsement by Darwin was crucial—it is what made Spencer's physiology so influential when other physiologies, Bain's, Kant's, Joubert's and Descartes' before them, had never generated much interest. *The Expression of Emotions* is not Darwin's best work and its discussion of laughter is particularly weak, but it is as a relative failure that it matters here, for it challenged others after him to try to explain what had eluded the great man. And it directed anyone after him who would take up the project to begin with the answers provided by Spencer.

The definition of laughter as an expression of joy was an obvious weak point—Darwin himself acknowledged in the discussion that it seemed also to be an expression associated with pain and with grief. His desire to say something new and to avoid the argument between Bain and Spencer led him away from his best scientific instincts. Neither could he explain "why the sounds which a man utters when he is pleased have the peculiar reiterated character of laughter." "We do not know," he admitted (205). What he did explain was the way in which laughter was an overdetermined behavior. There are three separate scientific principles contained in the book that are meant to account for emotional expression; laughter is a behavior compounded of all three. The Principle of Serviceable Associated Habits, Darwin's restatement of the principle of association held commonly in English psychology, explained that because bodily actions become associated with certain mental states, these mental states are later able to provoke the bodily actions, whether there is need for them or not. The Principle of Antithesis, Darwin's restatement of the principle of contradiction held commonly in German philosophy, explained that opposite states of mind produce opposite movements whether or not these opposite movements have any functional value. The Principle of Actions Due to the Constitution of the Nervous System, Darwin's restatement of Spencer's physiology, explained that excess nerve force would move into different outlets for discharge depending on the habit of the species and its physiological make-up. Thus laughter, the expression of joy, was like other expressions of joy through the principle of association, was unlike the expression of sorrow and grief through the principle of antithesis, and was an overflow of nerve force along habitual channels through the principle of the constitution of the nervous system.

There is nothing new here; Darwin's synthesis of German and English thought is weaker than Spencer's because it leads him only into restatement. The strength of the discussion is not in its theoretical explanations but in its meticulous observation and description—there is now a series of photographs illustrating different degrees of laughing and careful explanations of the contractions of muscles in the face. Curiously, it is this aspect of Darwin's work that is the most literary, with its physiognomy of laughing faces like Fielding's descriptions in "An Essay on the Knowledge of the Characters of Men" and its distinction between true laughers and false laughers like Addison's descriptions in the *Spectator* essays. But Darwin knew he had not done the subject justice and the book ends with two invitations to other scientists, one a general challenge about the general subject of the book, the other a specific challenge about laughter. "To understand, as far as possible, the source or origin of the various expressions . . . deserves still further attention, especially from any able physiologist," he wrote (366). And about laughter he suggested: "It is a curious, though perhaps idle speculation, how early in the long line of our progenitors the various expressive movements, now exhibited by man, were successively acquired. . . . We may confidently believe that laughter, as a sign of pleasure or enjoyment, was practised by our progenitors long before they deserved to be called human; for very many kinds of monkeys, when pleased, utter a reiterated sound, clearly analogous to our laughter" (360).

IV

THE DISCOURSE about laughter between Bain, Spencer, and Darwin ended here, although it continued about other subjects, and Bain acknowledged and used parts of *The Expression of Emotions* in the later editions of his psychology texts. There are two theories waiting to be used again, physiology and evolutionary biology, and one empirical method—the close observation of laughter. The first response to Darwin's challenge came in 1888, not from physiology or psychology but from literary criticism and philosophy—*Poetry, Comedy, and Duty*, by Charles Everett, a professor of theology at Harvard. The book is not really within the scientific discourse of the period—it rejects

Spencer as foolish and Bain as short-sighted, and it is almost as if through Everett the German philosophers had been given a chance to refute English psychology. The book is recycled Schopenhauer, Hegel, and Kant brought to bear against Spencer and Bain, but it is also an attempt to write a kind of Darwinian literary criticism. Comedy is one of three ethical and aesthetic attitudes to the world—the other two are poetry, meant to stand for beauty, and duty, meant to stand for ethics. Like Kierkegaard's three stages on life's way, Everett's three stages are equally important in the life of man, and like Kierkegaard's sense of the comic as superior to all stages except the religious, Everett's sense of the comic is superior to all but duty. The language of the book is sometimes Hegelian, with discussions of form/substance and the contradictions between them, and often it is explicitly an elaboration of Kant and Schopenhauer. But it ends as an answer to Darwin, with a fable about "the moment when our ape-like progenitors were becoming human," a comic story about "Great-grandfather Ape" outraging "the delicate and cultivated sensibilities of his descendants," about "servants caught wild in the forest to be initiated into the mysteries of the kitchen." Everett asks his readers to "excuse the levity of its form," because the story is meant both to celebrate the comic and to argue for the importance of laughter. The joke is a Darwinian joke, of course: the first attacks made on Darwin in the 1860s were that he was suggesting our grandfathers were apes—a point Huxley was to defend in his debates with Wilberforce. Everett turned it into a joke in Darwin's favor. At this time of evolutionary transition and stress, the time of the humanization of the ape, laughter was born—the point of origin of humor against Darwin becomes the point of origin of humor in the world. There comes "a strange sound through the wilderness" that seems like grief but is not. It comes "whenever one of those miserable awkwardnesses" occurs, and "the individual who made it seemed refreshed and exhilarated by what was crushing the life out of all others. While they pined he grew fat. His children inherited the habit which began with him, and with it inherited his cheerful strength; and thus, while other families dwindled and passed away, the descendants of the man who laughed alone endured, to form the race of man that laughs" (*Poetry, Comedy, and Duty*, 214–15).

The scientists ignored Everett's book—the praise of Darwin was not enough to excuse the attack on English psychology and on Darwin's favored theorist, Spencer. The return of psychology to the problems of laughter began in 1894 with John Dewey's essay "The Theory of Emotion" in the American journal *Psychological Review*. What prompted the return was William James's argument that emotions were not the origins of physical behavior but the opposite, that physical behavior caused the behavior. This is the so-called James-Lange theory of emotions named also after its other independent author, and it caused John Dewey to attempt to rewrite Darwin's theory of the expression of emotions. Laughter was one of Dewey's principal examples. Dewey, following James's inversion of the commonsense relationship between action and emotion, rejected Darwin's notion of antithesis as preposterous. "But there is something intolerable to the psychologist in the supposition that an opposite emotion can somehow select for itself channels of discharge. . . . Antithesis is made a causal force. Such an idea is not conceivable without some presiding genius who opens valves and pulls strings" ("Theory of Emotions," 566–67). Dewey was left with Darwin's other two principles, which he revised somewhat more gently. "*The reference to emotion in explaining the attitude is wholly irrelevant,*" Dewey cautioned (556). Because laughter would appear to be "one apparent exception" it is discussed in the essay at some length. "Now I am not so rash as to attempt to deal in detail with laughter and its concomitant features, but I think something at least a little less vague than Mr. Darwin's account may be given. I cannot see, even in the vaguest way, why pleasure *qua* feeling (emotion?) should express itself in uttering sounds" (556). What we are seeing, Dewey argued, was the "pleasure of a certain qualitative excitement or vivacity" breaking out (556). Turning back to Bain, Dewey wrote that laughter was only a "sudden relaxation of strain." "The laugh is thus a phenomenon of the same general kind as the sigh of relief"

(559)—Bain, however, was not credited. Turning back to Spencer, Dewey wrote that the laugh "marks the ending . . . of a period of suspense, or expectation, an ending which is sharp and sudden" (558)—Spencer, however, was not credited either. But now, turning back to James, Dewey insisted, "The laugh is by no means to be viewed from the standpoint of humor; its connection with humor is secondary" (558). Laughter is first a "sudden relaxation of strain," then and only then can it become humor; the physiology precedes the perception of the comic. The "rhythmical character" of laughter "seems to be simply a phase of the general teleological principle that all well-arranged or economical action is rhythmical" (559). Dewey meant by this to split the laugh off from humor. "The connection of humor with the laugh, and the ideas of relative superiority–triviality, and of incongruity, involved in humor, etc., seem to be simply more complex, and more intellectually loaded, differentiations of this general principle" (559). Ironically, Suzanne Langer was to use Dewey's very point and Dewey's very language to return the notion of the rhythm of the teleological principle of the laugh to literary criticism. She did it, however, without crediting Dewey.

Dewey's essay is the first attempt to isolate laughter from the comic; it is also the most purely psychological and scientific discussion of laughter written in the nineteenth century in Anglo-American psychology. For Bain, for Spencer, and for Dewey, laughter was a response to a series of different stimuli, the most important of which was the ludicrous. Although Darwin did argue for a sense of joy—no obvious relation to the ludicrous—his definition echoes Hegel's description of comic literature. If the James-Lange theory was true then the sense of the ludicrous came after the laugh and it was the laugh itself that was the crucial activity. The temptations of this theory were great at the time because it took the strength of Anglo-American psychology, the empirical observation of physical behavior, and maintained that this behavior was the cause of emotions and of consciousness. But such a position Stanley Hall set out to refute with special reference to laughter, in "The Psychology of Tickling, Laughing, and the Comic" in the *American Journal of Psy-*

chology in 1897. The title itself makes laughing the connection between the purely physiological tickling and the purely mental comic—Hall, who had studied philosophy and taught literature before he became a psychologist, would not allow James-Lange to break apart the connections. Coauthored by Arthur Allin, who assisted in the collection of the data (responses to over 700 questionnaires on the subject), the essay surveys many theories of laughter, many definitions of the comic, and many physiological studies of tickling and of general muscular response. Dewey's is not mentioned, but at the end of the survey a group of theories not worth elaboration is listed as "either utterly mistaken and misleading or entirely inadequate to the subtleties of nature" ("Psychology of Tickling," 41). And here is the "Lange-James" theory.

In the journal Hall founded and edited that rivaled *Psychological Review*, Hall answered his rival, James, and Dewey, his former student who had allied himself with his former teacher. He used Meredith without attribution to refute Dewey and James-Lange, combining ideas taken from Meredith's essay on comedy (which had just been republished in book form in 1897) with Darwin's theory of evolution. Hall was like Spencer in that he too wished to produce a synthetic psychology, but he had no use for Spencer's theory of laughter, since it had been appropriated already by Dewey. He turned instead to Spencer's rival, just as literary criticism was turning away from Spencer's rival. Bernard Shaw reviewed the republication of Meredith's essay in 1897, dismissing it with mocking sarcasm in the *Saturday Review* as hopelessly outdated, pompous, and absolutely wrong, of no possible use for an understanding of literature. "Comedy, indeed!" Shaw concluded, "I drop the subject with a hollow laugh" (*Comic in Theory and Practice*, 42). Meredith had pleaded in the essay on comedy against the hollow laugh. Discarded as literary criticism, Meredith's essay was reborn as the psychological study of laughter, reworked first by Hall in 1897, then by Meredith's friend James Sully in essays published between 1897 and 1901 that culminate in the massive *Essay on Laughter* in 1902. Sully took over Hall's project, the synthesis of Meredith and Darwin. The founder of the American Psychological Association and the founder of the British Psychological Society insist that laughter cannot be separated from the comic and rescue Meredith's ideas from the oblivion that was about to envelop them.

Literary critics do not as a rule read the *American Journal of Psychology* and psychologists do not as a rule read literary criticism, especially that written in the ornate style of George Meredith. Hall's peculiar essay of 1897 was published in the wrong journal for it to find its audience, if indeed there really was an audience for it that could simultaneously accept physiology and poetry. The essay is both encyclopedic and eccentric, a loosely organized study of every aspect of the subject: the physical act of laughing, the nature of tickling, the possible connections to the animal instincts, a classification of different types of laughing (from fear, at calamity, from practical jokes, at what is forbidden, at the naïve), and a classification of different rhetorical styles (humor, satire, wit, caricature, the comic). The questions that Hall and Allin set out are extensive and various, from "Is it true that satire and wit are declining and a sense of humor increasing?" (a matter of some debate within the popular journalism of the end of the century in England and the United States) to "Can or should we try to train ourselves or children to make prettier faces and noises when they laugh, or leave them all to nature?" (an issue that had been raised in a number of attacks on laughter); from "Why do the insane laugh?" (a reasonably medical question) to "Does a dog smile with its tail?" (a reasonably Darwinian question) ("Psychology of Tickling," 1–3).

The encyclopedic method allowed Hall to distinguish between laughter that had no connection to the perception of the comic or the ludicrous and laughter that depended on such perception. Dewey had been myopic. The responses to the wildly various questions essentially allowed Hall to conclude anything he wanted to conclude. He came to the precisely opposite answer that Dewey had. Laughter, he wrote "is in the majority of adults" an experience "which begins with the highest level in consciousness and with the finer muscles, and passes downward to lower levels and more fundamental and earlier developed musculature, although sometimes in children this order is exactly inverted" (8). Dewey, who argued for the inverted order, was of course, as Hall's student, also his academic child. What is "generated in the higher regions of consciousness" passes down "till circulatory, glandular and even intestinal and excretory activities are affected and the sphincters relaxed" ("Theory of Emotions," 8). Taking the antithetical position to Dewey, Hall adopted an antithetical prose style, Meredith's. "The mental horizon of expectation . . . narrows down to the most intense focalization upon the mirth-provoking object till the soul is, as it were, impaled on the sharp point of the jest." At this point, having impaled Dewey on the point of the jest, Hall breaks into rhapsody.

> The objective world has vanished and is forgotten, the proprieties and even the presence of others are lost, and the soul is all eye and ear to the one laughable object. Care, trouble, and even physical pain are forgotten, and the mind, as it were, falls back through unnumbered millennia and catches a glimpse of that primeval paradise where joy was intense and supreme, and where life and the joy of living were both inconceivably vivid and were expressed by the most generic, primeval and correspondingly energetic sounds and movements, from which all other and later human sounds and movements have sprung. ("Psychology of Tickling," 8)

Compare Meredith's argument in "The Idea of Comedy": "A perception of the Comic Spirit gives high fellowship. You become a citizen of the selecter world, the highest we know of in connection with our old world, which is not supermundane. . . . Good hope sustains you; weariness does not overwhelm you; in isolation you see no charms for vanity; personal pride is greatly moderated. Nor shall your title of citizenship exclude you from worlds of imagination or of devotion" (49). Hall's essay is an elaboration of this argument, but in its vacillation from scientific to poetic styles it resembles the narrative styles of *The Ordeal of Richard Feverel*. Hall can separate laughter from the comic in his scientific exposition, but in his odes to the comic spirit the two are magically combined. Laughter is for Hall the scientist a sign of many different kinds of experience, but for Hall the poet only one kind matters, the perception of the comic and entry into Meredith's experience of the elect.

If Hall's essay were simply a restatement of Meredith it would not have much value, but it is Meredith rewritten according to Darwin. The evolutionary importance of laughter is now directly considered and in a more substantial manner than in Everett's comic fable. The laughter of humor, Hall writes (that is the laughter of the sympathetic comic), is "an exercise for rudimentary organs of the soul which come into their unfrequent and evanescent functions before they are slowly transformed into higher ones" ("Psychology of Tickling," 26). Inverting Nietzsche's argument that the superman who will come will laugh harshly and mockingly, Hall writes, "Man is not the larva of an angel, but of a higher superman that is to be." The sign for this is wit and fancy, which show "present man . . . practicing for the higher man that is to be." The "possibilities opened by wit" have value for us as prophecy, Hall argues. They "bid us hope" (30). Meredith, the critic of comedy, had argued that the silvery laughter of the comic spirit would cure our follies whenever men "wax out of proportion, overblown, affected, pretentious, bombastical, hypocritical, pedantic, fantastically delicate; whenever it sees them self-deceived or hoodwinked, given to run in idolatries, drifting into vanities, congregating into absurdities, planning shortsightedly, plotting dementedly" ("Idea of Comedy," 48). The passage continues in this manner. Rewriting this praise as a scientist, Hall concludes his essay by insisting that "hearty laughing is a good thing for children, and might be listed among their inalienable rights. . . . it is good for the voice, lungs, diaphragm and digestion, produces needed increase of blood pressure to irrigate new forming tissues, develops arterial tonicity and elasticity, tends to range, flexibility and vigor of emotional life, gives an optimistic trend against its evils, and tones down into settled and less paroxysmal states and grades of pleasure as maturity advances." The final sentence of the essay concludes, as the field shifts suddenly back into human consciousness, that "it is possible that aesthetic pleasures generally, genetically considered, and even some of the joys of religion and virtue, are laughter diffused, tempered, properly alloyed with pain, and minted for general circulation through all our psychic activities" ("Psychology of Tickling," 41). Genetic is Hall's term for evolutionary. Rewriting Meredith according to Darwin, Hall ends up sounding like Rabelais in the prefaces to the books of *Gargantua and Pantagruel*—where there is similar praise of laughter as an elixir of health—but there is a significant difference. Rabelais was mocking the huckster's voice; Hall means this very seriously.

V

FOLLOWING from Hall's praise there have been a number of serious studies of the medical and spiritual values of laughter, particularly in the first three decades of the twentieth century— among them *Laughing* by Martin Armstrong in 1928, an argument for its political value; *Laughter and Health* by James Walsh in 1928, an argument for its medical value; and *Salvation by Laughter* by Dudley Zuver in 1933, an argument for its spiritual value. These are remarkable but strange books; Hall's exaggerations of praise lead only to greater and greater hyperboles after him. But Hall's more serious project—the reconciliation between science and literature effected through the synthesis of Darwin and Meredith—does result in one other similar project, that carried out by Hall's counterpart in England, James Sully. Hall's forty-one-page encyclopedic essay of 1897 is meticulously and gradually expanded by Sully, first in a series of essays from 1897 to 1901, then in *An Essay on Laughter*, which is massive, encyclopedic (it is 432 pages long), and wildly various. It is similarly written in a prose style that alternates between objective scientific exposition and Meredithian poetry—the dedication is "To my children and my pupils in the hope that if they cultivate both brain and heart, and have a quick ear for the muffled moanings along the road, they may hear also, above the deeper music, the blithe notes of laughter" (v). Sully wrote his essay in this manner, sometimes from his brain and sometimes from his heart. And as for the muffled moanings along the road, they were sounded after the book's publication by critics who had wished for more concise argument and greater clarity. Hall's co-writer Arthur Allin complained that "the reader is fairly deluged and swamped with lively adjectives and figures of speech. 'Blithely' tumbles merrily after 'sprightly' on every page, and 'floods of merriment' chase wildly the 'rillets of joy' of less significant dimensions" ("On Laughter," 306).

There had been nothing like it published in English, nothing as long, as extensive, as thorough. It reads very much like an *Encyclopaedia Britannica* entry on laughter written by Meredith to novel length. Written two years after Bergson's "Laughter" and three years before Freud's *Jokes and Their Relation to the Unconscious*, Sully's essay—longer than both of the other works combined—should have taken its place as the standard English critical text next to the French and the German, but its influence was much briefer (twenty years) and much more limited (to Anglo-American criticism). E. M. Forster may have been its chief beneficiary; he took several of Sully's arguments as the basis of the comic novels he wrote between 1905 and 1908. By the 1920s a great many shorter and better organized psychologies of laughter and the comic appeared, and Sully's book ceased being a standard work. It also virtually ceased being read. Certainly its control of theory is much weaker than "Laughter" or *Jokes*, but buried within its Meredithian prose style are a number of important arguments: an inversion of Meredith that anticipates Mikhail Bakhtin's argument in *Rabelais and His World* and an inversion of Darwin that anticipates Freud's *Jokes*. But it is primarily a compilation of all the conventional wisdom on laughter and the comic in 1902, and it should thus be contrasted to critical works like Fielding's preface to *Joseph Andrews*. But if Fielding's preface has value for precisely that reason, so does Sully's essay. It serves to close a discourse initiated by Bain, Spencer, and Darwin at mid-century, and which Hall began to connect to Meredith and the literary critical tradition. Sully's book does that as well and suggests new directions for the psychological study of laughter and the comic.

Fully titled *An Essay on Laughter: Its Forms, Its Causes, Its Development, And Its Value*, Sully's book considers in its ten chapters the physiology of laughing, smiling, and tickling; the evolutionary biology of laughing and its origins and values for the species; the evolutionary history of laughter, its major turning points, and its meaning for the species; the relationship between laughter and comic literature; a classification of laughter; and a classification of comic literary styles. It sounds sometimes like Darwin in its objective descriptions, more often like Meredith. It uses Bain and Spencer without attribution, and it takes its project from Hall without attribution. "We have seen a tendency to claim too much in the way of serious function for the laughter of comedy" (414), Sully cautioned, without identifying Hall's essay. And modifying the last sentence of Hall's essay, Sully suggested that "every one of the great directions of social evolution," intellectual, moral, political, economic, was closely tied to the evolution of "the laughing impulse" (254–55), but Sully did not make these developments *dependent* upon the laughing impulse as Hall had done. Rather it was the reverse—it was laughter that was dependent on these developments. But like Hall, Sully explained, "we find that we must resort to the genetic method, and try to explain the action of the ludicrous upon us in the modest scientific fashion" (154). This was the "biological point of view." "Laughter, looked at from this point of view, has its significance as a function of the human organism, and as spreading its benefits over all the paths of life" (21).

But to the question Darwin could not answer in *The Expression of Emotions* and which Sully rephrased—"By what process did the laugh, from being a general sign of pleasure, become specialised into an expression of the uprising of the mirthful, fun-loving or jocose spirit?" (155)—there was finally a clear answer. Unfortunately in the 430 pages of the answer, Sully delighted in writing like Meredith. "Some hearts of many chords, resonant to all the notes of life's music, might break but for the timely comings of the laughter-fay with her transforming wand" (424). Accepting Spencer's physiology as the explanation for one kind of laughter, Bain's notion of the release from restraint for another, and Darwin's notion of laughter as expression of joy for yet another, Sully in turn rejected the theory of superiority endorsed by Bain as the explanation for the mental cause of laughter, and the theory of incongruity endorsed by Spencer for the same. Rejecting all the theories of the German philosophers that he admitted he could not understand, Sully turned instead to another German, Karl Groos, whose books *The Play of Animals* and *The Play of Man* had been recently translated into English. Groos was also to be a major influence on Freud. Sully proposed Groos's theory of play and made it into his own answer to the challenge of James-Lange. Laughter was "born of play" (411), was the "offspring of the play impulse" (257), and was "spurts of joyous consciousness" that "are of the essence of play. To be glad with the gaiety of laughter, to throw off the stiff and wearing attitude of seriousness and to abandon oneself to mirth and jollity is, in truth, to begin to play" (145). This is Bain allied to Groos. While Dewey had argued that laughter came before a perception of the comic, and Hall that the perception came before the behavior, Sully created a dialectical interaction of the two. Born of play, laughter also produced play. It was both a physical process that oxygenated the blood and a spiritual process that brought about from these "deep, forcible chest-movements" "a sense of heightened energy, of a hightide of fulness of the life-current," and this is the expansion of consciousness (45). It was only right then that Sully would dance on the current of laughter like Meredith, his mentor, and write from the fullness of the current.

Following Meredith, who had defined the comic spirit as a muse of silvery laughter looking down on man, Sully described a "Comic Muse" (412) and defined "philosophic humour" as an experience of looking down "the vast time perspective" (403). Following Meredith, who had attempted to distinguish this comic laugh from its close variants—"Humorist and satirist frequently hunt together as ironists in pursuit of the grotesque, to the exclusion of the comic" (46)—Sully defined "the attitude of the humorist in its relation to that of the comedian and of the satirist" (410). And following Meredith, who had admitted that "laughter is open to perversion like other good things" (50), Sully described "these strange perversions of laughter" (49). But in the essay on comedy Meredith had argued that harsh and bitter laughter typical of the uncivilized could be replaced by the reasonable and clearsighted laughter of men and women in civilization. Sully inverted this: the essay on laughter maintains that the "choral laughter" (428) of primitive peoples and of England before industrialization had given way to harsh and soulless laughter—cruel, hollow, empty. Sully argued that the theory of evolution did apply to laughter but not exactly as Hall had imagined it—laughter was getting worse. Hall had asked the question, "Is mirth growing more or less bitter?" and had decided, after Meredith, that is was growing less bitter. Sully took the opposite position and proposed a "history of laughter" (258), which anticipates the one contained in Bakhtin's *Rabelais and His World* (written in 1940, published in 1965). For Sully the choral laughter that had united people, classes, masters and servants and that was healthy and celebratory had given way after industrialism to the hollow and bitter laughter of modern society. "Perhaps, too, in our terribly serious purpose of conferring the blessing of an incorporation into a world-wide empire upon reluctant peoples of all degrees of inferiority, we are losing sight of the conciliatory virtue of that spirit of amicable jocosity, the value of which . . . was known to some who had to do with savage peoples" (430). But within this soulless laugh of the modern society Sully saw one small hope: English humor, the pride of literary theorists in the eighteenth and nineteenth centuries which for Sully was the refined laugh of play that combined sympathy with clear perception. Sully's essay ends with the hope that this laughter of "private individuals" could redeem the history, but he is not confident. Bakhtin's history of laughter is more elaborate but follows Sully's closely—there is the same shift from medieval carnival laughter that unites classes to modern laughter that divides them, but while for Sully individual laughter (humor), is good against the laughter of the mass, for Bakhtin, a better Marxist, it is the laughter of the individual as individual that is alienated, a part of the divisions into class. Literary critics who value Bakhtin study this theory carefully. Sully is ignored. And it is not possible to know if Bakhtin had access to Sully's book, but it is reasonable to expect that he did. There is no attribution.

Inverting Meredith, Sully also inverts Darwin. Laughter does not allow for the survival of the strong but for the survival of the weak—and here Sully approaches the theory of humor that Freud was to produce in *Jokes and Their Relation to the Unconscious*: that humor is the response of powerless people to conditions beyond their control. Sully wrote: "The evolutionist has accustomed us to the idea of the survival of the socially fit, and the elimination of the socially unfit sort of person. But more forces are at work in the world than our men of science dream of. There is, oddly enough, a force which favours the survival of the unfit" (408), and this for Sully was laughter and play. This is how the weak have managed to survive, by turning harsh reality into a plaything not to be taken seriously. The joke is on Darwin but it is also on Nietzsche, who had argued in the 1880s that laughter was the force of the overman as he took power back from the herd mentality.

There is then a true Hegelian process at work in Sully's book in spite of his repudiation of Hegel in the book. The combination of Meredith and Darwin, Spencer, Bain, and Hall leads Sully into theories that are to become central to twentieth-century understandings of laughter and the comic. Neither idea is present in any substantial way in the criticism of the nineteenth century, although an anonymous author had considered the decline of laughter in an essay in the *Spectator* in 1891, and in 1897 Lewis Morris had argued in *Forum* that the hearty laughter of earlier periods had been replaced by the laughter of a weak and sniveling race.

William McDougall reviewed Sully's essay in *Nature* in 1903. "There is implied . . . throughout the book the assumption that

... in general we laugh because we are pleased" ("Theory of Laughter," 318). McDougall noted that virtually all of Sully's examples illustrated the opposite point, that we laugh because we are displeased, because of physical deformity, small misfortunes, indecencies, pretenses. This required McDougall to rewrite Sully, which he did in two pages. "Being but imperfectly adapted to the world in which we live" (318), and surrounded by what is often displeasing, we are endowed by nature with the ability to laugh so that we are not destroyed by our sympathy to pain and humiliation. The point is really not so different from Sully's argument that laughter is the tool by which the evolutionary weak turn the world into play and therefore survive, although there is greater emphasis here on laughter as defense mechanism. McDougall also noted that Sully's theory did not support James-Lange, and he therefore corrected: "Laughter is not an emotion, but a state of physical organism (producing certain effects in consciousness) that may accompany almost any emotional state" (319). The "laughter reaction" developed as a corrective to the natural feelings of sympathy and therefore preserved sanity "for the power of sympathy is so great that in the absence of this corrective the spectacles, which meet us on every hand and which we call the ludicrous, might well destroy us" (319). The much vaunted sense of humor that Sully had praised was of course the celebration of sympathy.

Hall's response to Dewey is now mirrored and inverted by McDougall's response to Sully. McDougall restates the position taken by Dewey in 1894 that started the discourse between these four men—the notion of sudden relaxation of strain elaborated by McDougall has its origin in Dewey and in Bain. But if Sully-McDougall reflect Dewey-Hall, the entire discourse between 1894 and 1903 reflects that of 1859 and 1860. What begins with Bain and then with Spencer and his mirror inversion of Meredith ends with Hall and Sully and their mirror repetitions of Meredith, and Dewey and McDougall, and their mirror repetitions of Bain. The scientific discourse on laughter between 1859 and 1903 is very distant from Meredith in 1859. But everything is not simply repetition. Sully and McDougall argue over the ways in which laughter and the comic protect us from pain and suffering, while a half century before, Bain and Spencer argued over internal physiological dynamics. The evolutionary *psychology* of laughter has now been established on the foundations of the evolutionary *physiology*. The notion that melancholics find relief in the comic is present in the critical literature as early as Burton's *Anatomy of Melancholy*, but at the turn of the century Sully and McDougall make the position scientific. Darwin is almost completely answered and so is Spencer. It is not simply the physiology that matters but the effects within human consciousness. The conventional wisdom of the eighteenth and nineteenth centuries was that the comic was either an expression of superiority deriving from Hobbes or of sympathy deriving from Addison and Shaftesbury. Humor was the great pride of English letters, the comic of sympathy. The conventional wisdom of the twentieth century is that the comic is a defense against pain and suffering. Sully's and McDougall's work and Freud's 1905 study of *Jokes* mark the turning point of this idea.

It is with Freud that the next chapter is concerned. Although the discourse in Anglo-American psychology continues after Sully and McDougall, it is not nearly as intellectually rigorous, however, or as important—in the period between McDougall's first statement of his theory in 1903 and his last in 1937 there were what he himself characterized as "many ludicrous theories of the ludicrous" (*An Outline of Psychology*, 165). What remained to be explained were the specific physical movements of laughter—the shaking head, the moving hands, the sounds themselves. All Spencer had suggested was that the discharge of excess energy would travel through the habitual paths used by the body. In the first three decades of the twentieth century, between 1903 and the dominance of the experimental method in the 1930s, Anglo-American psychology and those critics who accepted its principal tenets attempted to explain the evolutionary value of the specific movements. The group includes physicians, literary critics, and journalists. In 1916 George Crile, an American professor of surgery, suggested in *Man: An Adaptive Mechanism* that the movements had evolved when we still lived in trees, and that their evolutionary value was that we would be able to hold on tightly to tree limbs while we laughed and thus not fall to the ground below where we would be devoured by wild animals. Anthony Ludovici, Nietzsche's English translator, argued in *The Secret of Laughter* in 1932 that the movements had evolved when we were still fighting for survival by showing our teeth and that laughter remained this kind of primitive display of fangs. At the same time, this discourse struggled to find more "scientific" explanations of the comic perception that appeared to trigger the movements, but for the most part these are little more than simple repetitions of early theory. And when they are not—as with the notion of the "interrupted love reaction," for example—they are too often just silly. The model inherited from Darwin and Spencer is becoming exhausted.

8

Jokes and Their Relation to the Unconscious:
Freud's Play with Play

IN 1905 Freud published his study of joking, the comic, and humor, *Jokes and Their Relation to the Unconscious.* Like Hall's 1897 essay on tickling, laughing, and the comic, and like Sully's 1902 essay on the forms, causes, development, and value of laughing, humor, and the comic, Freud's *Jokes* is a combination of a scientific content and unscientific form. For Hall and Sully scientific theory is elaborated and sometimes obscured by literary style; for Freud scientific theory is placed within philosophic structure. The nineteenth-century study of the comic in German philosophy is layered onto the nineteenth-century study of laughter in Anglo-American psychology, and the result is an elegantly playful synthesis. Nothing in these two very different kind of arguments about the comic is discarded, and from their skillful combination Freud produces a new explanation. The psychoanalytic study of the comic, equally scientific and philosophic, is a substantial contribution to the history of comic inquiry—on it much twentieth-century criticism of the comic depends, and on it much of Freud's later psychoanalytic theory also depends. Although the issues considered in the book on jokes are complex, Freud the scientist sees no labyrinth, nothing unclear or confusing. But Freud the philosopher is confused often and notes his uncertainties at the same time that he devises an elegant labyrinthine structure for his scientific explanations, one that both reveals and hides the full truth of his argument/demonstration.

Jokes and Their Relation to the Unconscious is a peculiar book and for most students of Freudian thought a marginal one as well. Ricoeur devotes a few paragraphs to it in his massive *Freud and Philosophy: An Essay on Interpretation*, acknowledging it as a "brilliant and meticulous essay" but then dismissing it for its narrow interest in the pleasures of laughter (167). Sulloway gives it a page and a half in his six hundred-page *Freud, The Biologist of the Mind*, explaining that it is "one of Freud's least-read books today, although it was well received upon publication and sold relatively well. Much of it is difficult to translate, at least without ruining the jokes, and many of the jokes are no longer as humorous as they were in Vienna at the turn of the century" (357). Intellectual historians like Gay and Rieff give it little or no attention, and even critics who have argued for its importance have found it to be a difficult and elusive text. Reik, who wrote more material about the comic than any psychoanalytic commentator after Freud, wrote toward the end of his life that the "psychological profoundness" of *Jokes* had "not yet been fully appreciated" (*The Search Within*, 35). Given Reik's own attempts to understand the comic from 1913 to 1962, the statement is a confession of his own limited success. And Lacan, who praised Freud's book as the clearest demonstration of psychoanalytic methods, wrote that the text had been ignored for good reason—for its ambiguity, its sophistry, its play with annihilation, and its "admirably compelling detours" ("Function of Language," 33). That Freud's clearest text should also have been exceedingly murky is, of course, a playful Lacanian notion, its own play with annihilation, but while what Lacan describes can be seen as the greatest of temptations for a good Lacanian critic, virtually everyone who has read the text carefully has been concerned with these deficiencies, from orthodox analysts like Kris and Reik, who picked up small parts of the book for correction, to Lacanians like Mehlman and

Weber, who pick up larger conceptions and flaws in the text for their own revisions and returns to Freud.

Mehlman's essay "How to Read Freud on Jokes: The Critic as Schadchen" follows and corrects Ricoeur's failure to discuss *Jokes* in *Freud and Philosophy*, which includes a subsection titled "How to Read Freud." It argues that reading Freud is also a matter of laughing at/with Freud, of understanding the wit but not the comicality of Freud's texts. More recently, Weber has made *Jokes* a major text for his *Legend of Freud*, which traces the nuances of Freud's failure there to come to a coherent and unified set of conclusions. For him *Jokes* becomes a kind of shaggy dog tale, a story without a point, a tangled knot, which raises questions that Weber cannot answer and to which he finally responds with his own joke. The critic must become a joker, Mehlman wrote; Weber takes on the challenge.

The issue is whether the flaws in the text are to be amended or celebrated, whether the limitations of Freud's text are to be taken as an occasion for embarrassment or pleasure—or indeed are so great that the book is better left ignored. There is nothing perverse in all of this, but nevertheless something extremely important has been lost, an understanding of the text through its strength. While *Jokes* is necessarily imperfect and therefore "flawed," it is also coherent, unified, and intellectually rigorous, the traits that Weber would deny to it, and which most of its other critics have not seen at all. Freud certainly *meant* the book to be so coherent—the previous theories of the comic, he wrote, are "*disjecta membra*, which we would like to see combined into an organic whole" (14). Weber argues that Freud "arrives here not so much at the organic whole he desired as at its shaggy fleece," and he asks, suggestively but rhetorically, "Has Freud's theory turned out, once again, to be corrupted by unsavory wit, the very malady it was designed to cure?" (*Legend of Freud*, 116). Weber refuses to answer his question, but the entire force of his argument has been to force the reader to one conclusion, that Freud's study of the comic is only an interesting failure.

The text achieves what Freud intended and announced to his

readers as his intention. It is a careful synthesis of the disjecta membra of nineteenth-century comic theory, specifically of the two radically different and often contradictory methods of interpretation that had given substantial attention to the problems of the comic, German writings on aesthetics from Kant and Schiller and English writings on physiology and psychology from Spencer and Darwin. To this material, Freud's intellectual inheritance, he brought his new understandings of dreams, the unconscious, and infantile sexuality, which can be seen as the occasion for writing the book, and also his immense collection of Jewish jokes which are lovingly scattered throughout the text and which were radically new material for comic inquiry. The result is not a hodgepodge, although it could have so easily become that, but intellectual rigor of very high order. In the synthesis Freud (1) rescued the concept of play from its purely aesthetic formulation and made it into a vital psychological concept, and (2) solved the unanswered problems of the comic for both German aesthetics and English psychology: the argument that had begun between Schlegel and Hegel on the need of the comic attitude to be both a free floating above reality and a close engagement and tie to reality, and the argument that had been provoked by Darwin and Spencer, that laughter, while it aided the survival of the species, produced only pointless and puzzling behavior. Freud's book answered those questons with finality and thus changed the nature of the questions asked about the comic and the assumptions made about it.

Yet it is precisely in the ways that the text appears mired in nineteenth-century thought that has made it difficult for twentieth-century readers, not the least of which is Freud's main point, that economy of expenditure of effort is the explanation of the pleasure that comes from the different forms of the comic. The idea has been useless for later critics of the comic for whom the laws of thermodynamics and the arguments of Helmholtz have no special charm or meaning. Some loyal Freudian critics, like Mauron, repeat the idea of economy, praise it with extravagance, and then go on to other matters, never using it; others, like Kris, simply dismiss it as an idea that does not interest them. Equally difficult for Freud's later critics is his elegant classification of the three varieties of the comic—wit, the comic, and humor—which he distinguishes both by internal functions and external requirements, a scheme that has been universally ignored, although Freud insists that this too is one of the major achievements of the book. What remains for the later critics are not these elements that help to control and unify the material, but small sections of text, fragments, which can be expanded upon, modified, and then applied either to comic behavior or comic literature: the relation of jokes to sexuality and hostility, the relation of the comic to play and childhood, the relation of humor to suffering. The text itself, Freud's organic whole, ceases to exist; indeed, it can no longer be perceived as an organic whole. The Central European critics exploit the fragments that remain while the Lacanians delight in discovering ever more subtle contradictions and ever more tangled knots in the fabric.

But no return to Freud is of any value without a return to Freud's sources, and no return to *Jokes* is of any value without a return to the critical issues Freud addressed in 1905. The explanation about the economy of psychic energy inside the human body would have been clear to any psychologist or physiologist in 1905, and the rigid classification into three mutually exclusive varieties of comic experience would have been clear to any German-trained aesthetician in 1905. And while such individuals must have been a part of Freud's original audience, there was only a nascent psychoanalytic audience, and few readers had backgrounds in both aesthetics and physiology. "Every joke calls for a public its own," Freud wrote in the book on jokes (151). The same is true for every book on jokes, and what *Jokes* calls for, what it attempts in fact to create, is this ideal reader who like Freud is equally schooled in science and in philosophy. The text was problematical from the beginning and by the time others did take up the project neither the assumptions of nineteenth-century psychology nor the methods of interpretation of nineteenth-century aesthetics were useful tools or meaningful tools for interpretation. The text then has only become increasingly problematical.

If the weaknesses of the text are the ways in which Freud was limited, necessarily, by nineteenth-century thought, the strengths are the ways in which he was able to synthesize and overcome these limitations, combining aesthetics and psychology-physiology. For aesthetics, deriving from Shaftesbury, Kant, and Schiller, the comic was a form of art and thus like all art an experience of free play and aesthetic judgment with no connection to basic life needs (although Schiller certainly did suggest that art had health-giving properties and thus had political importance for any ruler wishing to create a peaceful if not a perfect state). For psychology, deriving from Darwin and Spencer, laughter was a form of human behavior and thus like all human behavior an experience of instincts and impulses that had survival value for the species. Freud scolded the aestheticians for their assumptions about the comic in *Jokes*, specifically for their insistence that it is pure contemplation "which fulfils none of the other aims of life" (95), and not surprisingly he sided with the psychologists for their assumptions about laughter. But then he turned the psychological behavior back into the aesthetic object, arguing for the psychological importance of the comic form of expression, what allows the laughter to be created and released. A joke, he wrote, is a "physical factor possessed of power: its weight, thrown into one scale or the other, can be decisive. The major purposes and instincts of mental life employ it for their own ends" (133). From German aesthetics Freud took the concept of play developed by Schiller, but he made it into a psychological rather than an aesthetic idea. Play was not detachment and a pure sense of freedom, Freud argued, but rather the most basic characteristic of the unconscious, what he would later call primary process thinking. It was thus of the greatest importance and the deepest significance. And the joke, a literary form with origins in childhood play and in unconscious mechanisms, was equally important. In their social and political context Jewish jokes certainly showed momentary detachment, but they also showed clear connections to basic and vital needs, the needs of the community to survive. Freud must then count as a Darwinian literary critic, but in his method of combining disciplines he may better be characterized as a bricoleur, the critic who patches together and thus plays with serious things.

In this case what Freud was playing with was play itself, and it is in this sense at least that his book on *Witz* is witty, a characteristic that is obscured by Strachey's translation of the title as *Jokes* rather than *Wit*. The meaning of the word *Witz* as Freud would have understood it comes from Kant's discussion of the comic in the *Critique of Judgment*, where wit is defined as the "play of thought." "That which excites laughter," Kant wrote, is "different kinds of play with aesthetical ideas" (176). This, of course, is precisely what Freud's book on wit accomplishes. The meaning of the word *play*, similarly, is very different from Anglo-American conceptions, and play as Freud would have understood it derives from Schiller's discussion of play in his *Letters on the Aesthetic Education of Man*. "Man plays only when he is in the full sense of the word a man, and *he is only wholly Man when he is playing*" (80). This is a much wider sense of the term, and Freud follows it in his own claims for the unconscious as the place of play. For Schiller play was not only aesthetic contemplation but it was also the most important synthetic capability available to man, the delicate balancing of the most basic of Kantian antinomies, the real and the ideal, the sensual and the formal impulses, the demands of the natural world and the lures of absolute existence. All art allowed for an *Aufhebung*, for a reconciliation of what could otherwise not be reconciled, Schiller argued in the *Letters*, but in the essay "Naive and Sentimental Poetry" he praised comic art, satire, as the most effective. The argument, worked over by others, was basic to German romanticism: Schlegel defined romantic irony as the free floating between extremes; Richter described humor in much the same way; and then Kierkegaard placed all the varieties of the comic within the contradiction between the real and the ideal. For all of them, whatever the term, the comic experience was important because it led to the truth of existence, to the contradiction between the most basic of antinomies, and beyond that because it offered a way out, a way of understanding and then living with the human predicament. Freud, in his claims for the importance of the joke, of laughter, and of the other comic varieties, is making a similar argument, although he places it within the context of psychoanalytic materialism rather than German idealism. Writing about the comic in 1905, the antinomies for Freud were not the real and the ideal, but science and philosophy, the disciplines of Darwin and of Schiller. By reconciling them he was playing. The subject and the method of the book are identical. Derrida makes such a point in his discussion of *Beyond the Pleasure Principle*, in the essay "Coming Into One's Own," where he argues that the repetition compulsion of the fort/da game is also the shape of Freud's discussion of fort/da (115). In *Jokes* the invitation to play is perhaps more obvious but it is nevertheless dependent on an understanding of Freud's sources.

II

IN 1905 the attempt to merge psychology and aesthetics was not completely new or original nor was the attempt to effect that merger in a book on play. Freud found such a project in the publications of Karl Groos, a professor of philosophy at the University of Basel and the author of books on the play of animals and the play of man published in the decade before Freud's book. In *The Play of Man*, Groos discussed the comic very briefly as an aspect of play and argued that play was tied to biological needs because it was practice for the serious concerns of life. "Such practice," Groos wrote, "always responds to definite needs and is accompanied by pleasurable feelings" (5). Like Groos, Freud was to connect the comic to play and was to connect both to pleasure. Groos argued that play was both free and conscious activity *and* a natural impulse, though he hesitated to label it an instinct. He defined "the most significant feature" of the comic as the way the observer alternated between "an aesthetic feeling of inner imitation" and an "external sense of triumph," a far more psychological explanation (234). Like Groos, Freud was to describe the most significant feature of the comic as "ideational mimetics," a mental rehearsing in the mind of the comic perceiver of the energy wasted by the comic object. Built into Freud's sense of the comic then is also the concept of a triumph, although this was an element he wished to downplay. These notions in Groos are undeveloped since the comic for him was of only marginal interest. From them, however, Freud appears to have taken his project.

Curiously, though Freud discusses Groos at several points in *Jokes*, he never references these concepts he takes from *The Play of Man* nor any of the other aspects of his rather extensive intellectual debt. Among the arguments made but not elaborated by Groos, all of which become central to Freud, are the following: Wit often conceals serious meanings; there are both offensive and defensive forms of the comic, those that attack and those that ward off surprise; children develop a sense of the comic at a vaguely defined point in their development; civilized man is prohibited from the direct expression of sexual feelings, but often finds an outlet for them in laughter; love play is a kind of courtship by self-exhibition, and thus female spectators are necessary when this kind of mock combat takes place between men. But by far the most striking use Freud made of Groos's book is his appropriation of its structure. Freud's text is elegantly divided into three large sections: a first analytic part that is an extensive catalogue of the types of jokes and their forms; a second synthetic part that is a classification of tendentious jokes into four types, hostile, sexual, cynical, and skeptical; and a final third section or theoretical part that contains the connections between jokes and dreams, and the discussions of the other two variants, the comic and humor. *The Play of Man* is similarly divided into three large sections: the first, on playful experimentation, is an extensive catalogue of the types of play and their forms; the second, on the "Playful Exercise of Impulses of the Second or Socionomic Order," is a classification of play into four types, fighting, love, imitative, and social; and finally a third section, "The Theory of Play," contains Groos's arguments about practice. In the second section of the book, not only does Groos distinguish fighting play from love play, he finds a comic form of each, the comic of attack and the comic of sex.

It would be a mistake to see Freud's book only as an elaborate plagiarism (though its unacknowledged borrowings are extensive) and thus as a kind of joke on later readers. This would only relegate the book back to the margins of Freudian thought where it has languished for too long. What Freud did with the play theory that he took from Groos was to combine it with his own work on dreams and posit the unconscious as the location of psychic play within the self. Dreams and jokes reveal the unconscious to be governed by play, and the various manifestations of primary process thinking show that the unconscious plays with language, with thoughts, with rules, and with rationality itself. Groos's concept of play dealt with real objects in the physical world, and Freud's concepts of jokes, the comic, and humor kept that tie to the physical but also made a new connection to the internal psychic life of individuals and to the play of fantasy objects in the unconscious and preconscious as well as in the conscious. As dreams were a purposeful playing with the real in a nonphysical reality, so were jokes, and both rescued the individual from psychologically real objects, repressions, inhibitions, and other obstacles to mental health. Groos and other play theorists in the second half of the nineteenth century (including, in England, Herbert Spencer) had made play into physical recreation and practice for life; Freud made play into psychological re-creation and therefore life itself. It is as if Freud were seizing Groos's book and rewriting it: Freud's joke on Groos. Like Groos, Freud sought to situate himself between psychology and aesthetics, to play with play as Groos had done. But unlike Groos, Freud also sought to situate himself between the two extremes of the play theorists, to play with play as Groos could not have done. By rescuing the concept of play from the idea of recreation that was trivializing it, and by locating it in the unconscious lives of individuals, Freud found a way to play in a new way, to devise a concept that was both aesthetic and psychological, both a complex mechanism of philosophical detachment

and a pragmatic and simple process of recreation. Between philosophers and scientists, idealists and materialists, Freud played,
the middle man in a quadrant of extremes.

This is not a marginal position and neither is the book itself
marginal in Freudian thought. In *Jokes*, Freud reduced all forms
of the comic to play: a joke has its origins in play and is a way of
evading adult repressions and returning momentarily to childhood pleasure; the comic is the contrast between adulthood and
the recollection of childhood pleasure; humor is the victory of
pleasure and play over the most threatening aspects of reality.
Play and pleasure are inextricably bound, and although Freud
found a logical and mechanistic explanation for the generation
of pleasure in his notion of psychic economy, of far greater significance is the meaning of this connection for Freud's intellectual development. All the major aspects of Freudian thought can
in this way be reduced to the comic. The pleasure principle is
the play principle, and thus the opposition between the pleasure
principle and the reality principle that formed the basis of
Freud's early work is in fact the basic opposition revealed by the
study of the comic. A joke is the contribution made by the unconscious to the conscious; the comic and humor are similarly
generated by the contrast between adult realities and childhood
or childlike playful denials of those realities. Psychoanalysis itself is this contrast between play and nonplay. A joke is a psychic
structure of importance, Freud argued, and this is true not only
in the mental life of individuals but also true in the mental life
and intellectual development of Freud himself. The connections
apply to his later work as well—the notion of the repressive
demands of civilization has its origins in ideas first developed
in the book on jokes, where comic forms serve individuals as
compensations for these restrictions. The joke is the microcosm
of Freud's major beliefs about the nature of psychological and
cultural reality. The comic idea is elaborated into the totality of
Freudian discourse, and it is thus in the history of ideas about
the comic the most significant application of comic theory into a
systematic theory of man and society.

III

UNLIKE MANY theoretical studies of the comic, *Jokes* is not straightforward. By making play into both subject and technique, Freud creates the kind of text that readers of literature commonly find in complex narratives, and that almost twenty-five years after the publication of the book, Hesse was to create as *Steppenwolf.* The comparison is helpful, for what the reader is clued to pick up in the novel, he is clued to ignore in the work of criticism. The central character of Hesse's novel, Harry Haller, must find a way of reconciling the Kantian antinomies of the real and the ideal, and what he learns is what Schiller and the German romantics after him had described in great detail, that this can only be accomplished through play and humor. Harry learns how to play in the course of the novel, but although his friends urge him to learn how to laugh, this proves much more elusive and troubling. Hesse puts the reader in a similar situation, forcing him to read Haller's story simultaneously as the experience of real existing individuals and as an allegory of ideal types and abstractions. The reader must reconcile real and ideal, as Harry must, and like Harry, the reader finds nothing to laugh at in the experience, although he too hears the pleas for laughter. Laughter comes after play. (The point is Freud's.)

But while Hesse can only take his character and his reader through play up to humor, Freud takes his reader through play into humor and laughter. Freud's book is not only a play with play, it is also an alternation between invitations to laugh and explanations of the laugh, the narrative pattern of the comic/metacomic tradition that this book has studied. In the book there are both manifest jokes and latent jokes: the obvious jokes are introduced as those which Freud borrows, much as he borrows from Groos, and the jokes hidden in the text by Freud are the comic reversals on the previous studies of the comic. These are Freud's own creations. "*Humor,*" Kant wrote in the *Critique of Judgment*, from which Freud borrowed many ideas, "means the talent of being able voluntarily to put oneself into a certain mental disposition, in which everything is judged quite differently from the ordinary method (reversed, in fact), and yet in accordance with certain rational principles in such a frame of mind" (181).

Not only does Freud's book play with play then, it also jokes about jokes. No other theoretical work on the comic has this textual complexity and few others make such demands on the reader. But unlike comic and metacomic fiction the book contains no narrative to guide the reader, only a dazzling display of categories, classifications, and structures. Yet the critical readings of Freud's book have ignored these structures, fixating instead on the content of the argument, on what can be easily summarized and quoted, even though Freud argues in the text that it is form and not content that provides the key for understanding the texts he is interpreting, the jokes. It is in the tension between form and content that the joke comes into being. The same is true of the book on jokes. What makes the joke is the form, the contribution from the unconscious, for once the joke is summarized and reduced to pure content the joke disappears. This is a notion that Freud takes from Kant and Schiller, although he credits neither of them. In the *Critique of Judgment*, Kant discussed the comic as an aspect of the sublime, which he defined as the disparity between form and content. (Its opposite, beauty, was the harmony between form and content.) In *The Letters on the Aesthetic Education of Man*, Schiller argued that the basic Kantian antinomy of reason and nature was expressed in the opposition between form and content, which all art could mediate. "The real artistic secret of the master consists in his *annihilating the material by means of the form*, and the more imposing, arrogant, and alluring the material is in itself, the more autocratically it obtrudes itself in its operation, and the more inclined the beholder is to engage immediately with the material, the more triumphant is the art which forces back material and asserts its mastery over form" (106). Form is the essential control over unruly content and the essential element of art. "In a truly beautiful work of art the content should do nothing, the form everything." Immediately after making this point, Schiller explained that "the most frivolous subject must be so treated that we remain disposed to pass over immediately from it to the strictest seriousness. The most serious material must be so treated that we retain the capability of exchanging it immediately for the lightest play" (106). The opposition between form and content gives way here to the opposition between joking and seriousness. The most frivolous subject must be so controlled by the artistic form that the beholder passes into the strictest seriousness.

Jokes is such a text, the victory of form over content, in this case over the imposing, arrogant, and alluring material of the jokes themselves and their connections to both hidden psychic structures and repressed sexuality. Freud's presentation of this disturbing material is tightly controlled and structured; its effect is to convert the frivolous into the strictest seriousness. The text is divided into the three large sections—analytic, synthetic, theoretic—taken from Groos; jokes are divided into innocent and tendentious, or purposive, a distinction taken over from Kant, who had divided the *Critique of Judgment* into the aesthetic and the teleological. Jokes are further divided up into a tripartite psychogenesis, beginning as play, developing as jest, culminating as joke, a sequence of stages taken over from Schiller, who had argued that individuals develop first through a physical condition, then through an aesthetic condition, and culminate in a moral condition (*Aesthetic Education*, 113). And just as Freud altered Schiller by translating a pattern meant to describe all behavior into a pattern meant to describe only comic behavior, so too did he alter Kant, for Kant had argued that the comic was a form of aesthetic judgment and thus nonteleological. Freud demonstrated that there were both teleological and nonteleological jokes, thus translating a pattern meant to describe all judgment into a pattern meant to describe only comic judgment.

Freud's original contribution to this frenzy of forms, structures, and patterns is the three-fold division of *Witz*, the comic, and humor, which he justified by both internal and external evidence. A joke required three persons: the teller, the object of the joke, and the listener; the comic required two persons: the individual perceiving the comic and the individual in which it is perceived; and humor required one: the individual who makes light of his own predicament. All three save energy, but do so differently. A joke saves energy otherwise spent in maintaining repressions; the comic saves energy otherwise spent in what Freud awkwardly called ideational mimetics; and humor saves energy otherwise spent in painful emotional affect. (The concept of ideational mimetics, which Jack Spector regards as "potentially" Freud's "most valuable contribution to aesthetics and the best bridge leading from his psychoanalytic views on art to the general field of aesthetic appreciation" [*Aesthetics of Freud*, 119], comes to Freud not only from Groos but also from Schiller in his discussion of satire in "On Naive and Sentimental Poetry." The purpose of all of these structures, imposed on the text itself and on the jokes and other comic variants, is to make the text an aesthetic object, to do what art was supposed to do. The fact that virtually all of the structures are borrowed from these same writings on aesthetics makes Freud's project somehow safer, more legitimate, and it also makes it seem artistically correct. Most of the content is the contribution made to the study of jokes by psychology. If most of the form is the contribution made to the study by aesthetics, then *Jokes* is in yet another way a reconciliation of the field.

Freud's classification into *Witz*, the comic, and humor is the weakest structure in the book, and although it is theoretically elegant and overdetermined in the best psychoanalytic manner, Freud was forced to admit that the evidence did not always fit the scheme. The comic, for example, could be present in only one individual, and then the individual would have to be regarded as splitting in two. The comic and the joke, absolutely different, could nonetheless be present in the same verbal form, and then distinguishing between the two became a matter of constant referencing back to Freud's definitions. And a situation could be comic to an adult but humorous to a child, or, more confusing yet, comic to an adult but laughable to a child in a way no longer accessible or even understandable to an adult, a sign of the "lost laughter of childhood," for which the adult comic sense was only an imperfect substitution. The classification created as many problems as it was designed to solve, which Freud freely admits through the book, confessing again and again that he is puzzled and does not have the material fully under his control. The form controls the content and then is destroyed by that same content. Again Freud repeats in his text the patterns of the jokes he studies there, for while the joke is made by the form, it is in the end destroyed by the content, when in the telling and not in the summarizing the content is given permission to burst forth from repressions and find both conscious expression *and* approval. The joke form gives way to formless laughter, the sign of the released energy. The more the joke deals with emotional content the greater the laughter and the greater the explosion of the content. Although Freud never states it as explicitly as this, what he is working toward in his study of comic forms is a more interactive and dialectical version of the form/content opposition.

IV

THE IMPOSING, arrogant, and allusive content remains: the barely expressed sexuality of laughter and the latent Jewish joke at the core of the text. Combining aesthetic concepts with psychological concepts, Freud plays with pure content. The now peculiar notion of psychic economy is such a playful synthesis of Kant's description of the aesthetic gratification of the comic, Spencer's notion of physiological energy overflowing a closed system in laughter, and the self-demeaning aspects of the Jewish joke. For Kant, the comic was a form of gratification deriving from ideas but having bodily effect, a confounding of the judgment that allowed for the free play of sensations, and from that, the oscillation of the internal organs, which produced a feeling of health and "the furtherance of vital bodily processes" (*Critique of Judgment*, 177). Without mentioning Kant, Freud wrote: "We differ in our explanation of comic pleasure from many authorities who regard it as arising from the oscillation of attention backwards and forwards between contrasting ideas. A mechanism of pleasure like this would seem incomprehensible to us" (188). Instead, he took the notion of the physiology of laughter proposed by Spencer—that laughter was the overflow of nervous energy let loose inside a closed system that tended naturally to equilibrium. Spencer believed that overflow to be purposeless. "Strong feeling, mental or physical, being, then, the general cause of laughter, we have to note that the muscular actions constituting it are distinguished from most others by this, that they are purposeless" ("Physiology of Laughter", 200). As an afterthought Spencer suggested that they might aid digestion, since Kant after all had located the oscillation of organs in the intestines. But Freud did not believe that laughter was purposeless, and combining Kant's notion of gratification with Spencer's notion of energy flow, he developed his own concept of the pleasure from economy. To do this he had to invert both Kant and Spencer. Kant had argued for the priority of ideas, that the body was excited by ideas; and Freud argued for the priority of the body, "the dependence of . . . mental functions on bodily need" (202). Spencer had argued that the important physiological element was excess, while Freud insisted it was economy, a savings of energy rather than a wasteful spending. This forced Freud into a much more complicated scheme, the demonstration of the greater energy that was spent maintaining repressions and the lesser energy that was spent escaping repressions.

Freud makes the point about economy insistently throughout the book, and although he appears to mean it quite seriously, it is difficult not to see this revision of Spencer as his own hidden Jewish joke, a joke at his own expense. The gentiles believe that laughter is the joy at waste, but the Jew knows better, for what would a Jew celebrate, waste or economy? What would the gentile stereotype of the Jew love more, spending or saving? For Freud the special value of the Jewish joke is that the maker demeans himself in a loving way and so diffuses criticisms and attacks from gentiles. Freud worried about the reception of his collection of Jewish jokes among gentile readers, justifying his presentation again and again. The only time he presents a joke at all critical of priests, he apologizes for it profusely. Jewish jokes also build bonds between Jews, who can be defined as a network of mutual jokers—it is a special intimacy between them. And although the Jewish joke appears to take the Jew as the butt, it contains a more subtle criticism of gentile society for having placed the Jew in such a position. Freud's hidden Jewish joke is not about real Jews, but about the gentile stereotype. And Jewish jokes do express serious truths—there is wisdom in the wit. About Freud, Reik wrote: "In my thirty years of friendship with Freud, I heard him, of course, frequently tell a Jewish anecdote or quote a witticism, but it was never for its own end, never for mere amusement. In most cases the comical story was used as illustration to a point he had made. . . . It was as if he brought the joke forward as an example of how wisdom is expressed in wit, and—much more rarely, wit in wisdom" (*Search Within*, 36). It should not be surprising then that Freud would feel compelled to make his own special Jewish joke in the text that celebrated the specialness of Jewish jokes. The joke is overdetermined, if latent. The reader who has learned the value of jokes from a reading of *Jokes* should also be in a position to recognize Freud's joke and understand why it is a joke. Joking/seriousness is the basic opposition at the core of all of Freud's work. The text that makes this explicit is *Jokes*, at the core of which is the main point, the joke meant seriously, carrying serious content in spite of its playful form. The latent joke content of the manifest serious argument is a demonstration of Freud's understanding of the joke, what was hidden from Spencer, who could see only the obvious manifest behavior. Mehlman argues that "it is perhaps time to learn just *how* to laugh in reading Freud, to appreciate how *funny* (perversely allusive), how uncannily *uncomic* an author he is" ("How to Read Freud on Jokes," 461), but what Mehlman means by this playful invitation is that Freud's wit can only be seen by reading him intertextually, by jumping between the book on jokes and his other writings and making connections that are not in any single work. Funny for Mehlman means perversely allusive—Freud is *uncomic* at the same time because he does not show the victory of the ego, what an interpreter like Kris had made central to the psychoanalytic meaning of the comic ("How to Read Freud on Jokes," 461). In the process Mehlman is asking the reader for a very arcane and intellectual laughter, and this is certainly not the kind of laughter Freud was most interested in nor the kind of wit that the book illustrates again and again. It is time to learn how to laugh in reading Freud, but the invitations in the text are simpler than Mehlman suggests and do not require jumps into the essays on sexuality or narcissism.

The most common criticism of comic theory is that explication destroys the comic effect, the laughter. The joke is destroyed and the comic pleasure denied. But the very best theoretical studies of the comic are also attempts to teach an appreciation of the comic, and the reader of Freud's book is encouraged to laugh and to understand at the same time. He is constantly confronted with jokes. The joke at the center of *Jokes*, exactly like these manifest jokes, is no accident. Like Poe's purloined letter, it is only hidden because it is so obvious, the most anti-Semitic of all statements presented in all seriousness in Freud's first major celebration of Jewishness. In a beautiful work of art, Schiller had written, we pass back and forth between frivolousness and seriousness.

Taken seriously, Freud's main point appears biological, physiological—the explanation that comic processes depend on economy of expenditure of energy—but that is only the manifest reduction. The latent joke content of this biological explanation reduces it to play, to the aesthetic, to the form of the joke itself. The two approaches, the psychological and the aesthetic, cannot in fact be separated at all.

And just as the content includes both manifest jokes and a latent joke, so does the content include manifest discussions of sexuality and a latent discussion of sexuality. Freud is very direct when he explains the sexual content of many jokes, and the origins of these jokes in smut and the desire to seduce, but he is much less direct when he discusses laughter. When he explains how a small joke can produce great pleasure by upsetting the balance between the drive for pleasure and the drive to repress, he calls this small energy added by the joke "comic forepleasure." Freud stops his analogy here, although he does discuss laughter as the release of energy. What remains unstated though implied is that laughter is ejacula not of semen but of psychic energy and that the pleasure of laughing is analogous to the pleasure of sexuality, whether this laughter be at sexual jokes or much more innocent varieties. Again Freud's reduction appears to be finally biological and sexual, but the comic experience is only symbolic sexuality, the ejaculation of not yet formed words, mental lust. The physiological process becomes a psychological process, a rehearsing or mimicking of actual sexuality, and thus again a kind of aesthetic process, play, unreal except within the play frame of the unconscious. The answer to the problem posed by psychology and physiology returns to the concept of play adapted from aesthetics. What is real for psychologists, in this case the sexuality, appears condensed and displaced into the aesthetic category of play, just as what is free and detached for aestheticians, the removal from the practical affairs of everyday life, appears displaced and distorted into the psychological category of instinct, or basic biological need. Once again the two cannot be separated. There is no final reduction.

Jokes, the comic, and humor are symbolic action—there is no real seduction, sexuality, or ejaculation. But neither is it simply play in the trivial and limited sense of the word. Something of significance does happen. The sexual joke allows for the expression of a repressed sexual wish, and all jokes allow for a return to pleasure by their invitation to psychic masturbation. The benefit is to the individual and to his internal psychological states rather than to external social conditions. The joke does not change objective conditions of existence but it does alter subjective response. And here Freud's collection of Jewish jokes is crucial to the argument. While there had been other Jewish critics of the comic—Bergson, notably—undisguised Jewish material had never been introduced into the critical discourse on the comic. The material did not support the obvious point that slaves made jokes against their masters or that people living in periods of political repression tended to become good jokers, the point made by Shaftesbury in the early eighteenth century, but it allowed for the somewhat more complicated observation that slaves made jokes about themselves and thereby found a way of enduring their servitude. Both Jewish jokes and Jewish humor, to retain Freud's distinction, salvage pleasure from un-pleasure, but the position as victim is never denied—indeed it is given emphasis and exaggerated. This is masochism, and al-though Freud was writing about masochism at this same time, he did not identify Jewish jokes by this term. Doing so would have reduced what he saw as healthy coping mechanisms to mal-adaptive behavior. (It remained for psychoanalytic commen-tators after him to make the connections to masochism.) What was far more important to Freud was the stress on weakness in the Jewish material, that the symbolic action of the joke did not deny the real conditions of servitude but simply found a way of adapting to those conditions while remaining acutely conscious of them.

The introduction of Jewish material into the discourse on the comic thereby solved the unanswered problems of both aestheti-cians and psychologists in nineteenth-century comic theory. He-gel strongly attacked Schlegel for his notion of romantic irony as a free floating above existence, for what Schlegel celebrated as transcendental buffoonery. The true comic, Hegel insisted, must remain tied to reality. Kierkegaard took up this argument and proposed the comic as a position that was simultaneously free and bound, but it remained for him more of a theoretical possi-bility. He had the example of Socrates before him and a comic persona he tried himself to act out, but it remained something that was very difficult for him to explain. Freud's Jewish joke ex-plained it all. Here were actual existing people, in history, who had used the comic and had therefore become free and bound. The problem in nineteenth-century psychology was somewhat different. If laughter was an instinct or at least instinctive, then it had survival value for the species—a generation of psycholo-gists struggled with attempts to explain how laughter had sur-vival value in the second half of the nineteenth century and an-other in the first half of the twentieth century until the search was finally abandoned. Freud's Jewish joke explained it all—it was not in the laughter that there was survival value (in laughter there was only pleasure) but rather in the comic, of which laughter was only the immediate short-term result. The Jewish joke was a survival mechanism because it allowed for a psychological adaptation to difficult circumstances.

The conventional wisdom about the comic in the twentieth century is precisely this point, that the comic, regardless of its form, is a defense against suffering. *Jokes* is the work in which this shift is effected. Freud did it by taking the standard texts of the nineteenth century and combining, inverting, and destroying them—precisely what Fielding did in *Joseph Andrews* to the standard texts he inherited. But Freud did not change the understanding of the comic by himself. Groos's work allowed Freud to write the book, and in England, Groos's work had a somewhat similar effect on the psychologist and aesthetician James Sully, who wrote his *Essay on Laughter* in 1902 and proposed a play theory of the comic. Freud knew the text. Sully in turn provoked a theory of the comic as defense against pain and suffering from William McDougall, and this Freud appears not to have been familiar with—it was, at first, contained in a very brief review. But there is no unconscious in either Sully or McDougall, no material comparable to Freud's collection of Jewish humor, and no complex synthesis of an intellectual tradition. Neither Sully nor McDougall had any influence beyond the immediate years of their publications, but Freud, while he had to wait nearly twenty years for attention, has had the more lasting impact.

In *The Origins of Psychoanalysis*, Freud confessed, "I secretly nurse the hope of arriving by the same route"—medicine—"at my own original objective, philosophy. For that was my original ambition, before I knew what I was intended to do in the world" (141). To Freud's critics who believe that he never achieved a true synthesis of science and art, *Jokes* stands as a rebuke. For the critics of comedy who believe that there is either theory or practice but not a true synthesis, Freud's book stands as an open invitation and a great challenge. The comic idea is appropriated by a great many writers and critics and used in a great many ways. Rarely has it been mastered so brilliantly.

V

THE PSYCHOANALYTIC study of the comic began in 1905 with the publication of Freud's book on jokes, but although the book went through four German-language editions by 1925 and was translated into English by Brill in 1916, there was little interest in the subject among Freud's early followers. For two decades what attention the book did receive came almost entirely from critics working on the problems of the comic in other disciplines, individuals who had little understanding of Freud's concept of the unconscious and even less interest in the connections he was making between jokes and internal psychic structures. Max Eastman, for example, discussed Freud's theory at length in his *Sense of Humor*, published in 1921, and concluded that it was both silly and incomprehensible. Within the psychoanalytic group around Freud in this period there was not so much hostility as indifference, and Freud himself did little additional work on the subject. He lectured on jokes to the Prague B'nai B'rith in 1907 and made some minor additions to the second edition of the book in 1912 (Klein, *Jewish Origins*, 161). Only Ferenczi, Brill, and Reik showed any real interest in the subject: Ferenczi lecturing on Freud's book to the Budapest psychoanalytic society in 1911, Brill publishing a summary of *Jokes* in the United States in the same year, and Reik publishing essays on wit in Vienna in 1912 and 1913. Ferenczi also began an essay on the psychoanalytic meanings of laughter in 1913, but he never completed it; and these fragments were not published until 1939, several years after his death. Having failed to interest his psychoanalytic colleagues in the subject, Ferenczi could not sustain his own study of the material.

Reik was more persistent, returning to the comic in the late 1920s with a series of essays that were then collected as *Lust und Leid im Witz* in 1929 and with a second series that became part of *Nachdenkliche Heiterkeit* in 1933. By the late 1920s there was finally some significant interest in the problems of the comic in psychoanalysis, an interest that can be dated to the fourth edition of *Jokes* in 1925. Jekels published a short study of the comic drama and its relation to the oedipal complex in 1926, which was the first attempt to consider comic literature beyond very brief discussions in the 1905 book; and in 1927 Freud revised his concept of humor, touched on briefly at the end of the book on jokes, with a paper that was delivered for him at the Tenth International Psychoanalytic Congress. The paper was published in 1928. In 1929 Reik's first set of essays was published in book form, and in 1930 *Jokes* was translated into French. In the 1930s more psychoanalytic critics took up the subject and since then it has continued to be a small but nevertheless sustained interest to the discipline.

The first critics to take up Freud's work in the 1920s and 1930s were a group of relatively orthodox analysts, first in Central Europe, then with the migrations of the mid-thirties in the United States: Reik, Winterstein, Dooley, Bergler, Kris, Jekels. Following Freud's emphasis on the practical benefits of laughing and joking, these critics concentrated on refining and modifying Freud's argument on humor as defense and joking as offense. Later critics in the 1940s and 1950s—Feldman, Grotjahn, Jacobson, Wolfenstein, and others—were to reconsider the origins of the comic in childhood development, the meanings of laughter during analysis, and the connections of the comic to psychological illness. Their work is uniformly scholarly and serious and often more rigorously analytical than Freud's. But the translation of *Jokes* into French in 1930 had the opposite effect in France, where Freud's ideas were taken quite playfully, and by artists and artist-critics rather than by scholars raised in talmudic traditions. The surrealists incorporated Freud's discussions of the comic into their art just as they had done with his discussions of dreams and the unconscious, demonstrating his method rather than continuing his inquiry. Breton's *Anthologie de l'humour noir* published in 1940 is the most explicit literary example of this use of Freud, for not only does it acknowledge the debt directly, it also illustrates the comic in the selections themselves and beyond that in the playful and obscure principles that govern the selection.

A second generation of relatively orthodox critics took up Freud's work on the comic in the 1950s and 1960s; they were trained like the earlier group in Central European methods of interpretation but were now interested in the problems of comic art, an issue of the most minor concern to the earlier group. Only Jekels and Kris had offered psychoanalytic explanations of comic art to any significant extent in the earlier period, and it is from a group of essays Kris wrote in the 1930s—one in collaboration with Gombrich—that all the later work derives. When Kris collected these essays as *Psychoanalytic Explorations in Art* in 1952, gaining for them a much wider audience, he took Freud's analysis of the joke as the model for all forms of psychoanalytic criticism of art, not simply comic art. Others have followed this lead: Gombrich, in his own study of Freudian aesthetics in 1966, and Holland, in *The Dynamics of Literary Response* in 1968. Jekels's early essay on comedy and the oedipal complex was repeated by Grotjahn in his *Beyond Laughter* in 1957, and it was then developed and combined with ideas taken from Kris in Mauron's *Psychocritique du genre comique* in 1964. This work is strictly limited to comic art. All of these critics regardless of nationality write within the context of Central European orthodoxy and seriousness, and like the first generation of serious critics, these two have been opposed by a far more playful group of artist-critics who originate in France, the followers of Lacan. In his study "The Function of Language in Psychoanalysis," delivered in 1953 and published in 1956, Lacan praised Freud's study of the comic as "the most unchallengeable of his works because it is the most transparent, in which the effect of the unconscious is demonstrated to us in its most subtle confines" (33). What Kris took as the royal road back into art in 1952, Lacan took as the royal road back into Freud in 1953; and as Lacan's writing has gained a following, most recently in the United States, a number of later critics have followed this line of inquiry, applying the psychoanalytic method of reading the joke to the problem of reading Freud more generally. Thus Mehlman explicates Freud by a method very similar to that which Kris uses to explicate art, although the result for the Lacanians is not so much to extend Freud's inquiry into the comic as it is to develop a new understanding of Freud's critical texts. The critic, Mehlman argues, must be a joker. A generation earlier the surrealists had argued that the artist must be a joker.

The readers of *Jokes* can be divided between the jokers and the nonjokers, between those trained in Central European methodologies who pick up on the rational project of the book and those trained within French methodologies who pick up on its irrational content. Freud's book is a synthesis of the rational and the irrational, but it has not been a synthesis that critics working after Freud have been able to sustain. A joke, Freud explained, was a celebration of irrationality that served rational purposes, a return to a state of childhood pleasure and free play that helped preserve the sanity of the adult. Moreover, a joke was a highly irrational verbal form, the contribution made by the unconscious, but nevertheless one that could be understood by another highy rational verbal form, the book itself, a carefully structured and intellectually rigorous work. The book seeks to demystify and to preserve the irrationality of the comic, to bring rationality into the service of irrationality. But there has been little appreciation of this tension among Freud's followers, who have instead focused upon one or the other of these qualities. Mehlman bitterly attacks Kris for misreading and misrepresenting Freud as a rational ego psychologist, but he fails to see his own similarities to Kris. Their methods are almost the same, although their objects are significantly different; and Mehlman's central argument, that the critic must be a joker, is close to a notion put forward by the equally orthodox Reik in the 1930s, that the psychoanalytic method is comparable to the techniques of the joke ("Psychogenesis"). Reik made his point apologetically, worrying that his colleagues would not think him sufficiently serious; Rieff made a similar point in passing in *Freud: The Mind of The Moralist* some twenty years later; Mehlman makes the point the most important part of his argument another fifteen years later, and finally it is made with confidence.

The Central European and the French critics have made unequal contributions to the psychoanalytic study of the comic, for while both have extended (and therefore inevitably changed and distorted) Freudian analysis and both have added to the understanding of Freud's book as a text, only the Central European group has extended the inquiry into the problems of the comic. Surrealists are more important in the history of art than the history of comic theory, and Lacanians more important in the history of ideas and the history of analysis than the history of comic theory. The Central Europeans however, perhaps because they have been far less playful, have been much more concerned with the rational study of play and with the comic as such, with developing Freud's own study of the comic both in art and in lived experience. While they have used the book for larger concerns, taking from it a model for all aesthetic interpretations, they have also always kept the comic itself under careful scrutiny.

Freud's work on the comic has had influence well beyond the psychoanalytic community, particularly on comic theorists of literature like Frye, Barber, and Bentley, and on experimental psychologists like Hom and O'Connell, who have attempted to test psychoanalytic theory in laboratory conditions. This project has sometimes itself been comic. In one experiment individuals were subjected to increasingly strong electric shocks as they looked at cartoons. If humor was a defense against suffering as Freud had argued, the experimenter reasoned that individuals would laugh increasingly vigorously as the shocks increased. When they did not he announced that Freud was thereby disproved.

Afterword

ANYONE who enters a university library looking for simple answers to basic questions about comedy and laughter finds a labyrinth of contradictory explanation and a morass of terminology from which there is no escape. Like the reader of *Tom Jones* or *The Ordeal of Richard Feverel*, he wanders through an almost perfect symmetry of binary oppositions, of mirrored and inverted arguments, and of flawed and unreliable guides. Virtually everything that could be said about the subject has been said—every position, its counterposition, and their synthesis. Between Meredith's essay "The Idea of Comedy and the Uses of the Comic Spirit," first delivered in 1877, and the present, critics have argued that comedy is a force for civilization (Meredith) and a force of nature against the repressions of civilization (Freud, Santayana); that the comic corrects aberrant behavior (Bergson) and that the comic does not correct aberrant behavior (Smith); that comedy celebrates what is (Scott) and that it celebrates what should be (Feibleman); that it represents detachment from life (Bergson) and that it represents engagement with life (Burke); that it is an irrational attitude (Sypher), a rational attitude (Swabey), and a force both rational and irrational (Gurewitch); that it is politically left (Feibleman) and politically right (Cook); that it affirms freedom (Kaul, McFadden) and that it de-

nies freedom (Girard); that it shows the victory of the individual
(Torrance) and that it shows the victory of society over the individual (Bergson, Duncan); that its subject is carnival (Santayana) and that its subject is everyday life (Kaul); that it requires self-consciousness (Burke) and that it requires a lack of
self-consciousness (Mack). Who speaks the truth in this discourse? For most Anglo-American literary critics in this period
comedy is a positive subject—the integration of society (Frye),
the elan vital of biological life (Langer), the victory of civilization (Meredith). For most European critics, however, comedy is
much more negative and unpleasant, a sense of constantly being
off balance (Pirandello), an adjustment to painful situations that
cannot be avoided (Freud), existence in boundary situations
(Plessner).

There is virtually no agreement even at the level of basic terminology. For Sully, writing in 1903, humor means genial and
loving laughter in contrast to the harsh laughter of the modern
world, while for Freud in 1905 humor is this harsh modern
laughter, the defensive response to pain and suffering. For Pirandello in 1908 humor is another name for German romantic
irony, a kind of mocking insight into the nature of reality, although for him it is mixed with despair and a sense of paralysis.
For Rourke in 1931 humor is the tradition of American tall
tales, the pleasure not of clear sight but of deliberate obscurity.
For Freud, humor is the strategy of survival for the weak while
the comic is a mental process, an intellectual saving of energy of
much less importance for the psychic lives of individuals. For
Burke in 1937 comedy is the strategy of survival, a loving acceptance of the nature of the world, while humor is the dangerous
emotional error, a misjudgment of the seriousness of reality. For
both Freud and Burke, humor and the comic are separate and
contrasting terms, while for Kierkegaard a century before, humor and irony are both special varieties of the comic. Burke
claims most comedians are actually humorists; Thompson
claims Pirandello means irony when he uses the word humor;
Moses claims Meredith means irony when he speaks of the
comic spirit. But what then can we make of a sentence like this

from Meredith's essay on comedy? "Humorist and satirist frequently hunt together as ironists in pursuit of the grotesque, to the exclusion of the comic" ("Idea of Comedy," 46). This sentence is a model of the clarity that exists in the study of the subject.)

For the literary critic who turns to comic theory for some assistance in interpreting the novels of Jane Austen or the plays of Samuel Beckett, the discourse on comedy and laughter is a paradox of arguments. The alternatives have been to dismiss the discourse altogether as hopelessly muddled (Knights), as irrelevant (Leacock), as pompous (Kaul), and as general (Blistein); to accept a handful of critics as correct (Caputi, Henkle, Kern, Robinson); or to attempt a systematic evaluation of the entire field (Gurewitch, Heilman, Holland, McFadden). Those who simply dismiss the field lose the most—avoiding tough critical problems rarely seems a praiseworthy activity. Those who accept a few theorists as correct simply follow the judgments of others and are guided by their own ethnocentric loyalties and prejudices: Anglo-American critics privilege Frye and the Cambridge anthropologists Cornford and Harrison; French critics privilege Baudelaire and Bergson; Italians privilege Croce and Pirandello; Germans privilege Kant, Hegel and Schopenhauer. And while nearly everyone does use Freud, at least presently, this one point of contact has been itself subject to the fluctuating prestige of the author in other fields. Those who take the last alternative, the thorough evaluation of the field, become either comic theorists in their own right or at the very least scholars of theory.

Few literary critics come to this material with backgrounds from which they can adequately judge the approaches that the theorists juggle. Because comedy and the comic touch so many aspects of experience, work on the subject goes on simultaneously in many disciplines. On the margins of discourse in literary criticism, psychology, philosophy, sociology, anthropology, folklore, biology, physiology, and theology, even occasionally in political and historical analysis, comic theory is central in none. A hybrid of texts with different critical languages, methodologies, and assumptions, it is a babel of academic voices, a set of separate discourses within these disciplines, full of multiple references to and borrowings from earlier works on the subject. The literary critic who would understand the inquiry is led backward from text to text, finally to Plato and Aristotle, and it is here too that the psychological, philosophical, and sociological critic is led. The separate discourses have a common origin. "Each domain, in its own systematicity, circulates an autonomous type of truth," Michael Serres explains in *Hermes*; "each domain has a philosophy of the relations of its truth to its system and of the circulation among these relations" (xiv). For Serres, and for those whom he has influenced, the problem is seeing the domains of literature, philosophy, and science in relation to each other and finding a way of rising above the limitations of any single discipline. This study of comedy and the comic has attempted such a project: to understand the common interests shared by these domains and to illustrate how the subject itself demands interdisciplinary scholarship.

"I see you are waiting for an epilogue," Stultitia tells her followers at the end of *The Praise of Folly*, "but you are crazy if you think I still have in mind what I said, after pouring forth such a torrent of jumbled words." Erasmus's mock encomium ends appropriately enough in self-mockery, then in a mockery of the audience. Modifying a Roman proverb for her own purposes, Stultitia explains, "*I hate a listener with a memory.*" She bids her listeners farewell, asking them only to "clap your hands, live well, drink your fill, most illustrious initiates of Folly" (138). They are finally left on their own to make sense of her torrent of jumbled words—those with a memory will understand that it is no jumble at all, but a carefully and elaborately structured sequence of three arguments about folly, the first comic, the second satiric, the third religious. These constitute a dialectic: an initial position, a counterstatement, then a synthesis that combines them both and moves to a new level of meaning. But Folly will not choose between them for her listeners and will offer no epilogue or conclusion. All of the positions are correct, of course; that is what Folly would have us understand. Folly is universal—every explanation of her meaning contains at least part of the truth. The best explanation of folly is the most universal. It is only by understanding the complex, contradictory nature of all the answers that we begin to understand the subject itself. From Plato and Aristotle to the present, writers and critics have argued over the nature of comedy and the comic, humor, laughter, and mockery, and they have agreed on very little. Read as a series of attempts to answer unanswerable questions about the meaning of comedy and the nature of laughter, the inquiry into the comic appears as 2,500 years of interesting failure. But read as intellectual history, the inquiry into the comic is a rich and exciting discourse, a series of remarkable attempts to understand the most essential characteristics of very difficult material. Some of these attempts are more successful than others, more carefully thought out, and more influential. The best of them, like Erasmus's *Praise*, have attempted to include as many critical positions as possible, by classifying variants, by relating stages, by devising dialectics. The best of them have also masked their analyses in mockery, sometimes so thoroughly that there can be no simple reading of their intentions. It is with these that this book has been concerned.

To Wayne Booth's familiar concept of the unreliable narrator, then, we need to add a concept of the unreliable critic, and in the inquiry into laughter and the comic the best critics are unreliable. Fielding's critical statements as presented in his essays are contradicted by his novelistic practice, and even the preface to *Joseph Andrews* does not describe the novel. Kierkegaard presents every possible position toward the comic in the stages on life's way of his pseudonyms. Thackeray's essays on humor are far more sentimental than his novel on humor, and Meredith's essay on comedy radically different from his novels on comedy. Such discrepancy between what the writer says about laughter and the comic and what he demonstrates extends beyond the novelists and philosophers studied here and appears to be so widespread that it is part of the tradition of the comic. The prologue to *Volpone* urges us to laugh heartily until our cheeks be "red with laughter," but what we are asked to laugh at is a play in which the central character is led to his downfall because he laughs until his cheeks are red with laughter. Jonson's prologue is another apparently didactic trap, actually a parody of didacticism. In the preface to *Tartuffe* Molière wrote that individuals so fear public ridicule that they will reform rather than endure it, but in the *Miser* Molière presents the opposite position. When Harpagon learns that he is the general object of laughter, instead of reforming he becomes even more ridiculous and beats the man who has been his informant. Sterne begins *Tristram Shandy* with the clear and explicit statement: "I live in a constant endeavour to fence against the infirmities of ill health, and other evils of life, by mirth; being firmly persuaded that every time a man smiles, —but much more so, when he laughs, that it adds something to this Fragment of Life." But in the novel that follows mirth is shown to be the cause of many of the infirmities of life and health that plague Tristram, and laughter is shown to be an action just as likely to subtract from the fragment of life as add to it. What Sterne praises without reservation as an authority on the comic, he demonstrates to be a far more difficult matter as a comic author. In fact, since Tristram's story is a demonstration of the operations of mirth, it is Sterne the critic who is proved too simpleminded. And when Parson Yorick appears to die only because he laughs and smiles, we must understand that the position in the dedication is a critical trap. Sterne, like Molière and Jonson before him, is only echoing the conventional wisdom on the subject, and mocking it.

There is an important lesson to be learned here: it is only when we do not take comic theory seriously that we can understand the complexities of its comedy and the meanings of its mockery. When comic theory is reduced to a handful of homilies it seems neither interesting nor intellectually meaningful, but when those homilies are rightfully seen as part of larger and far more elaborate efforts to understand the meanings of the comic, even the most banal statement takes on new significance. The intellectual history of the comic is thus ready for a major reinterpretation. This book has been a first step in that process.

Works Cited

Abrams, M. H. *The Mirror and the Lamp: Romantic Theory and the Critical Tradition*. New York and London: Oxford University Press, 1953.

Addison, Joseph. *Spectator*, no. 35, Tuesday, 10 April 1711. In *The Spectator*, edited by Donald F. Bond, 1: 145–48. Oxford: Clarendon Press, 1965.

Allin, Arthur. "On Laughter." *Psychological Review* 10 (1903): 306–15.

Alter, Robert. *Partial Magic: The Novel as a Self-Conscious Genre*. Berkeley and Los Angeles: University of California Press, 1975.

"Anatomy of Laughter." *Chambers' Edinburgh Journal* 8, no. 208 (25 December 1847): 408–9.

Armstrong, Martin. *Laughing*. London: Jarrolds, 1928.

Bain, Alexander. *The Emotions and the Will*. London: John W. Parker and Sons, 1859.

———. *The Emotions and the Will*. 2d ed. London: Longmans Green and Co., 1865.

———. "Wit and Humour." *Westminster Review* 48 (1847) 47–59.

Bakhtin, Mikhail. *Rabelais and His World*. Translated by Helene Iswolsky. Cambridge: M. I. T. Press, 1968.

Battestin, Martin C. *The Providence of Wit: Aspects of Form in Augustan Literature and the Arts*. Oxford: Clarendon Press, 1974.

Baudelaire, Charles. "On the Essence of Laughter, and, in General, on the Comic in the Plastic Arts." In *Comedy: Meaning and Form*, 2d ed., edited by Robert Corrigan, 311–23. New York: Harper and Row, 1981.

Beer, Gillian. *Meredith: A Change of Masks: A Study of the Novels*. London: University of London, Athlone Press, 1970.

Bergson, Henri. "Laughter." In *Comedy*, edited by Wylie Sypher, 60–190. Garden City, N.Y.: Doubleday, 1956.

245

Blistein, Elmer. *Comedy in Action*. Durham N.C.: Duke University Press, 1964.

Breton, Andre. *Anthologie de l'humour noir*. Paris: Jean-Jacques Pauvert, 1966.

Brill, A. A. "Freud's Theory of Wit." *Journal of Abnormal Psychology* 6 (1911): 279–316.

Burke, Kenneth. *Attitudes Toward History*. New York: New Republic Press, 1937.

———. *Language as Symbolic Action*. Berkeley and Los Angeles: University of California Press, 1966.

Caputi, Anthony. *Buffo: The Genius of Vulgar Comedy*. Detroit: Wayne State University Press, 1978.

Carlyle, Thomas. "Jean Paul Richter." In *Critical and Miscellaneous Essays*, 1: 1–26. London: Chapman and Hall, 1899.

———. *Sartor Resartus*. New York: E. P. Dutton, 1973.

Carpenter, William. *Principles of Comparative Physiology*. Philadelphia: Blanchard and Lea, 1854.

Coleridge, Samuel Taylor. "On the Distinctions of the Witty, the Droll, the Odd, and the Humorous; the Nature and Constituents of Humor; Rabelais, Swift, and Sterne." In *The Complete Works of Samuel Taylor Coleridge*, edited by W. G. T. Shedd, 4:275–85. New York: Harper and Brothers, 1853.

Cook, Albert. *The Dark Voyage and the Golden Mean: A Philosophy of Comedy*. Cambridge: Harvard University Press, 1949.

Cornford, F. M. *The Origins of Attic Comedy*. London: Edward Arnold, 1914.

Crile, George. *Man: An Adaptive Mechanism*. New York: Macmillan, 1916.

Darwin, Charles. *The Expression of Emotions in Man and Animals*. 1872. Reprint. New York: Philosophical Library, 1955.

"The Decay of Laughter." In *Spectator*, no. 67 (1891): 672–73.

Derrida, Jacques. "Coming Into One's Own." Translated by James Hulbert. In *Psychoanalysis and the Question of the Text. Selected Papers from the English Institute, 1976–77*, edited by Geoffrey Hartman. Baltimore and London: Johns Hopkins University Press, 1978.

Dewey, John. "The Theory of Emotions." Part 1. *Psychological Review* 1 (1894): 553–69.

Duckworth, Alistair. *The Improvement of the Estate: A Study of Jane Austen's Novels*. Baltimore and London: Johns Hopkins University Press, 1971.

Duncan, Hugh Dalziel. *Language and Literature in Society*. Chicago: University of Chicago Press, 1953.

Eastman, Max. *The Sense of Humor*. New York: Charles Scribners, 1922.

Edwards, P. D. "Education and Nature in *Tom Jones* and *The Ordeal of Richard Feverel*." *Modern Language Review* 63 (1968): 23–32.

Erasmus, Desiderius. *The Praise of Folly.* Translated by Clarence Miller. New Haven and London: Yale University Press, 1979.

"Eutrapelia: An Omniumgatherum Literarium, Chiefly Illustrative of Barrow on Wit." *The New Monthly Magazine* 108 (1856): 362–69, 460–68; 109 (1857): 176–83, 346–54, 451–61; 110 (1857): 78–89, 201–13; 424–35.

Everett, C. C. *Poetry, Comedy, and Duty.* Boston: Houghton Mifflin, 1896.

Ewbank, David R. "Structure of *The Ordeal of Richard Feverel.*" *English Studies* 57 (1976): 348–52.

Feibleman, James. *In Praise of Comedy.* 1939. Reprint. New York: Horizon Press, 1970.

Ferenczi, Sandor. "Laughter." In *Final Contributions to the Problems and Methods of Psycho-Analysis,* edited by Michael Balint, translated by Eric Mosbacher et al., 177–82. 1955. Reprint. New York: Brunner Mazel, 1980.

———. "The Psychoanalysis of Wit and the Comical." In *Further Contributions to the Theory and Technique of Psycho-Analysis,* edited by John Richman, translated by Sanie Suttie et al., 332–44. 1926. Reprint. New York: Brunner Mazel, 1980.

Fielding, Henry. *Champion,* 12 January 1739/1740. In *Miscellaneous Writings,* vol. 15 of *The Complete Works of Henry Fielding,* edited by William Henley, 150–52. Frank Cass and Co., n.d. Reprint. New York: Barnes and Noble, 1967.

———. *Champion,* no. 52, Thursday, 13 March 1740. In *Miscellaneous Writings,* vol. 15 of *The Complete Works of Henry Fielding,* edited by William Henley, 240–43. Frank Cass and Co., n.d. Reprint. New York: Barnes and Noble, 1967.

———. *Common Sense: or, the Englishman's Journal,* 21 May 1737. In *Henry Fielding: The Critical Heritage,* edited by Ronald Paulson and Thomas Lockwood, 102–5. London: Routledge and Kegan Paul, 1969.

———. *The Covent-Garden Journal,* no. 10, Tuesday, 4 February 1752. In *Miscellaneous Writings,* vol. 14 of *The Complete Works of Henry Fielding,* edited by William Henley, 111–15. Frank Cass and Co., n.d. Reprint. New York: Barnes and Noble, 1967.

———. *The Covent-Garden Journal,* no. 56, 25 July 1752. In *Miscellaneous Writings,* vol. 14 of *The Complete Works of Henry Fielding,* edited by William Henley, 218–22. Frank Cass and Co., n.d. Reprint. New York: Barnes and Noble, 1967.

———. "Essay on Conversation." In *Miscellaneous Writings,* vol. 14 of *The Complete Works of Henry Fielding,* edited by William Henley, 243–77. Frank Cass and Co., n.d. Reprint. New York: Barnes and Noble, 1967.

———. "Essay on the Knowledge of the Characters of Men." In *Miscellaneous Writings,* vol. 14 of *The Complete Works of Henry Fielding,* edited by

William Henley, 279–305. Frank Cass and Co., n.d. Reprint. New York: Barnes and Noble, 1967.

——. *The History of Tom Jones, A Foundling*. Edited by Fredson Bowers. Middletown, Conn.: Wesleyan University Press, 1975.

——. *Joseph Andrews*. Edited by Martin C. Battestin. Middletown, Conn.: Wesleyan University Press, 1967.

Freeman, Kathleen. *Ancilla to the Pre-Socratic Philosophers: A Complete Translation of the Fragments in Diels*, Fragmente der Vorsokratiker. Oxford: Basil Blackwell, 1948.

Freud, Sigmund. "Humor." In *The Complete Psychological Works of Sigmund Freud*, translated by James Strachey, 21:160–66. London: Hogarth Press, 1961.

——. *Jokes and Their Relation to the Unconscious*. Translated by James Strachey. New York: W. W. Norton, 1960.

——. *The Origins of Psychoanalysis: Letters to Wilhelm Fliess: Drafts and Notes: 1887–1902*. Edited by Maria Bonaparte, Anna Freud, and Ernst Kris. New York: Basic Books, 1954.

Frye, Northrop. *Anatomy of Criticism*. Princeton: Princeton University Press, 1957.

Gay, Peter. *Freud, Jews and Other Germans*. New York: Oxford University Press, 1978.

Girard, Rene. "Perilous Balance: A Comic Hypothesis." *MLN* 87 (1972): 811–26.

Gombrich, E. H. "Freud's Aesthetics." *Encounter* 26 (1966): 30–40.

Groos, Karl. *The Play of Man*. Translated by Elizabeth Baldwin. New York: D. Appleton and Co., 1901.

Gurewitch, Morton. *Comedy: The Irrational Vision*. Ithaca and London: Cornell University Press, 1975.

Hall, G. Stanley, and Arthur Allin. "The Psychology of Tickling, Laughing, and the Comic." *American Journal of Psychology* 9 (1897): 1–41.

Hazlitt, William. "Lectures on the English Comic Writers." In *The Complete Works of William Hazlitt*, edited by P. P. Howe, 6:1–168. London: J. M. Dent and Sons, 1931.

Hegel, G. W. F. *Aesthetics. Lectures on Fine Art*. Translated by T. M. Knox. Oxford: Clarendon Press, 1975.

——. *Phenomenology of Spirit*. Translated by A. V. Miller. Oxford: Oxford University Press, 1977.

Heilman, Robert. *The Ways of the World: Comedy and Society*. Seattle and London: University of Washington Press, 1978.

Henkle, Roger W. *Comedy and Culture: England 1820–1900*. Princeton: Princeton University Press, 1980.

Hesse, Hermann. *Steppenwolf*. Translated by Basil Creighton. Revised by Joseph Mileck and Horst Frenz. San Francisco: Rinehart Press, 1963.

Hilles, Frederick. "Art and Artifice in *Tom Jones*." In *Imagined Worlds: Essays* on *Some English Novelists in Honor of John Butt*, edited by Maynard Mack and Ian Gregor, 91–110. London: Methuen and Co., 1968.

Holland, Norman. *The Dynamics of Literary Response*. New York: Oxford University Press, 1968.

Hom, George. "Threat of Shock and Anxiety in the Perception of Humor." *Perceptual Motor Skills* 23 (1966): 535–38.

Hunt, Leigh. "On the Combination of Grave and Gay." In *Leigh Hunt's Literary Criticism*, edited by Lawrence Huston Houtchens and Carolyn Washburn Houtchens, 559–66. New York: Columbia University Press, 1956.

———. *Wit and Humour Selected from the English Poets*. London: Smith, Elder, and Co., 1846.

Hunter, J. Paul. *Occasional Form, Henry Fielding and the Chains of Circumstance*. Baltimore: Johns Hopkins University Press, 1975.

Iser, Wolfgang. *The Implied Reader: Patterns of Communication in Prose Fiction from Bunyan to Beckett*. Baltimore: Johns Hopkins University Press, 1974.

Jekels, Ludwig. "On the Psychology of Comedy." In *Selected Papers*, 97–104. New York: International Universities Press, 1952.

Kant, Immanuel. *Critique of Judgment*. Translated by J. H. Bernard. New York: Hafner Press, 1951.

Kaul, A. N. *The Action of English Comedy*. New Haven and London: Yale University Press, 1970.

Kern, Edith. *The Absolute Comic*. New York: Columbia University Press, 1980.

Kierkegaard, Soren. *The Concept of Irony*. Translated by Lee Capel. Bloomington: Indiana University Press, 1968.

———. *Concluding Unscientific Postscript*. Translated by David F. Swenson and Walter Lowrie. Princeton: Princeton University Press, 1941.

———. *Crisis in the Life of an Actress and Other Essays on Drama*. Translated by Stephen Crites. New York: Harper and Row, 1967.

———. *Either/Or*. Vol. 1. Translated by David Swenson and Lillian Marvin Swenson. Princeton: Princeton University Press, 1959.

———. *Johannes Climacus or De Omnibus Dubitandum Est*. Translated by T. H. Croxall. Stanford: Stanford University Press, 1958.

———. *Philosophical Fragments*. Translated by David Swenson and Howard Hong. Princeton: Princeton University Press, 1962.

———. *The Point of View for My Work as an Author*. Translated by Walter Lowrie. New York: Harper and Row, 1962.

———. *Repetition*. In *Fear and Trembling. Repetition*, translated and edited by Howard V. Hong and Edna H. Hong, 125–231. Princeton: Princeton University Press, 1983.

———. *Søren Kierkegaard's Journals and Papers*. 7 vols. Translated by Howard Hong and Edna Hong. Bloomington: Indiana University Press, 1967–1978.

————. *Stages on Life's Way*. Translated by Walter Lowrie. New York: Schocken, 1967.

————. *Training in Christianity*. Translated by Walter Lowrie. Princeton: Princeton University Press, 1941.

Klein, Dennis B. *A History of Scientific Psychology: Its Origins and Philosophical Backgrounds*. New York and London: Basic Books, 1970.

————. *Jewish Origins of the Psychoanalytic Movement*. New York: Praeger, 1981.

Knights, L. C. "Notes on Comedy." In *Theories of Comedy*, edited by Paul Lauter, 432–43. Garden City, N.Y.: Doubleday, 1964.

Kris, Ernst. *Psychoanalytic Explorations in Art*. 1952. Reprint. New York: Schocken, 1964.

Lacan, Jacques. "The Function of Language in Psychoanalysis." In *The Language of the Self*, translated by Anthony Wilden, 1–87. 1968. Reprint. New York: Dell, 1975.

————. "The Mirror Stage as Formative of the Function of the I as Revealed in Psychoanalytic Experience." In *Ecrits, a Selection*, translated by Alan Sheridan, 1–7. New York and London: W. W. Norton, 1977.

Langer, Suzanne. *Feeling and Form*. New York: Charles Scribners, 1953.

Lauter, Paul, ed. *Theories of Comedy*. Garden City, N. Y.: Doubleday, 1964.

Leacock, Stephen. *Humour: Its Theory and Technique*. London: John Lane, 1935.

Ludovici, Anthony. *The Secret of Laughter*. London: Constable and Co., 1932.

Macaulay, Thomas. "Leigh Hunt." In *Critical, Historical, and Miscellaneous Essays*, 350–411. New York: Riverside Press, 1866.

McDougall, William. *An Outline of Psychology*. 6th ed. London: Methuen and Co., 1933.

————. "The Theory of Laughter." *Nature* 67 (1903): 318–19.

McFadden, George. *Discovering the Comic*. Princeton: Princeton University Press, 1982.

Mack, Maynard. "Introduction to *Joseph Andrews*." In *The Comic in Theory and Practice*, edited by John J. Enck, Elizabeth T. Forter, and Alvin Whitly, 100–101. New York: Appleton Century Crofts, 1960.

Malantschuk, Gregor. *Kierkegaard's Thought*. Translated by Howard Hong and Edna Hong. Princeton: Princeton University Press, 1971.

Martin, Robert. *The Triumph of Wit: A Study of Victorian Comic Theory*. London: Oxford University Press, 1974.

Marx, Karl. *The Eighteenth Brumaire of Louis Bonaparte*. New York: International Publishers, 1963.

Maturin, Charles Robert. *Melmoth the Wanderer*. Lincoln: University of Nebraska Press, 1961.

Mauron, Charles. *Psychocritique du genre comique*. Paris: Jose Corti, 1964.

Mehlman, Jeffrey. "How to Read Freud on Jokes: The Critic as Schadchen." *New Literary History* 6 (1975): 439–61.

Meredith, George. *Celt and Saxon*. Vol. 4 of *The Works of George Meredith*. Standard Edition. London: Constable and Company, 1910.

———. "The Idea of Comedy and the Uses of the Comic Spirit." In *Comedy*, edited by Wylie Sypher, 3–57. Garden City, N.Y.: Doubleday and Co., 1956.

———. *The Ordeal of Richard Feverel*. Edited by C. L. Cline. Boston: Houghton Mifflin Co., 1971.

———. *The Poems of George Meredith*. Edited by Phyllis B. Bartlett. 2:755–60. New Haven and London: Yale University Press.

———. *Sandra Belloni*. Vol. 14 of *The Works of George Meredith*. Standard Edition. London: Constable and Co., 1914.

Morris, Lewis. "The Disuse of Laughter." *Forum* 24 (1897): 319–24.

O'Connell, Walter E. "The Adaptive Functions of Wit and Humor." *Journal of Abnormal and Social Psychology* 61 (1960): 263–70.

Paulson, Ronald. *Satire and the Novel in Eighteenth-Century England*. New Haven and London: Yale University Press, 1967.

Peacock, Thomas Love. *Nightmare Abbey*. Edited by Raymond Wright. New York: Penguin Books, 1969.

"Philosophy of Laughter." *Chambers' Edinburgh Journal*. 17, no. 438 (22 May 1852): 321–22.

Pirandello, Luigi. *On Humor*. Translated by Antonio Illiano and Daniel Testa. Chapel Hill: University of North Carolina Press, 1974.

Plautus I. 5 vols. Translated by Paul Nixon. Edited by T. E. Page, E. Capps, W. H. Rouse. Loeb Classical Library. New York: G. P. Putnams, 1930.

Plessner, Helmuth. *Laughing and Crying: A Study of the Limits of Human Behavior*. Translated by James Spencer Churchill and Marjorie Grene. Evanston, Ill.: Northwestern University Press, 1970.

Reik, Theodor. *Lust und Leid im Witz*. Wein: Internationaler Psychoanalytischer Verlag, 1929.

———. *Nachdenkliche Heiterkeit*. Wein: Internationaler Psychoanalytischer Verlag, 1933.

———. "The Psychogenesis of Analytical Interpretations and of Wit." In *Surprise and the Psychoanalyst*, translated by Margaret Green, 62–72. New York: E. P. Dutton, 1937.

———. *The Search Within: The Inner Experiences of a Psychoanalyst*. New York: Jason Aronson, 1974.

Richter, Jean Paul. *Horn of Oberon: Jean Paul Richter's School for Aesthetics*. Translated by Margaret Hale. Detroit: Wayne State University Press, 1973.

Ricoeur, Paul. *Freud and Philosophy: An Essay on Interpretation*. Translated by Denis Savage. New Haven and London: Yale University Press, 1970.

Rieff, Philip. *Freud: The Mind of a Moralist.* 1959. Reprint. New York: Doubleday, 1961.

Robinson, Daniel. *An Intellectual History of Psychology.* Revised Edition. New York: Macmillan, 1981.

Robinson, Fred Miller. *The Comedy of Language: Studies in Modern Comic Literature.* Amherst: University of Massachusetts Press, 1980.

Rourke, Constance. *American Humor: A Study of the National Character.* New York: Harcourt Brace and Co., 1931.

Sahakian, William. *History and Systems of Psychology.* New York: John Wiley and Sons, 1975.

Santayana, George. "The Comic Mask" and "Carnival." In *Theories of Comedy,* edited by Paul Lauter, 414–23. Garden City, N.Y.: Doubleday, 1964.

Sartre, Jean Paul. *L'Idiot de la famille: Gustave Flaubert de 1831 à 1857.* Paris: Gallimard, 1971.

Schiller, Friedrich. *Naive and Sentimental Poetry* and *On the Sublime.* Translated by Julius A. Elias. New York: Ungar, 1966.

———. *On The Aesthetic Education of Man in a Series of Letters.* Translated by Reginald Snell. 1954. Reprint. New York: Ungar, 1965.

Schlegel, Friedrich. *Lucinde and the Fragments.* Translated by Peter Firchow. Minneapolis: University of Minnesota Press, 1971.

Schultz, Duane. *A History of Modern Psychology.* New York and London: Academic Press, 1969.

Serres, Michel. *Hermes, Literature, Science, Philosophy.* Edited by Josue V. Harari and David F. Bell. Baltimore and London: Johns Hopkins University Press, 1982.

Shaw, George Bernard. "Meredith on Comedy." In *The Comic In Theory and Practice,* edited by John Enck, Elizabeth Porter, and Alvin Whitley, 38–42. New York: Appleton Century Crofts, 1960.

Smith, Willard. *The Nature of Comedy.* Boston: Gorham Press, 1930.

Spector, Jack. *The Aesthetics of Freud: A Study of Psychoanalysis and Art.* New York: McGraw Hill, 1972.

Spencer, Herbert. "The Physiology of Laughter." In *Illustrations of Universal Progress,* 194–209. New York: D. Appleton and Co., 1889.

Sulloway, Frank J. *Freud, Biologist of the Mind: Beyond the Psychoanalytic Legend.* New York: Basic Books, 1979.

Sully, James. *An Essay on Laughter: Its Form, Its Causes, Its Development, And Its Value.* London: Longmans Green and Co., 1902.

Swabey, Marie. *Comic Laughter: A Philosophical Essay.* New Haven: Yale University Press, 1961.

Swift, Jonathan. *Intelligencer,* no. 3. In *Irish Tracts 1728–33,* vol. 12 of *The Prose Works of Jonathan Swift,* edited by Herbert Davis, 32–37. Oxford: Shakespeare Head Press, 1955.

———. *Swift's Polite Conversation,* edited by Eric Partridge. London: Andre Deutsch, 1976.

Sypher, Wylie. "The Meanings of Comedy." In *Comedy*, edited by Wylie Sypher, 191–255. Garden City, N.Y.: Doubleday, 1956.

Tave, Stuart. *The Amiable Humorist: A Study in the Comic Theory and Criticism of the Eighteenth and Early Nineteenth Centuries*. Chicago: University of Chicago Press, 1960.

Thackeray, William Makepeace. "Charity and Humour." In *The English Humourists and the Four Georges*, 267–86. New York: E. P. Dutton, 1912.

———. "The English Humourists." In *The English Humourists and the Four Georges*, 3–263. New York: E. P. Dutton, 1912.

———. *Vanity Fair: A Novel Without a Hero*. Edited by Geoffrey Tillotson and Kathleen Tillotson. Boston: Houghton Mifflin, 1963.

Thompson, Alan Reynolds, *The Dry Mock: A Study of Irony in Drama*. Berkeley and Los Angeles: University of California Press, 1948.

Thompson, Josiah. *The Lonely Labyrinth: Kierkegaard's Pseudonymous Works*. Carbondale and Edwardsville: Southern Illinois University Press, 1967.

Torrance, Robert M. *The Comic Hero*. Cambridge: Harvard University Press, 1978.

Wadlington, Warwick. *The Confidence Game in American Literature*. Princeton: Princeton University Press, 1975.

Walpole, Horace. *The Correspondence of Horace Walpole*. Edited by W. S. Lewis, Warren Hunting Smith, and George L. Lam. Yale Edition. New Haven: Yale University Press, 1967.

Walsh, James. *Laughter and Health*. New York: D. Appleton and Co., 1928.

Weber, Samuel. *The Legend of Freud*. Minneapolis: University of Minnesota Press, 1982.

Welsford, Enid. *The Fool, His Social and Literary History*. 1935. Reprint. New York: Doubleday, 1961.

Willeford, William. *The Fool and his Scepter: A Study in Clowns and Jesters and Their Audience*. Evanston, Ill.: Northwestern University Press, 1969.

Wilt, Judith. *The Readable People of George Meredith*. Princeton: Princeton University Press, 1975.

Woolf, Virginia. "The Novels of George Meredith." In *The Second Common Reader*, 245–56. New York: Harcourt Brace and Co., 1932.

Wright, Andrew. *Henry Fielding: Mask and Feast*. London: Chatto and Windus, 1968.

Zuver, Dudley. *Salvation by Laughter: A Study of Religion and the Sense of Humor*. New York: Harper and Brothers, 1933.

Index

Abrams, Meyer, 12
Addison, Joseph, 17, 209; and Darwin, 187, 194; and Fielding, 17, 21, 23, 28, 30, 36, 72; and Thackeray, 126–27
Allen, Ralph, 60
Allin, Arthur, 198, 203
Alter, Robert, 18, 73
Amadis de Gaul, 142
American Journal of Psychology, 197–98, 199
Ariadne, 10–11. *See also Joseph Andrews*, Kierkegaard, Labyrinth, *The Ordeal of Richard Feverel*, *Tom Jones*, *Vanity Fair*
Aristophanes, 4; and Fielding, 22, 27, 59; and Meredith, 141, 143, 167
Aristotle, 15, 242; and Fielding, 28–31, 41, 42, 70–71, 156; and Meredith, 141, 155–56, 176, 180
Armstrong, Martin, 202
Austen, Jane, 6–7, 119, 123, 142–43

Bain, Alexander, 1, 184–87, 208; comic theory, 179, 188–90, 192, 197; and Dewey, 196–97; and Everett, 195; and Hobbes, 192; and Kant, 189–90; and Spencer, 192; and Sully, 205, 207
Bakhtin, Mikhail, 13, 15, 17–18; on fools, 92, 95; and Sully, 203, 206–7
Barber, C. L., 237
Barnes, Peter, 4
Battestin, Martin, 53–55, 68
Baudelaire, Charles, 8, 241; and Mer-

edith, 140, 141, 142, 155, 156, 164–65, 180
Beckett, Samuel, 7
Beer, Gillian, 157–58, 166
Bentley, Eric, 237
Bergler, Edmund, 234
Bergson, Henri, 4, 7–10, 15, 203, 239, 240, 241
Blistein, Elmer, 241
Booth, Wayne, 243
Boswell, James, 179
Breton, Andre, 8, 234–35
Brill, Abraham, 233
Buckingham, George, 27
Burke, Kenneth, 13–14, 239, 240
Burton, Robert, 31, 209

Camus, Albert, 8
Caputi, Anthony, 241
Carlyle, Thomas, 15; and Meredith, 143, 163, 167, 181; and Spencer, 181; and Thackeray, 132
Carpenter, William, 180, 191
Carroll, Lewis (pseud.), 169
Cervantes, Miguel de, 16, 17, 18, 73; and Fielding, 6, 17, 22, 23, 28, 38, 39, 49, 50, 59, 72; and Kierkegaard, 96; and Meredith, 142, 143, 146, 174
Chambers' Edinburgh Journal, 143, 164, 176
Cibber, Colley, 26, 28, 45–46, 57, 72, 145
Cicero, 11, 28, 29, 30, 68, 69, 176